International Standards for Design and Manufacturing

International Standards for Design and Manufacturing

Quality management and international best practice

Nick Rich

F Tegwen Malik

KoganPage

Publisher's note
Every possible effort has been made to ensure that the information contained in this book is accurate at the time of going to press, and the publishers and authors cannot accept responsibility for any errors or omissions, however caused. No responsibility for loss or damage occasioned to any person acting, or refraining from action, as a result of the material in this publication can be accepted by the editor, the publisher or the authors.

First published in Great Britain and the United States in 2020 by Kogan Page Limited

2nd Floor, 45 Gee Street
London
EC1V 3RS
United Kingdom

122 W 27th St, 10th Floor
New York, NY 10001
USA

4737/23 Ansari Road
Daryaganj
New Delhi 110002
India

www.koganpage.com

ISBNs

Hardback 978 1 78966 043 2
Paperback 978 1 78966 042 5
Ebook 978 1 78966 053 1

British Library Cataloguing-in-Publication Data

A CIP record for this book is available from the British Library.

Library of Congress Cataloging-in-Publication Data

Names: Rich, Nick, author. | Malik, F. Tegwen, author.
Title: International standards for design and manufacturing : quality management and international best practice / Nick Rich, F. Tegwen Malik.
Description: London : New York, NY : KoganPage, 2019. |
Includes bibliographical references and index.
Identifiers: LCCN 2019036527 (print) | LCCN 2019036528 (ebook) | ISBN 9781789660432 (hardback) | ISBN 9781789660425 (paperback) | ISBN 9781789660531 (ebook)
Subjects: LCSH: Production management–Standards.
Classification: LCC TS155.8 .R53 2019 (print) | LCC TS155.8 (ebook) | DDC 658.5002/18–dc23
LC record available at https://lccn.loc.gov/2019036527
LC ebook record available at https://lccn.loc.gov/2019036528

Typeset by Integra Software Services, Pondicherry
Print production managed by Jellyfish
Printed and bound by CPI Group (UK) Ltd, Croydon, CR0 4YY

To all the people who support the promotion of standards around the world and those who work with them on a daily basis. To the patience of our families for putting up with this 'labour of love'. Thanks to Mel, Dan, Josh, Conor, Tyler and our two families from Nick. Thanks to Bronwen, Naz and Iqbal from Tegwen.

CONTENTS

ABOUT THE AUTHORS

Nick Rich is a Professor at Swansea University and focuses his research on the design of high-performance and highly reliable organizations. Nick is a polymath and his research interests range from high-performance manufacturing and service operations to healthcare and safety-critical systems. He was trained in lean ways of working whilst researching with Toyota Motor Corporation of Japan and has worked with many of the world's leading businesses. He also has research interests that cover the design and improvement of processes operated by Highly Reliable Organizations (HRO) including health and care provision.

Tegwen Malik is an academic at Swansea University and focuses her research on biomimetics for product design and innovation (for all applications including the life sciences sector). She started her career as a 'world class' elite squash player and has combined her sporting career with academic excellence in scientific and management disciplines. She was awarded a Bristol Red for her world-class sporting achievements, reaching world ranking of number 16 whilst studying Physics at Bristol University. She went on to carry out research in the field of oncology within the medical physics sector before immersing herself in project and process management.

ACKNOWLEDGEMENTS

A book is much more than a series of pages and information – it is the result of a lot of influences and events that have shaped your thinking and desire to publish. This book was born from need – our students needed a textbook and half the managers we worked with did not really know what standards were or how to exploit them for competitive advantage. Some managers even saw standards as a bit of a chore and something that was a 'necessary evil' because customers wanted it and therefore the business would 'do it'. The scenario was quite sad. For our students, there wasn't a resource that would help frame their studies and at the same time we found that managers seemed to take a negative view of standards rather than the view I (Nick) had experienced as an engineer at Toyota in Japan and in the UK. Toyota suppliers had studied the ISO systems and decided they were useful in establishing and building upon the Toyota Production System. As such, the systems were embraced strategically and many Toyota suppliers (some of the most efficient companies in the world) introduced ISO 9001 and ISO 14001 and made huge savings. The Toyota supplier attitude is the right one – what can it do for us and how can we use it? What they did was use it to find more savings than the systems cost to introduce and audit (using external third-party businesses). It is that type of spirit we hope to engender to give students a great experience wherever they are studying standards or using them.

We are very lucky to be surrounded by some great and fascinating people, who – as part of our daily lives as researchers – have helped to shape our thinking and shared their experiences with us. It is our pleasure to name a few people who have influenced us and to pay respects to their contributions. Our research sponsors are a great source of support and innovative thinking and so too are the staff at the British Standards Institution known affectionately as the 'BSI' (as well as their many committees, working groups and their membership). The UK is very lucky to have such an influential national body to represent its interests. BSI staff and committee members are the dynamos that make sure existing and new standards are there to support organizations improve and learn to improve. It is a very worthy cause.

We would like to thank the following staff at the BSI. Sally Swingewood, Matthew Chiles and Sara Walton have supported our courses and our research. The work they do with technical committees and the educational sector is great and collectively they are 'walking encyclopaedias' of the how, what and why of the standards world. Thank you for your help with our classes and research projects. Also, Martin Cottam and David Smith, who we watched as they led committee meetings and allowed us to observe the process in action, and to Dr Scott Steedman (CBE) and his impact on standards globally – you guys are awesome! We hope you like the book and will forgive us when we have simplified issues.

The staff at Swansea University, and the School of Management in particular, deserve a special mention. We would like to acknowledge the help and support of Bev John and Beks Mannion for their input into the book – two very lovely colleagues who have been so supportive and insightful. As co-researchers we share a broad research agenda at the university and would therefore like to formally recognize the staff of the Bevan Commission and Bevan Academy which promotes leadership, quality and transformation for healthcare processes. Some previous 'International Standards' students and support staff also deserve a mention in this section. These include Kauthar Al-Bartamani, Cynthia Wong, Yolanda Song, Octor Dong, Chaio Li, Lily Wang, Lucas Hao, Sian Brown, Laura Male, Kim Howell, Sarah Warren, Amy Jones, Diana Stoycheva-Pavlova, Eftychia Petasi, Helen Keogh, Asma Altamimi, Harrison Lyons, Emily Miles, Adam O'Sullivan, Paige Jones, Megan Payne, Ollie Holloway, Rose Forehead, Christina Johnson, Malwina Badzio, Tom Poles, Jack Meredith, Jamie Bradford, Patrycia Szczerba, Gabriella Radford, Joe Kempster, Nicholas Pinocci, Ahmed Bashaykh, Carys Evans, Connor Boylan, Amanda Xu, Demi Griffiths, Khalid Alabdullatif, Chris Arnot, Gavin DSousa, Adam Loader, Catia Lopez-Araujo, Ali Moosa, Jac Morris, Brian Muchiri, Bridie Phipps, Thomas Reynolds, Thomasz Sledz, Bee Tan, James Thomas, David Wilson, Sin Nga Wong, Amanda Xu, C Li, Mariam Abu-Gharieb, Yanny Chunphakdee, Jonathan Bradfield, Shengnan Sun, Lowei Hills, Joe Tucker, Hannah Williams, Katie Bray, Angela Fung, Mike Straw, Malachi Casey, John Georgi, Sarah Bray, Luke Whitmore, Matt Gray, Lauren Jones, Katie Skinner, Yue Liang, Viv Mrema, Ashley Jiang, Shannon Stevens, Bo Liu, Kate Edmond, Tom Hooper, Heidi Zhu, and Ariel Yin of our alumnae. Also Hanze Liu, Rhys Rowberry, Tiri Kunga, Syed Tanvir Wahab, Salma Begum, Egle Bubelyte, Tawonga Banda, Ho Man Tam, Zi Jun Dou, Xi Liu, Guo Yu Xu, Zelin Chang, Lawrence Done, Michael Fletcher, Hongren Wang, Shen Li Xu, Yanjun Fang, Aleksei Daniliuk, Chan Tsz Wing and Chang Long Zhuang of the class of 2018/19. These are all great students and a credit to the university; they were always a pleasure to teach.

Finally, we would like to say thanks to a few lifelong friends and really lovely people including Professor Sharon Williams, Dr Annie Esain, Professor Pauline Found, Professor Maneesh Kumar, Professor John Bicheno, Dr Thomas Bortolotti, Dr Stefania Boscari, Beverley John, Emeritus Professor Andy Graves, Sion Charles, Helen Howson, the Bevan Commissioners, our PhD students and the Professoriate and staff of Swansea School of Management.

Thank you everyone for all your help and support! Any omissions and errors from this book are purely ours. We hope you enjoy the book!

Professor Nick Rich
and Dr F Tegwen Malik

LIST OF FIGURES

All figures drawn by author.

LIST OF TABLES

KEY TERMS

The following is an alphabetical list of terms or short-hands, along with their definitions, which have been used throughout this book. The world of standards has many terms (these words are scrutinized by every standards committee to ensure they are correct!) and here is a summary of some of the popular ones.

Annex SL: The original name given, by the ISO, to the high-level structure that makes writing and employing standards easier for the ISO, for commercial users, and auditors.

Aspect/Impact Risk Matrix: A risk matrix which reviews the environmental impacts of a business and applies a risk analysis to convert environmental impacts into a priority score. The higher the score for an environmental risk, the greater its significance and the need to eradicate/contain the negative impact.

Audit: The process and principles of checking to see whether a business conforms to the certification standard operated by a certified company or as part of the process of gaining certification (gap analysis). ***First-Party Audit:*** Audits of working practices against a standard that are conducted by employees of the organization. ***Second-Party Audit:*** Audits of working practices against a standard that are conducted by customers of the organization. ***Third-Party Audit:*** Audits of working practices against a standard that are conducted by an independent and qualified auditing organization.

BSI: British Standards Institution. The national standards body of UK which operates with a royal charter to promote standards.

BS 5750: The first quality management standard, which was developed and introduced by the BSI and later became the international standard ISO 9001.

BS 7750: The first environmental management standard to be introduced by the BSI and which later morphed into the ISO standard ISO 14001.

Certification: The process of independent (third-party) testing and investigation which results in a technical decision as to whether a business meets all the necessary conformity criteria and clauses of a given standard to the degree that the company can be awarded the ISO certificate.

Clause: An element of a conformance standard to which a business must conform or it will receive a non-conformance notice and requirement to improve its performance and business processes in order to conform.

Compliance: The term is not used often by the ISO but it concerns the fulfilment of legal and statutory/regulatory requirements of a business. It is not a word or legal term used for international management systems.

Conformity: The demonstrable and tested fulfilment of a requirement (clause) of a conformance standard. The opposite is a non-conformity and non-fulfilment of a stated requirement.

Draft International Standard: A technical document that has been processed by an ISO technical committee in the process of offering the standard to the world. The lifecycle of stages are, in order:

- Preliminary draft.
- The Working draft, which is reviewed by the ISO Working Group; it is not balloted on but consensus is required to move to the next stage (CD).
- Committee Draft (CD); the documents are sent to the wider Technical Committee (TC) for comment and ballot.
- The Draft International Standard (DIS) stage, is where the draft is sent out for public consultation, to all participating National Standards Bodies (NSB) and through them to the wider stakeholder community for comment. The NSBs then, deciding on the ballot position, approve/disapprove/abstain from the adoption of the standard.
- Any technical changes made as a result of the DIS comments lead to a Final Draft International Standard (FDIS). If there are no technical changes to be made and the ballot reaches more than 66 per cent approval and with less than 25 per cent disapproval, the standard goes to publication.

Emergency Preparedness: The set of procedures that are pre-written by an organization to specify the exact tasks and sequence of tasks needed to recover a business from a catastrophe. It is a key feature of the ISO 14001 conformance standard.

High-Level Structure (HLS): The common and systematic way in which a standard is written using key themes; such an approach makes reading and interpreting standards easier. It also allows multiple standards to be managed and operated simultaneously with much less duplication or administrative effort.

ISO: International Organization for Standardization, known often as the International Standards Organization; the central coordinating secretariat and Non-Governmental Organization (NGO) based in Geneva.

ISO 9000 Series: Quality Management System standard (ISO 9001) and guides for better quality management by businesses.

ISO 14000 Series: Environmental Management System standard (ISO 14001) and guides for business.

Non-Conformity: A discrepancy between the working practices employed by an organization and the requirements (clauses) of a given standard. Includes grades of non-conformance, specifically an *observation* (an issue that the auditor suggests a company could look at and address as it is of benefit to them). *Minor non-conformity*, where there are deficiencies in a process but the process is not wholly conformant with a standard. A *major non-conformity* is a major failing in a critical business system which shows the certified company (or company seeking certification) is operating business processes that do not conform nor fulfil major requirements.

Normative References: These are reference documents that should be read and are of indispensable assistance in how to optimize and exploit the advantages of a certification standard. The documents that are named in the Normative Reference section of Annex SL are often termed 'guides' by the professional management community.

P-Member: Participating and active member bodies that are fully engaged with the publishing (and voting to publish) international standards.

Registration: The US terminology used to describe the European process of certification.

Requirement: The written and stated business practices that must ('shall') be operated by an organization in order to conform to a standard.

Revision: The updating and improvement of a standard or guide so that the most up-to-date 'good practice' information (and requirements for conformance standards) are built into every document.

Scope: The scope of a standard determines what the standard covers when it is applied to an organization.

Standard: A standard is simply a document. A certification standard is structured with a series of requirements that must be fulfilled in order to gain third-party certification to a specific contemporary ISO standard. Guidance standards that are provided to help managers are also known as standards. Most management conversations and presentations will focus on the certification standard and conformity to the requirements laid out in that document using the High-Level Structure.

LIST OF ABBREVIATIONS

3D	Three dimensional
6σ	Six Sigma
ADKAR	Change management acronym: Awareness, Desire, Knowledge, Ability and Reinforcement (registered trademark of Prosci Inc.)
AJ	After Japan (Ford Motor Company programme)
ANNEX SL	The 2015 High-Level Structure
AXELOS	UK Cabinet Office and Capita joint venture
B2B	Business to Business
B2C	Business to Consumer
BCM	Business Continuity Management
BCMS	Business Continuity Management System
BCP	Business Continuity Plan
BMIS	Business Information Management System
BSI	British Standards Institution
C2C	Cradle-to-Cradle
CAB	Conformity Assessment Body
CAP	Certified Authorization Professional
CB	Certification Body (see also CAB)
CCFP	Certified Cyber Forensics Professional
CCSP	Certified Cloud Security Professional
CD	Committee Draft
CEN	The European Standards Body
CFM	Cross Functional Management
CG EIT	Certified in the Governance of Enterprise IT
CIA	Confidentiality, Integrity and Availability of data
CISA	Certified Information System Auditor
CISM	Certified Information Security Manager
CISSP	Certified Information Systems Security Professional
CLIPS CFM	Eight quality principles of customer focus, leadership, involvement of staff, process approach, systems thinking, continuous improvement, fact-based management and mutually beneficial relationships.
CM	Capability Maturity

CMMI	Capability Maturity Model Integration
CMMI SVC	Capability Maturity Model Integration for Services
COBIT	Control Objectives for Information and Related Technology
COPIS	Customer – Output – Process – Input – Supplier Analysis (Six Sigma method)
CRISC	Certified in Risk and Information Systems Control
CS SLP	Certified Secure Software Lifecycle Professional
CSX CSXP	Cyber Security Nexus
DFA	Design for Disassembly
DFD	Design for Disassembly
DFE	Design for the Environment
DFM	Design for Manufacture
DFMC	Design for Mass Customization
DIN	Deutsches Institut für Normung
DIS	Draft International Standard
DMADV	Six Sigma improvement methods for Define, Measure, Analyse, Design and Verify for new products and processes
DMAIC	Six Sigma improvement method for existing processes and products consisting of Define, Measure, Analyse, Improve and Control
DPMO	Defects per million opportunities
DRIFT	Do It Right First Time
DTO	Design to Order
EASO	Environmental Assessment of Sites and Organizations
EFQM	European Foundation for Quality Management
EMAS	Eco-Management and Audit System
EMAS II	Eco-Management and Audit System II (2001 version)
EMS	Environmental Management System
EN	European Standard
FDIS	Final Draft International Standard
FSA	First-Stage Assessment
GDPR	General Data Protection Regulation (EU Regulation 2016)
GE	General Electric Inc.
HCISSP	HealthCare Information Security and Privacy Practitioner
HLS	High-Level Structure

HR	Human Resources department
I4.0	Industry 4.0
IEC	International Electrotechnical Committee
INTERPOL	International Criminal Police Organization
IOS	International Organization for Standardization – see ISO
IoT	Internet of Things
IoT CM	IoT Conceptual Model
IoT RA	IoT Reference Architecture
IoT RM	IoT Reference Model
IP	Internet Provider
IRS	Incident Response Structure
ISACA	Information Systems Audit and Control Association
ISC2	Cyber Security Certification Organization
ISMS	Information Security Management System
ISO	International Standards Organization
ISO or IOS	International Standards Organization
ISO/IEC	International Organization for Standardization and the International Electrotechnical Commission
ISO/PC	ISO Project Committee
ISO/TC	ISO Technical Committee
IT/ICT	Information Technology/Information and Communications Technology
ITAF	Information Technology Assurance Framework
ITIL	Information Technology Infrastructure Library
ITSM	Information Technology Service Management
IWA	International Workshop Agreement
JIT	Just in Time
JUSE	Japanese Union of Scientists and Engineers
KPIs	Key Performance Indicators
LCA	Lifecycle Analysis
LO	Learning Organization
M2M	Machine to Machine learning
MAO	Maximum Acceptable Outage
MBB	Master Black Belt
MBNQA	Malcolm Baldrige National Quality Award
MJR NC	Major Non-Conformance
MNC	Minor Non-Conformance
MS	Management System

MTP	Maximum Tolerable Period
NATO	North Atlantic Treaty Organization
NATO AQAP	NATO Allied Quality Assurance Publication
NCN	Non Conformance Notice
NB	National Body
NGO	Non-Governmental Organization
NIST	National Institute of Standards and Technology
NSB	National Standards Body
NWIP	New Work Item Proposal
OH&S	Occupational Health and Safety
OP	Operational Plan
OpEx	Operational Excellence
OSH	Occupational Safety and Health
OSR	Overall Significance Rating
PAS	Publicly Available Specification
PCI DSS	Payment Card Industry Data Security Standards
PDCA	Plan–Do–Check–Act
PII	Personally Identifiable Information
PPM	Parts Per Million
POLCA	Paired-Cell Overlapping Loops of Cards
QA	Quality Assurance
QC	Quality Control
QFD	Quality Function Deployment
QMS	Quality Management System
QRM	Quick Response Manufacturing
RA	Risk Assessment
RATER	Reliability, Assurance, Tangibles, Empathy and Responsiveness service quality methodology
RESILIA	RESILIA cyber security training portfolio
SA	Supplier Association
SAGE	Strategic Advisory Group on the Environment
SDCA	Standardize–Do–Check–Act cycle (post improvement)
SIPOC	Suppliers–Input–Operation–Output–Customer chain
SME	Small and Medium-Sized Enterprise
SMS	Service Management System
SOP	Standardized Operating Procedure
SPC	Statistical Process Control
SSCP	Systems Security Certified Practitioner
SSL	Secure Socket Layer

SWOT	Strengths, Weaknesses, Opportunities and Threats analytical method
TC	Technical Committee
TMB	Technical Management Board
TPM	Total Productive Maintenance
TPS	Toyota Production System
TQM	Total Quality Management
TWI	Training Within Industry
UNCED	United Nations Conference on Environment and Development
USB	Universal Serial Bus
Val IT	Governance framework to exploit value from IT investments
WC	Warning Communications
WCED	World Commission on Environment and Development
WD	Working Draft
WHS	Workplace Health and Safety
WHO	World Health Organization
ZD	Zero Defects

PREFACE

It is a significant advantage that international standards exist because they are conceived and designed by practising managers and experts (who make up every technical committee) in the field – they are then converted through an international engagement of promotional national bodies to ensure that organizations operate the right processes to support their business objectives (to make money!).

These objectives could be to operate within a quality standard, to develop a competence in environmental management, or any of a wide range of other standards that demonstrate competence to the world. Competence is a big issue – conforming to ISO standards means a business has invested in organizational processes that are the best current knowledge of how to manage a management system. Without standards the world would be chaotic and uncertain, and business would not be quite so easy to facilitate within a country and across borders.

Big or small, private or public, organizations with standards are far better at managing processes and improving than others. Certified businesses are learning organizations and are sensitive to exploiting the opportunities of their environments, stakeholder engagements, and learning from audits (and gaps created by non-conformances). Far from seeing a non-conformance or an auditor's observations as criticisms, these businesses see these issues as learning opportunities to actually help drive continuous improvement processes. These businesses understand the power of learning and adaptation in the modern dynamic marketplace.

The modern competitive environment is not the same as in the 1950s, where competition was not so intense and businesses were not quite so exposed to today's rate and severity of technical and societal changes. Today there are few industries that can survive without learning and harnessing the talent of their staff to innovate and reinvent the business year after year.

And here is a big irony – some industrialists believe standards are bureaucratic and do not promote innovation. This is simply not true and is an old and outdated mantra! This statement says more about the industrialists and the culture that their organization has developed rather than any standard. It shows that there is a gap in executive-level knowledge and a misconception of what a standard is and how it should be introduced. Standards are bureaucratic if you make them! How can a standard, based on best practice, promote anything other than innovation and staff engagement? Standards are not clunky and cumbersome with tonnes of paperwork anymore! Standards support good thinking, great processes and engaged staff in a world that is increasingly digital. Standards are a great support for the modern learning organization competing globally.

Standards are everywhere and they serve a very valuable purpose. They need to be cultivated, resourced and nurtured, then exploited. They add value to the selling aspect of an organization as well as the delivery processes and strategic management thinking.

Today organizational buyers and consumers alike just assume and implicitly accept that everything is subject to a standard. Britain must be proud of its influence on standards – from early ones that allowed the industrial revolution to occur, right through to the 1980s and the first organizational quality (BS 5750) and environmental (BS 7750) standards. These innovations, the output of the British Standards Institution (BSI), set in process a new revolution for international business standards. These first two standards started an evolutionary process that has witnessed many revisions of each standard and the internationalization of standards to almost every country in the world.

This book was conceived as a response to a need. There are few books in this subject area that are accessible and useful to managers and students. Shelves of books exist on individual standards but few books address the standards community and 'the system'. No student or manager can ever know enough about standards, their background and how everything fits together. We are very proud of our students and how they have progressed in the world; they are our customers, some of whom (over the years) have gone on to work with standards in their respective areas of expertise.

To be customer focused is a common feature of all world-class organizations – and aspiring ones! Students are 'customers' and when your customer says, 'Wouldn't it be good if there was one textbook for our course', it would be wrong of us not to oblige them. At the same time, we have interacted with managers and employees who have said they would benefit from such a resource. And so this project began. What soon became clear was just how much fun the book writing would be as we wrote each chapter and could bring in the experiences of our friends from the manufacturing, service, health and charitable sectors. So we are very grateful for those who practise the standards. There are now more than 22,000 different standards available to organizations and many are now being combined so multiple standards are operated and practised simultaneously. More effective organizations means safer ways of working, better health and safety, better quality, better regulatory compliance and better environmental performance, and each of these vital areas of management has a standard. Each standard demands employee engagement and innovation to make the standard relevant to each specific organization that implements it. The practice of standards is very much a winning formula for businesses of all types.

The universal appeal of the standards is reflected in the number and diversity of organizations that have gained these awards for management competence. It does not matter if the business is fiercely competitive or whether it doesn't focus on profit (maybe because it doesn't really understand profits) but understands that public service management is key to helping the quality of life of the people served. A standard is just that, a benchmark of the organization against meaningful practices of good management. Any management team worth their salt would naturally look to see how these systems can support learning and standardization of working practices by looking at how to improve processes so things are better tomorrow than they are today. Standards are therefore practical, relevant to strategic goals and suitable to modern requirements, from product design processes to order fulfilment.

Thus our book was born – great students and a great relationship with business came together and we decided it was about time we put everything in one place so that professionals and students (those at Swansea University and beyond) could take advantage of what we do and how we see the world. We do hope you will like the book and feel comfortable to give us feedback – after all, we are firm believers in continuous improvement too! Thank you.

The importance of standards 01

Welcome to the fascinating world of standards. It is a world that rarely stands still and a world that has a profound impact on our lives and everyone around us. So, let's begin to discuss the process of standards development and management that literally does change the world!

LEARNING OBJECTIVES

At the end of this chapter, you should be able to:

- understand the concept of competitive advantage and operational excellence;
- understand the strategic importance of quality management for competitive advantage;
- understand the importance of operating an organization using standards from:
  - the consumer perspective;
  - the buyer's perspective;
  - the producer perspective;
  - the supply chain perspective;
  - the sector perspective;
  - the national perspective.
- describe what is meant by a standard;
- understand the essential logic of improvement and standards.

Introduction

It is difficult to imagine a world without any standards but it did exist. Thankfully our world is now so very different. Can you imagine having to make everything you need so you can actually complete a product? Standards cover almost everything, but let's take as our example the humble 'screw' or bolt fastener. Many products are held together by bolts or screws. They are not extraordinary items – they are extremely common and can be found in products everywhere from battleships and supersonic jets to microwaves and televisions, laptops and gaming consoles, household lights and thousands of other items.

For traditional manufacturing businesses (of the 1800s), small volumes of screws and bolts were needed, and making them yourself was not such a problem – a craftsperson would use their skills to solve the problem and make the few you needed.[1] As demand increased and products started to sell in bigger quantities (and automation meant machinery was available to make bolts and screws in large batches) demand for bolts and screws soared but the variety of types was far too high to make economic sense. The answer was to reduce variation and to introduce a standardized screw.

Inevitably, the profits to be made from a standard product meant that a factory was built to make such screws, and J and W Wyatt in 1760 patented a screw with a standardized thread and began to make them. Standardized screws with standardized sizes and lengths made life a lot easier for people making products and building machines during a period of rapid industrialization in the United Kingdom. At long last a catalogue existed and screws could be bought to order by anyone who needed them. But the Wyatt family soon had competition and more manufacturers emerged to mass produce this type of fastener.

Then along came Joseph Whitworth. A notable engineer, inventor and philanthropist, he passionately collected all the different screws and bolts from all the different factories who had each designed their own standard bolts[2] to offer to the market. By 1841 his research led him to propose the standardization of all fasteners (diameter of bolts, angle of the thread of the bolt and the number of turns for a given length of bolt) and in the 1860s his ideas became mainstream; shortly after that the United States and Europe standardized too. And so the standard was born. This is a product standard but today management standards also support the manufacturing of screws and every other product imaginable. This book concerns management standards and the organizational systems that support effective design and manufacturing of products.

Some would say the standardization breakthrough was not really 'earth shattering' but it was. For the first time, engineers could ask purchasing staff to get them packs of screws/bolts with the certainty that they could be used

Figure 1.1 The common bolt

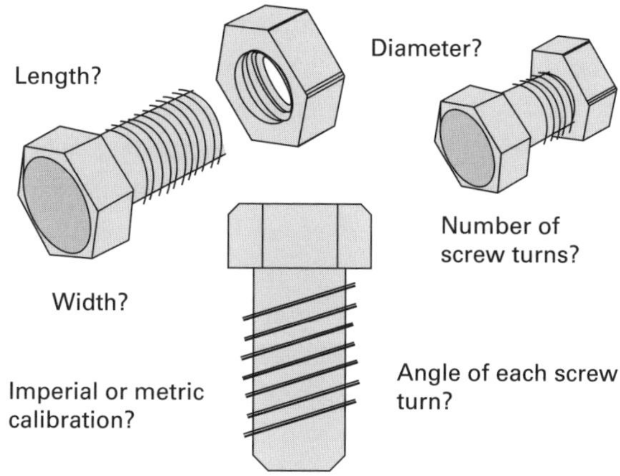

right first time and no production time would be lost trying to correct deficiencies or getting bolts to fit. Engineers could then focus on generating real value for an employer by working with designers to create attractive products.

Standardized fasteners meant they could be selected from a catalogue and only a small amount of inventory of a limited range of fasteners was needed. Product and machinery designers could therefore specify such bolts in the manufacture and assembly of their products and interoperability of these bolts spread. The standardization of '*the humble bolt*' has literally changed the world in the same way that the advent of the automobile would later do, meaning we could travel freely for work and pleasure. Ironically, the automobile relies upon standard products and still has, even with robot welding, a significant number of bolts. Sir Joseph Whitworth (his lifetime of standardization was rewarded with a knighthood!) would have been overjoyed that standardized bolts still exist today in multiple standard formats, and management systems have been standardized too.

What we have explored is a technical standard that has benefited industry worldwide. Whitworth created the 'Whitworth scale' by which bolts were measured and specified for years (the British Standard Whitworth scale for imperial bolts). Today only a few standards exist that span the world, and they are mainly metric now. That is not the point though – standardization of products is great but the standardization of organizational and management systems using the latest known good practices of contemporary management is equally important. The right product made in the right way!

But that isn't where the story ends. Product and technical standards have evolved to help shape the way in which we manage entire businesses and their interactions with customers, suppliers and the consumer, and such standards go far beyond just product manufacturers. Service providers, charities, governments and many other stakeholders and organizations use management standards. This book focuses on management standards and those documents (a standard is a document) that shape the organizational practices used to deliver great products and services. Product and technical standards are great but most people in this world will experience management standards. We must be grateful for product standards and the Kitemark but it is organizational management and international standards that are critical to business and profitability.

The following are some different types of standard:

- The **Kitemark** originated in the UK when in 1903 the British Standards Mark was used to identify safe tramway rails after the entire sector of tram constructors had standardized the specification of rails from 75 different sizes to just five. The British Standards Institution (known as the BSI) owns and operates the Kitemark system (and trademark). The logo certificate is awarded to products and services that meet stringent British and international safety standards – including motorcycle helmets, smoke alarms and suchlike. The Kitemark is awarded for product safety.
- **BS standards** are UK-developed standards and a company that displays the actual standard is declaring the product has been made in accordance with the demands of the named British Standard.
- **BS EN ISO standards** are standards that indicate the product was developed to a European (EN) and International (ISO) standard and was then adopted by the UK as a British Standard (BS). BS EN standards are developed by CEN (the European Standards Body) and then adopted in the UK. These are known generically as international standards.

What is an international management standard?

According to the International Organization for Standardization (known as the ISO), a standard is a document (or family of documents) that provides the requirements, guides, specifications and characteristics that can be used consistently to ensure materials, products, services and organizational processes are 'fit for purpose'.[3]

An ISO standard is typically numbered (unique number for that exact standard) and each management standard is universally applicable (other standards are very specific and apply to certain settings or organizations). The distinguishing number is unique. For ease, there are two major forms of 'standard', the first being a *conformance standard*, which is what companies must conform to by introducing the working practices outlined in the document (such as ISO 9001 for quality or ISO 14001 for environmental management). The second form of document is a *guide* and again will have a unique reference number – such as ISO 9004 – which is a specific guide to help an organization's management to develop and sustain a quality management system. All standards are guides and also have a date associated with the document which denotes whether the standard or guide is the latest revision. So ISO 9001:2015 was released in the year 2015 and replaced ISO 9001:2008 which was operational until 2015. To reiterate, conformance standards denote the exact set of requirements (known often as 'clauses') that a company must meet if it is to gain that certification. Conforming to the standard is validated by audits and assessment by an independent 'third party' company that is competent to do so and award certifications. These third-party companies are independent businesses that specialize in certification and are not part of the ISO organization nor connected to the business that is seeking to be certified.

Failure of a company to meet the requirements of a standard means that it must undertake improvements and investments in working practices to prove it is competent to meet the standard and conform. Once an organization meets a standard and passes the audit, it will be awarded the certificate which will include the ISO logo and number of the standard it has attained (such as ISO 9001:2015). This logo may be displayed on company websites and documentation for as long as the company maintains its independent audits and continues to pass them (maintains conformance). The logo and achievement of certification are causes for celebration for any business and their supply chain partners.

The documented standards – such as ISO 9001 for quality management systems – are available for purchase in every country that adopts the standard (and from the ISO itself) and a company may purchase and implement the standard themselves (this is very feasible yet proper advice tends to create a more effective and quicker certification route) or seek the services of the expert third party who can act as a consultant and also conduct the certification audit. Third-party auditors/certification businesses are known as Certification Bodies (CBs) or Conformity Assessment Bodies (CABs). Companies can, if they choose, buy the standard because it contains a portfolio of good practices and implement every requirement but not seek certification to the standard set by a third-party CAB. Standards are not written for certification but instead to improve an organization with or without certification. For some businesses, certification may be too expensive, but the methods will be introduced as a means of a business's 'self-declaration of conformity'.

Gaining the certificate containing the blue ISO logo for a given standard has many benefits and offers a confidence to those businesses that trade with or interact with the certified company. Benefits extend to customer confidence, supplier confidence, staff engagement with best practices, and systems that support learning and continuous improvement. Quite simply, standards make great business sense and support the strategic direction of an organization by equipping it with the working practices needed to be effective and efficient.

The implicit principles of an ISO standard

Every standard addresses a key aspect of management – ISO 9001 addresses organizational quality management and ISO 14001 focuses on organizational environmental quality but there are many more. Other standards set out the requirements for occupational health, information security, business continuity planning – over 22,000 more ISO standards exist.[4] Each management standard is different (there should not be duplication or overlap of standards) but it is possible to detect some underlying principles. These implicit principles concern effective business management and are similar to the principles of Total Quality Management (TQM).[5] The principles include:

- **Customer focus** – the organization must recognize its customers and stakeholders so that management systems support the profitable generation of value for stakeholders. Value means earning profits and contributing to the sustainability of the economic and environmental ecosystem within which the business operates.
- **Leadership** – this is a deliberate term that reinforces the importance of strategy and executives who lead by example and reinforce the importance of generating value and profits through the use of Total Quality principles within the standard they aspire to achieve.

- **Involvement of the workforce** (and extended workforce) so that every worker is engaged with the standard and actively seeks to improve performance through using the standard and learning how to improve or problem-solve. The best-designed management systems are useless unless you have the 'buy-in' and motivated engagement of the employees.
- **Continuous improvement** using standards to document current business processes and learning, which reduces problems and waste in the organization through problem solving. Problem solving involves all employees (as well as customer and supplier staff) to reduce problems and increase performance. Continuous improvement implies learning how to do the right things, do things right and then to challenge the way things are done to do things better but differently.
- **Process management** is a key principle. Organizations have traditionally been designed around business departments. Each department would serve its own purposes, develop its own measures and try to maximize its own efficiency. But this is isolated thinking – customers need good process management and a process (like quality) is impacted by every department and cannot be owned by any individual department. How can you hold just the quality department only responsible for quality? The quality department is dependent upon the discipline and attention to quality shown by the purchasing of supplied materials that could be substandard and defective. The quality department is dependent on the operations teams and even the design department. So processes such as new product introduction, order fulfilment, quality, safety and the like must all engage with the quality agenda – it is everyone's responsibility. Quality is a process and one that generates value for customers – customers do not care much about departments!
- **Systems thinking** promotes the idea that the business is not the only thing you must think about when making decisions involving standards; a much broader view of the business and its context must be undertaken if all decisions are to be effective. The needs of customers, suppliers and other stakeholders must be incorporated in all business decisions in order to make better decisions that mutually support all businesses in growing and making a better economic return. This type of thinking is very valuable because both customers and suppliers have an interest in members of the supply chain doing well, selling more products and making more profit. This type of thinking lowers risks and generates mutually beneficial relationships so 'the system' and the entire supply chain of trading partners can be optimized through collaborating together.

- **Cross-functional management (CFM)** engagement means managers working together to change business processes. In the past, departmental management was practised (functional management), whereas cross-functional management is related to working across departments so that work is conducted in the most effective and optimized way. It is a practice that promotes customer focus and internal collaboration so that the flow of work and operations is optimized by sharing responsibility for the delivery of outputs that are needed to achieve and maintain the ISO standard. Cross-functional working could include designers, supply chain, operations and engineering teams working together to bring products to market quicker and therefore working across departments to build robust processes.
- **Fact-based management.** Intuition is not very scientific when running a manufacturing business, growing it and protecting the jobs of the workforce. Scientific evidence is needed so that decisions are based on good data. Standards demand data is collected and managers in the business must use this data to make better decisions. Data helps to pinpoint what needs to be improved and what aspects of the standard need to be made more robust. Measurement leads to focused and effective investments in time and resources to improve a business.
- **Mutually beneficial relationships** with customers and suppliers. Any organization will only survive if it works with the right type of customer and supplier businesses. Traditionally, buying organizations saw suppliers and customers as adversaries and would try to win every negotiation to lower supplier prices or raise their own prices to customers. But long-term business is about all companies winning. If just one supplier goes bankrupt because their prices were squeezed to the point of financial collapse, then no one has actually won. Let's face it – without light bulbs or fuses you cannot assemble cars! So, car assemblers will ensure that everyone in the supply chain to the customer and consumer benefits from the trading relationship and over the long term.
- **Risk-based thinking.** More recently, the concept of risk-based thinking has joined the principles of standards writing. This stresses that the systems approach needs to look more deeply at the alternatives for any decision and build procedures that minimize risks in the system and decisions; it promotes the use of analyses to assess the impacts of any decision for the business and its stakeholders.
- **Transparency and communication.** As businesses operate in complex markets and contexts it is important that they invest in internal (staff)

communications and greater communication with its stakeholders (trading partners, local community, government, interest groups, regulators and such like). This principle promotes the view that a system works best when it uses frequent and quality information exchanges to keep all stakeholders informed. The basic idea is that businesses and their stakeholders cannot ever know enough about each other to help and support one another.

These core principles of management standards provide the essential logic of international standards even though they are not formal aspects of the standards development process and how standards are configured (including recent changes to the main sections and language used by each modern standard – known as the High-Level Structure (HLS)). These essential elements were presented because they are also the foundations of business improvement and high-performance business models such as lean or Six Sigma. Management standards therefore help to focus thinking in the same way that Whitworth's system attempted to standardize the 'humble' screw and bolt. The difference is that management standards are voluntary and less prescriptive. Instead of addressing a technical aspect of the bolt (eg length or diameter), the management system standards set generic requirements for the leadership of the business and demand that senior managers demonstrate they are playing an effective role for the leadership of quality (ISO 9001), environmental management (ISO 14001), occupational health and safety (ISO 45001) or any of the ISO management standards in which the business seeks certification.

You now know the underlying good business principles that are embedded within each standard. Standards are used to make businesses better and make great businesses even better. So, before we go any further, we need to explore how businesses get better and how standards can be used to provide foundations for higher performance.

How do standards support high performance and highly reliable organizations?

It is often said that there is a standard for everything, and this is probably true, but before we begin to explore the key standards and how best to introduce/exploit a single standard we need to arm ourselves with more logic: business logic.

Traditionally, business leaders thought superior technology would lead to profits and sustainable competitive advantage over their competitors. Well, that isn't exactly true because technology can be bought on an open market and changes so quickly that any advantage would be short-lived. Some business leaders thought their products were the source of competitive advantage, but sadly it takes only a matter of days before a competitor can buy, strip and copy your products. Even copyright laws do little to protect businesses from infringement. So competitive advantage is less about technology and products and more about the people employed and the processes they manage/the designs of products they invent. People drive improvement and innovation. People are the thinking and delivery capabilities for what a business does, and they are the vital ingredients to sustainable competitive advantage. Interestingly, according to Liker and Meier (2007), the 'world class' manufacturer/vehicle assembler Toyota does not just produce great cars, it also produces great people.[6] The ability to attract and retain great people is probably the reason why Toyota excels in markets such as cars, forklift trucks, lorries, sewing machines and housing to name but a few.

People make businesses work and people work with management standards. Even the best design for a business or product will be ineffective if the people who make it do not care and are not nurtured to be the best they can. The same is true in the world of standards – engaged and innovative staff will embrace standards and make the most of them. Engaged staff will innovate and will be keen to use standards to improve the business and its performance.

One of the lessons you rarely receive at university is a lesson in commercial logic; instead students and early-career managers are left to themselves to make sense of the manufacturing world that they might aspire to manage and lead in the future. Every manager and every student should be equipped with the logic of high-performance and highly reliable manufacturing businesses, so we will now take a couple of pages to review it.

Making sense of how manufacturing (and service) operations are designed to become robust and high-performance businesses relies on the understanding that the traditional fixation with managing for cost minimization incurs a series of business-threatening trade-offs. That is quite a bold statement and some readers will get emotional and angry to hear it. But if a leadership team or management team focus exclusively on lowering costs week after week then they risk damaging their business! Think about it:

- If I lower my costs, I will look to buy from cheaper and less quality-assured suppliers:
  - if the parts used in production are inferior, then more defects will happen and that will push my costs up. I may even have to pay to dispose of the defects too!

- If I lower my costs, I will make in big batches:
  - but the stock I make will go into a warehouse without necessarily having an order for the products. That stops my cash flow. So I am really investing lots of money in slow-moving stock! That is not good for business.
- If I lower my costs, I will invariably treat my workers as automatons:
  - trying to squeeze every second of every minute out of the workers will burn them out over the long term and they may leave for a more enlightened employer. So another way needs to be found as the result of high productivity is the production of lots of stock.

Today's markets mean that customers do not want cheap and defective products either; the people who supply such products will not be around for long. So, what if we start with safety and quality as the basis of managing a business?

- Being safe means staff are protected and all the management processes are in place to protect this most important asset.
- Being proficient in quality means:
  - fewer defects, meaning more productive use of the manufacturing time available;
  - less stress as the business works without problems;
  - a greater ability to work to customer orders one at a time rather than making batches;
  - employees will be engaged in training, auditing and innovating in the workplace.

Now, if safety and quality are under control then doesn't that mean your costs will come down? Of course it does. So here is a lesson: if you exploit everyone for cost minimization then your costs will go up. If you emphasize safety and quality, then the outcome is reduced total costs to your business. The issue is that a safety and quality agenda will lead to no trade-offs. There are very few world-class manufacturing businesses that go to the market to say they are the cheapest! They go to the customer/consumer and promote high quality.

So, let us extend our initial lesson a little and show you more commercial logic – you will then be able to make a better selection of the International Management Standards you will (and may) need to support your business.

The commercial business logic is a process and a journey of mastery. You master safety and quality before moving to higher levels of mastery. So you could say it is like a sport, as you go from basic levels of control to higher proficiency. Each layer adds new skills and builds on the previous level. The levels in business start with safety and morale and this model is an adaptation of the 'sand cone' model proposed by Ferdows and DeMeyer (1990).[7] The model was drawn from their observations of what high-performance businesses (from the food processing sector) had achieved but the same observations hold true of most industries.

Our model starts with a foundation layer of good management practice, which is to engage the workforce and align their interests with the business by setting and communicating the direction of the business and nurturing staff to become experts and work as teams within it to help achieve the goals of the business. The engagement of staff is key to competitive advantage as we have seen, so to work on issues that relate to staff morale is a good place to start. You will also note that it is one of the key principles of the ISO standards too. The best ways to harness the morale of staff is to engage them and set up organizational processes for basic safety management. During this stage it is okay for staff to moan about the organization, its processes and its management – that is fine. Staff who moan are doing so because they still care. Think about it – if you didn't care about something you would not moan! The staff are asking for and contributing to the change agenda of the business. It is when the workforce goes quiet that the problems really start because that workforce doesn't care. Uncaring staff are highly unlikely to be customer focused and to really understand the key principles and behaviours needed to make the most of business standards.

It is not much to ask that staff work in an environment that is engaging and basically safe – so that is the first layer. In effect, staff come to work (if they hate work, they will find ways of avoiding coming to work) and they bring their talent to do a good job – they do not leave it with their coats as they enter the building. So the first stage is to enable that to happen.

Some staff will believe that the workplace is basically safe but when an international standard is applied it can bring an uncomfortable sense of inadequacy. This is the foundation and basic competence level of a system. Workplace safety is often forgotten or taken for granted, which is a pity. Staff that complain should not be ignored – they should be encouraged, and managers should not see this form of behaviour as offensive to them; it is not personal and they should welcome staff input. When managers ignore staff then they stop learning and will not want to change or have any faith that the management team will do anything to help them. In a business, all employees depend upon each other to achieve the highest levels of customer satisfaction and profitably, so it makes sense to invest in the skills for better safety, quality, delivery and flexibility needed to compete.

The high-performance organizational layer model

To be listened to at work is a reasonable request; to be able to work in a safe environment and to act safely in the workplace are equally reasonable. So this is the beginning of the high-performance manufacturing model and its relationship with international standards. The layers are (see Figure 1.2):

1 **Safety and morale level (Layer 1)**. This level promotes engagement of staff and the practices needed to make international standards work effectively. Efforts to influence morale will include teamworking, developing a team identity in each area of the facility, developing the skills needed for interdepartmental working, and basic understanding of

Figure 1.2 The layered approach

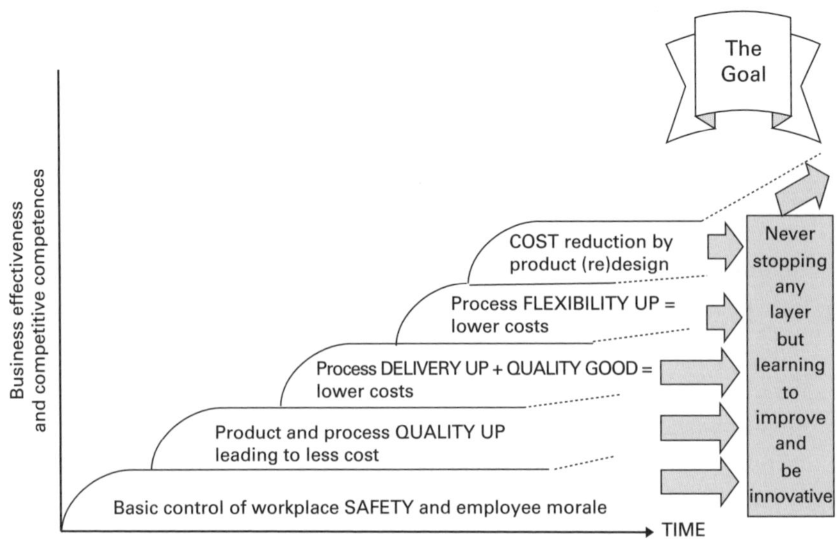

business. The focus on safety management practices, to embed good practice, focuses on the workplace, the factory and the systems/procedures for safety to be conducted effectively and embedded with an engaged and committed workforce. If morale improves, staff will come to work and absenteeism will decline. If safety improves then morale will improve and the costs of harm, litigation and lost production etc will reduce. The outcome of mastering this level (and we do not mean being fully expert but to have mastered the control of these safety- and morale-based processes) is key. If these processes are absent, then trying to deliver products in shorter and shorter times is foolhardy, as the business systems will not cope and inevitably there will be an event that causes a catastrophe.

2. **Quality systems and improvement level (Layer 2)** involves the focusing of staff attention on the processes that regulate quality (from suppliers to end customers) and especially internal quality systems. Just as better morale and safety will lower costs for a business, so too will improved quality. This layer is useful as it links working practices with superior customer performance and positive feedback. The positive feedback heightens pride and morale and reinforces the importance of learning how to increase quality.
3. **Delivery and timeliness level (Layer 3)**. If an organization has good and effective processes that manage the quality of the organization it is then possible to adjust the way in which the business operates to compete on time. Time compression can only happen when quality has been mastered because making a team work closer to actual orders, become more agile or work to just in time requires great quality. Speeding up an unreliable quality process just creates chaos as defects are made quicker and given to customers quicker too! So, when quality is mastered then the management of an organization can question the need for excessive stocks and large batches of product. 'World class' manufacturers know all about time-based competition and offering shorter lead times to increase sales. This level of competence is used to reduce time from order placement to order fulfilment and from initial product design concept to actual product.
4. **The flexibility level (Layer 4)**. With high levels of quality and products moved around the factory/to customers/from suppliers in a timely manner, the next stage is to invest in process flexibility and to make a greater variety of products in the production time available. This layer focuses on reducing equipment changeovers and making the minimal amount of product necessary to support the customer (to order or at a

rate of production that equals the rate of sales). The logic is to produce a greater variety of products and be better able to absorb customer demand without holding excess stocks. Again, the costs of the operation will reduce as flexibility displaces large warehouses of stock and long runs of production batches.

5 **The innovation and cost reduction level** (Layer 5). When manufacturing competence reaches Layer 5, there is almost no waste to remove from operational performance, as every minute of production is used to make perfect products in a timely manner and to customer order. Staff have the skills to enjoy working at this level of performance: teamwork, rapid problem solving, knowledge to proactively manage the process, and an unprecedented closeness to the customer. The focus of the teams is then on removing any further unnecessary costs that inevitably will return to product design and innovation. Such activities will include a renewed attention to design for manufacture, design for environment, mass customization and other activities associated with product innovation (including new technology exploitation).

The layered approach builds a robust and high-performance organizational system that is better able to cope with the demands of modern markets and also supports the phased introduction of multiple ISO standards. It is therefore no surprise that each layer of the model can be supported by international standards that help build the working practices and, because standards are designed by industry experts, performance improvement will result. It can be no surprise then that ISO 9001 Quality Management Systems, ISO 14001 Environmental Systems and ISO 45001 for Occupational Health and Safety are some of the most popular standards in industry today and the bedrock of modern business. The effectiveness of these standards relies entirely on the capability of organizational management, the staff and culture of working together/improvement, and how the standards are exploited for business success. International standards are therefore strategic investments made by a business and not just 'something we do because customers like it'. International standards are the bedrock and skeleton of high-performing and highly reliable businesses.

In summary

International Management Standards are all around us; they support business to improve, they have helped make this book, and, quite literally, standards support good business. They are so embedded in what we do, what we buy and how we are treated, yet we don't often see them. It can be no surprise that rarely do students or professional managers take time to consider what they are and why they are instrumental aspects of world-class business models. This chapter has presented a general history of standards, the contribution of Whitworth in starting a trend to standardize parts (in his case bolts), and the BSI introduction of the Kitemark in the early 1900s. Product standards are important and especially so for product designers. Designers/engineers are one element of the modern manufacturing business and they operate processes that also can be standardized through the introduction of International Management Standards and guidance as well as actual conformance standards that cover all aspects of business operations. The achievement of management standards is equally important to product standards and these help businesses to introduce 'best current known practice' to their organizations.

This chapter has also provided an insight into the principles that are implicitly embedded in every international standard – principles associated with Total Quality Management and an approach to business that believes great people (staff) produce great products using standardized and effective processes. The logic of business has also been explained in terms of the layers of organizational competence needed to engage staff, make more money, reduce costs as an outcome of good management practices, and master the competences needed to compete and gain a competitive advantage in the modern marketplace. This chapter should leave little doubt that international standards are important and exploiting them is good for business, profit, cash flow, security and most of all for customers, employees, suppliers and national governments. The next chapter will explore Total Quality Management and how improving organizational and product quality is the key to generating superior business performance.

Seminar topics and examination questions

Every chapter has been designed to help introduce managers and students to a subject and learn more. We have added seminar topics for students, but these questions are equally relevant to managers who, over a coffee, can think a bit deeper about the issues raised or help with note taking. As you progress through the book, the answers to these questions will become clearer.

- Is it possible to standardize every business? Making chocolate bars is not the same as making nuclear fuel rods, surely?

- What are the most popular standards for organizations and why would a business adopt them? (Think manufacturing.)
- Doesn't the intention of standardization contradict with getting staff to be more innovative?
- Don't standards mean we spend all our time writing reports, being audited, and being too busy documenting things rather than making money by making products/services that we sell?
- Does a good business need standards to prove it is good?
- Are using standards an efficient way for Western governments to protect themselves against cheap imports from developing countries?
- What are the penalties of having poor-quality organizational processes?

Further reading

Websites and pages move all the time – so it is quite difficult to name exact pages for the reader. Instead it is worth searching the ISO website as well as BSI in the UK. There are a few books on the life of Sir Joseph Whitworth but there are many good sources of information on the internet too. There are many sources of information concerning ISO standards which will be explored in later chapters.

Notes

1 Womack, J and Jones, D (1996) *Lean Thinking*, Simon and Schuster, New York
2 There are a number of publications that concern the life of Whitworth and resources such as www.whitworthsociety.org (archived at https://perma.cc/UA9P-R9KX)
3 ISO (nd) Standards [online] Available at: https://www.iso.org/standards.html (archived at https://perma.cc/N7VM-XGAQ) [accessed 17 April 2019]
4 See www.ISO.com (archived at https://perma.cc/N4G8-E3EQ)
5 Deming, W E (1986) *Out of the Crisis*, MIT Press, Massachusetts
6 Liker, J and Meier, D (2007) *Toyota Talent: Developing your people the Toyota way*, McGraw Hill, New York
7 Ferdows, E and DeMeyer, A (1990) Lasting improvements in manufacturing performance: in search of a new theory, *Journal of Operations Management*, 9 (2), pp. 168–84. doi: 10.1016/0272-6963(90)90094-Ts

The evolution of Total Quality Management (TQM) 02

The difference between Total Quality Management (TQM) and an international standard is that TQM develops the cultural aspects of a business and its working practices whereas a management system will develop the processes of an organization (including structuring and measuring them). Hence TQM makes more sense when it comes to the intangible daily work of employees, managers and business leaders as it requires individuals within the organization to collaborate and ISO standards to make sense of what processes and issues staff should collaborate on. ISO standards differ from TQM in that they have a certification requirement and a need for conformance whereas TQM is cultural, less prescriptive and more grounded in the behaviours of staff. TQM and standards are therefore highly compatible, and the principles of TQM underpin every standard.

The key principle of continuous improvement and the methodology, known as the 'plan, do, check and act cycle', can be seen in every requirement to certify to a given standard. Also, just a quick internet search will reveal how most world-class businesses that have pursued TQM have also (in Europe and internationally) adopted international management standards.

LEARNING OBJECTIVES

At the end of this chapter, you should be able to:

- understand the principles of TQM;
- understand the evolution of quality thinking;
- discuss the key ideas generated by each phase of the TQM evolution and name the most influential figures of each era;

- differentiate the features of quality control and quality assurance-based systems and contrast them with TQM business features;
- understand the significance of international standards and how TQM principles are inbuilt to modern standards.

Introduction

Most modern senior managers and business owners aspire to build their organization into a Total Quality Management (TQM) enterprise,[1] and that's not an easy undertaking. It makes perfect business sense as we have already seen – improving business performance is based on the application of effective standards, making it a great place to work too. It also makes perfect sense for organizations that are not motivated by profit but seek to provide the best quality to their customers, patients, citizens, clients, and such like. Therefore, the service aspects of manufactured products (which are increasingly part of the customer offering) need to be integrated with the international standards of the business in order to generate a profit or surplus of income (for charities and social ventures).

Who would not want to be an employee of a business on the journey to becoming a TQM exemplar?

Imagine a business that believes in 'customer-centricity', process management, empowerment of staff to solve problems and 'collaboration' that happens within and beyond the organization. What a great employer and a great place to work. These features of TQM change a drab and boring workplace into a source of pride and fulfilment – where everyone's brains are exercised daily and even if there are no workplace problems to solve, the skills of staff turn towards new innovations and learning. TQM and standards rely on thinking staff, so the Toyota expression stating that 'great people create great products' clearly indicates the importance that the company attaches to people development and their role in sustaining the drive towards total quality and the ultimate perfection of profitable customer service.[2]

Interestingly, the staff employed at Toyota are also comfortable that they really are the business's 'number one asset' and, whilst products may come and go, staff will adapt, learn and relearn new duties over a lifetime of employment for a business that wants to be successful at everything it does.

Highlighting Toyota is no coincidence. The business believes wholeheartedly in TQM and was instrumental in the early experimentation of the approach; Toyota has not yet (after 80 years) achieved perfection but it has never given up. The journey from a business that started to manufacture cars when it had no idea how to make them, to the globally recognized giant it is today has been built on strong TQM principles and the power of staff seeking to make tomorrow a better day.

Where did these influential TQM ideas come from? And how have they changed over time?

These questions are often forgotten when business leaders get caught up in the here and now and forget it is their role to design an organization that is fit to compete. Failing to think about how the business is resourced and aligned with the capability to provide profitable value to customers now and in the future is fatal. Many business managers forget the importance of thinking and reflecting (these are part of the value adding that managers provide) and resort instead to buying 'best practices' that they implement and which fail.[3] Lack of senior management engagement to work out how best to design a quality organization results in little support and direction to the business. Importantly, they miss the enormous respect the leader of an organization gets when they ask others what they think and empower them to deliver the change. Such empowerment is a characteristic of a TQM organization where senior managers engage and show respect to the employees around them. After all, everyone has an interest in the future of the organization and being in a secure workplace that is safe and committed to providing the best quality it possibly can.

It may seem strange to dedicate this chapter to TQM and many readers will equate TQM to international quality management standards (such as the most popular standard ISO 9001) but the arguments presented here concern the design of the organization to implement any standard (occupational health and safety, information security, or any other). The principles of TQM support all standards – not just quality!

The art of TQM is to take a systems view of the organization and its context. Emulating best practices is an interesting discussion point – TQM companies learn from the best practices of others, but their natural tendency is to question why such a practice is important. What does it solve? And how it could be used? This means they will take an idea and work out what the practice was designed to solve and what organizational factors support its sustainability as an improvement if it was to be adopted. The lessons of TQM are hard to grasp at first sight – they are simple so long as it is understood that they are counterintuitive. Hence once understood, people rarely look back and will see the new wisdom as 'common sense' for organizational success. Unfortunately, common sense is not that common, so this chapter was prepared to provide a context and background to international systems and their use for the modern business.

This chapter will present the historical twists and turns that have resulted in modern TQM; the reader must understand that each evolution of thinking did not throw away the ideas that came before it, but built upon the previous stage.

Defining organizational TQM

In management history, organizational quality has evolved to become known as Total Quality. These stages of evolution vary by country but have generically followed (see Figure 2.1):

1. the era of the individual worker (up to 1900s);
2. the era of Quality Control (from 1900s);
3. the era of Quality Assurance (from 1950s);
4. the TQM Era (from 1980s+) and the Western TQM Emulation stage (from 1990s+);
5. the modern complex adaptive system stage (2000s+).

The era of the individual worker

The modern business can trace its roots to the efforts of skilled individuals and engineers who operated in an era of craft production (craft being the term for a person with specialist skill such as a carpenter, mechanic, and such like). These individual workers served apprenticeships to learn their trade and tended to be engaged in bespoke project work with other individual crafts to deliver a finished product. The best example is early car production,[4] where skilled individuals with specialist knowledge to

Figure 2.1 The evolution of TQM

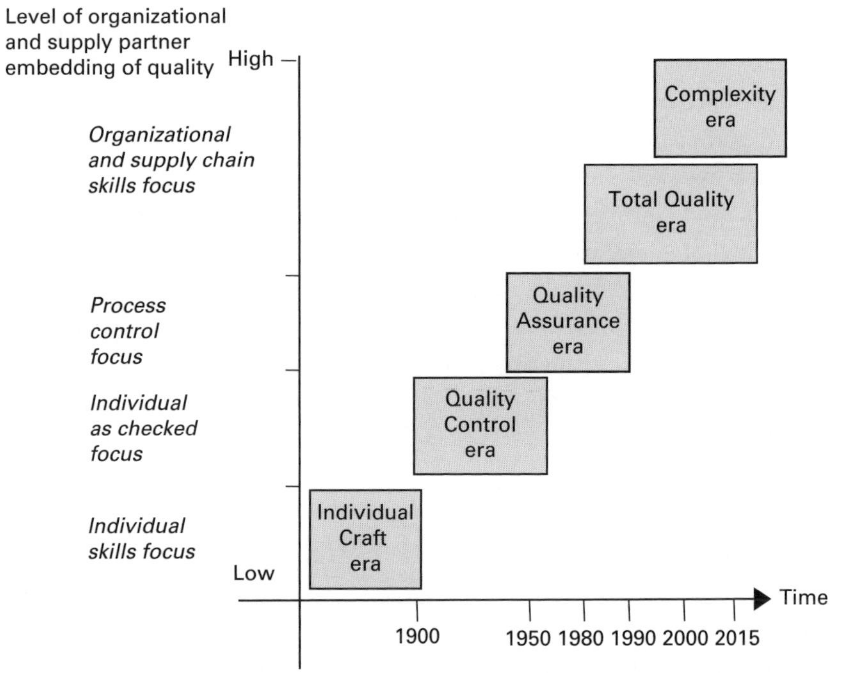

build engines, make wheels, 'fit out' the vehicle upholstery, and so on came together to build a unique vehicle from start to finish, usually for the very wealthy.

In this stereotyped era, every product was personalized and the worker – as a specialist – would use their diagnostic skills to great effect as they solved problems to create a final product, such as fitting the steering to a vehicle that others had built and without a blueprint or reference document. In this era, quality management existed only in the standards imposed by the individual on their own work and possibly the requirements of a comparatively unsophisticated customer (or certainly a customer who lacked power relative to the crafts personnel who built the product).

In this era there were few documented standards and the quality of work was learned through personal skill and personal standards (knowing why things work). This form of production relied heavily on individual and team diagnostic skills and teamworking to achieve a goal – this is ironically what businesses want of employees today! The modern need is for employees that are great team workers, collaborating and sharing knowledge in order to successfully support the organization in achieving its goals. This era may be characterized as the individual knowing what to do as a result of technically 'knowing why' things work and through building relationships with others, so the combined skills of a team are used to create a great-quality solution to a customer need. Industrialization soon de-skilled this type of worker, which meant that the crafts moved to bespoke sectors.

The era of quality control

When the factory system was developed, entire countries began to standardize practices and automate. The role of the worker changed. American ideas (often coming from the Ford Motor Company) were imported by countries in Europe and elsewhere. The new approach to management was based on the operating model of mass production. Mass production, led by General Motors and Ford, was internationalized and built in to subsidiary factories across the world.

The management of the mass production factory was vastly different to that of 'the craft era' and experts with knowledge (engineers were formed into specialist departments) around the making or assembling of products were disconnected from the engineer by this type of job being de-skilled so that any new worker could perform the task. Specialist departments provided centres of expert skills and unquestionable authority; workers were not allowed to improve tasks – this was the role of the specialist. These experts worked in offices and 'the workers' were recruited to conduct tasks that were designed by the specialists. In this period, thought leadership promoted a rational worker who could be motivated by being paid by 'piece rate' to maximize their daily earnings – thus individuals produced as much as possible as fast as possible so they could take home more money![5]

The expert would design tasks and monitor the worker to ensure they conformed (supervisory role). At the heart of the specialists was the quality control department, which housed specialist workers with access to the design documents and product part standards that had been produced by specialist industrial engineers. These documents described every task for every worker's job and every product at every stage of its manufacture. These specialists did not deal with vagueness; their role was clear – to differentiate the good products from the bad products and to determine what would happen next to any defective product. Could the product be reworked to meet the set standard, or would it be scrapped? This question was the exclusive responsibility of the quality control department.

Therefore, engineers designed the job and quality control measured the critical dimensions of the outputs of workers against a design template. If the physical product did not meet standard, then the worker was considered at fault. Ironically, the worker may well have known they were getting close to producing a defect but without the empowerment to stop production and raise the issue they would just plough through. Worse still, some businesses motivated workers by paying them on output produced in a shift and therefore some workers would make as much as they could even if they knew that half of what they produced was defective. If a worker persisted in producing defects they were exited from the business.

Ironically, the modern world still needs good quality control (QC) systems and standards. The documented work procedures are a good discipline but deploying QC responsibilities to the worker rather than preventing the worker from checking their own work (or the preceding operation) ensures only good product is made and reactions to deviations can be undertaken quickly when defects are detected. The modern business still needs standards but operates these within a context of valuing workers and deploying greater empowerment and responsibility to those who do the job, combined with an expectation of continuous learning and continuous improvement. Documented and auditable task standards are a feature of the modern business and are vital for the effective performance of a person when conducting a task.

The era of quality assurance

As the 'company quality specialist' role developed, it was soon apparent that QC was reactive and was not an effective use of such skills; instead, the specialist needed to provide process quality assurance so that monitoring process performance and variations was more important than condemning products that had been made. By moving from the end of a production line to monitoring the process meant that quality specialist and staff could direct their attention to correcting variances in key aspects of the machine so defects were not produced. The era of quality assurance (QA) therefore shortened the time to react to potential problems and again this activity is one that is highly prized by modern businesses. As (QA) grew and greater controls were imposed (in terms of measuring processes and sometimes one in every five products during the production process) learning increased and when reviewed process information could also be used to influence product designs – especially the good practice of design for manufacture.

The ability to learn how to control processes and product designs adds to the QC era and increases the control that can be exercised over business processes through measurement. QA also broke down the barriers that existed between the quality department and the worker. In effect, knowledge was transferred from the specialist to the worker – knowing what needed to be controlled to assure good outputs. The 1960s saw a switch in general management thinking towards greater empowerment and ownership of production by operators[6] and greater levels of responsibility (including quality reporting) were deployed to supervised teams.

The Total Quality Management (TQM) era

The TQM era went further still (in the 1980s for the West – an era which started in the 1950s/60s in Japan) and statistical process control measures were expanded from the process into every aspect of company performance. Measuring processes was fine but the root cause of variation needed to be traced and this was not always in the skill set of the operator or quality professional. These root cause issues could be traced to asset maintenance, the quality of supplier materials, ineffective designs, poor training of human resources and such like. The rate of global competition had risen steadily throughout the 1970s and into the 1980s, which saw the rise in dominance of Japanese producers and brands. The success of these businesses was undoubtedly the result of the attention to quality rather than the 'cost minimization' approach taken by mass producers in the West. At this stage of quality thinking, TQM developed in the West (it was already well established in Japan) and the knowledge of specialists, many of whom went to technical colleges and universities to gain such knowledge, was starting to be shared and deployed to all workers. The Western adoption of Business Process Re-engineering[7] and de-layering of organizations[8] meant that departmental silos were reduced and removed, which did much to promote cross-functional working, though it also led to many job losses of managers with good experience and vital skills.[9]

Knowledge sharing – the sharing of knowledge to solve problems and satisfy customers – is a hallmark of TQM, such that the future prosperity of the organization could be assured through the acceptance of teamwork and high dependency between all members of the organization (as well as its suppliers). Another interesting side-effect is that when specialists get involved with knowledge sharing and transfer, they change their own role to that which is far more value adding and challenging to them as individuals. Let us take the role of the maintenance technician or engineer with TQM – by helping operators and other staff safely understand the way in which a machine works and the little signs that it is deteriorating towards a breakdown, skills are deployed to the operator. The operator is more aware and will call for help when these signs are detected.[10] By the maintenance technician not having to check for signs of failure every day, the organization effectively releases time for these technicians to get involved with bigger and more complex engineering projects such as the redesign of the machine to prevent its failure.

The engagement with projects appeals to the high level of diagnostic skills of the college-trained technician. The same release of time is therefore available to quality specialists who move to facilitators and mentors of staff under TQM, accountants who can help staff understand the costs of failure, supply chain specialists who can help staff understand why frequent deliveries of smaller numbers of materials mean that defects can be spotted more easily and such like. Further still, in the TQM era there was a drive to place quality at the heart of company strategy and move it from a departmental issue to a source of competitive advantage. For some this was to catch up with the Japanese in cars, electronics, consumer goods etc, and for others it was a need to improve performance.

During the 1990s, an approach called 'competitive benchmarking' fuelled industrialists' thirst to learn more about world-class performance and the performance of competitors. Studies repeatedly showed a competitive advantage for the Japanese[11] and this resulted in many visits to see their ways of working and experiments that copied the more visible aspects of their production systems. Sadly, the visible methods did not help Western manufacturers understand the softer and organizational culture-related issues such as leadership that enabled TQM to work effectively and sustain. The period of emulation resulted in copying of best practices, fuelled greatly by the advent of lean production and its reliance on quality as a basis for competitive advantage and superior operational efficiencies. The lean model brought with it a confirmation and prioritization of process flow (from goods in to finished goods) rather than the artificial definitions of departments. In effect, the specialists were brought (often physically) closer to the actual place where production was undertaken and the traditional 'staff office' was eliminated. Breaking down physical walls and integrating specialists with the flow of work sped up decision making and responsiveness and was used to compress time (to improve cash flow and the time from order placement to receipt of the goods/services).

TQM and the modern complex adaptive organization

The latest evolution of TQM has occurred in an era of massive changes to the internet and internet-linked technologies, such as 3D printing and

Industry 4.0. In the modern era, quality remains a strategic priority but now many more manufacturing organizations are adding services to their manufactured products, or leasing them rather than selling to a customer, taking responsibility for the quality of a product from the beginning of its life to the end of its lifecycle/reuse and even printing products to the exact specification of the customer 'on demand' 24 hours a day.[12] The current era is now TQM in an era of the complex and adaptive organization; international management systems remain critically important, as does an expansion in the number and issues posed for product standards when making bespoke products. However, the constancy of management system standards provides a vital structure for businesses to engage with new models of adding value and extracting a profit from consumers in the modern and hyper-competitive environment.[13]

The last stage of TQM goes beyond the emulation of best practices in quality and business standards to create an organization that is best suited to the new 'hyper competitive' environment. The priority for management is to build a business that can cope with a rapidly changeable market environment and use the internet and Internet of Things (IoT) with new technologies to make money and deal with new trading partners and suppliers operating in different continents and in different time zones. The modern competitive environment places an even greater emphasis on the soft aspects of TQM and the process focus of international management standards.

In summary

The evolution of quality thinking is certainly an interesting one and ideas have evolved and are interwoven into the very fabric and design of the modern organization and its use of international standards.[14] The modern era calls for the best aspects of each of the stages of evolution. It requires:

- the diagnostic skills, sharing, and collaborative teamwork involved in craft production;
- the documented standards associated with quality control;
- the techniques for managing processes and identifying variations in performance of quality assurance as well as the release of experts for greater levels of project work;
- the learning and innovation processes of modern TQM.

Why look back into history?

The remainder of this chapter will review the developmental phase of TQM and the figures that have influenced TQM thinking since the 1940s. These figures reached a critical mass in the 1960s and 1970s in Japan, and the 1980s in the United States and Europe. An understanding of the historical development of TQM is important for modern business managers and those professionals seeking to build a resilient and competitive business. Today's systems and standards have evolved and are underpinned by the core principles of TQM. Even though international standards will guide you in how to build a robust management system, the principles of TQM will provide insight into the values and leadership issues that need to be foremost in your mind. To repeat an important message from the previous chapter, there are a number of key TQM principles that have endured over time; it will become quite obvious that ideas came from the ideas of the gurus Dr Deming and Dr Juran. Originally there were just eight key principles of TQM:

Customer focus.

Leadership.

Involvement of people.

Process approach.

Systems approach to management.

Continual improvement.

Factual approach to decision making.

Mutually beneficial supplier relationships.

Modern additions:

Risk-based thinking.

Transparency and communications.

The reason for repeating this lesson is important and the eight principles used to be known as CLIPS CFM (the first letter of each principle). The eight old principles are therefore design aids that help senior management (plus the new risk-based thinking and transparency). In summary, the principles demand that an effective business always remains focused on its customers; customers place orders, they drive cash flow and determine the long-term success of the business. Leadership – rather than management – is a key principle and is needed to drive the quality agenda throughout the organization. It is important that the most senior management of any business 'walks the talk' and reinforces the application of quality daily as well as showing the direction of change needed to keep up with customers and to grow the business. Customer focus and leadership are worthy activities but the most progress is made when every member of the organization (and its supplier and customer organizations) is engaged, well trained and actively seeking improvements as simple changes and as the result of innovative transformations. It is important to note that the involvement of people goes well beyond specialists and includes everyone.

Traditionally, every employee worked for a department and their loyalty remained in that department with others who were trained and thought the same way. But customers rarely care about departments – they want products and/or services. Products and services are the result of departments coming together to satisfy the customer; purchasing and supply chain, operations, quality, distribution, and customer services are all dependent upon each other when satisfying customers. Therefore, great products and services come from collaborations and following the process of designing products for markets and from the fulfilment (delivery of customer satisfaction) of customer demand. This collaboration concerns the process of providing great products and services – 'process thinking' in short. Processes generate satisfied customers (internal or external), loyalty and profits. So engaged people who are working together to deliver customer value must focus on the process and its improvement.

Processes are linked beyond the organization too. Customers and suppliers do not stand still and neither does the competition. The external environment changes constantly and new laws are introduced, pressure groups add new constraints (including exposing poor company performance – using the internet to send this message globally and instantly) and businesses need to react or pre-empt such changes. Therefore, any TQM business will assess these changes and how they impact on the business and its relationship with others; senior managers will use this system approach within the business to promote dependencies between staff so that change requirements can be seen from multiple stakeholder perspectives. This design principle concerns thinking about the organization in its totality.

Continual improvement means making tomorrow a better day and is a facet of the learning organization. Improvement is the result of learning about problems and taking a proactive risk-based approach to solving problems that have not yet happened. Think about it – it does make sense that your staff are building systems that stop a potential problem from happening.

To prevent an engaged workforce and every member of staff from just randomly improving in an unfocused manner, data and facts are needed. Such data is a justification for change and may include the number of defects produced per hour and that certain hours generate more defects than others. This would prompt greater investigation – does the worker get tired at these times? For example, a surgeon operating late at night might be naturally tired, or perhaps machinery is running too hot, which would prompt more data to be safely collected on the running temperatures of the machinery. Data leads to collation and this can be converted into meaningful management information when workers study it and make sense of what is happening.

So, it is important to substitute opinions for facts so that a convincing argument can be built for change and improvement to happen.

The final of the long-established design principles is mutually beneficial relationships with suppliers (and this should include customers and other stakeholders such as local communities). Mutually beneficial means a two-way series of benefits. Collaboration beyond the organization is key – it makes the systems approach work. In early history, suppliers were treated with suspicion and viewed as self-interested, which meant a supplier would try to exploit the organization if they could put their prices up. This suspicion is strange because both businesses need each other. The organization needs materials and services to satisfy the end customer and consumer, and the supplier wants to sell their materials or services to the organization.

Just as investing in employees is a good move, then so too is developing collaboration and trust with the trading partner of a business. Every organization can seek to learn more about the final customer. Having significant knowledge about what customers want is key to solving their needs, and solving needs is the very basis of TQM. Collaborating is a preferred approach because it involves sharing and working together as well as sharing risks between organizations. Collaboration is also important if the quality methods and approaches (even staff) are to be shared between trading businesses for the benefit of them both. This should be extended to customer organizations and others such as environmental pressure groups, trade unions, banks and other businesses that have a stake in the organization doing well. Risk-based thinking ensures great decision making and high levels of transparency. The eight old principles and two modern ones are linked together and create a system that supports the layered approach to business performance improvement. They are simple to understand but quite difficult to apply. Companies such as Toyota and others have continued to apply the principles decades after first employing them. They are the glue that binds international standards into a coherent management system and come from many innovators in TQM history.

The four stages of TQM evolution

There are four discernible periods in the development of TQM in the West:

1 The Second World War and its aftermath in the 1950s and 1960s – a period dominated by Early American models of TQM (ironically these Early Americans were to lead working practices in Japan).
2 The popularization of TQM by Japanese businesses and academics – an era of all-staff engagement, with applied tools and techniques for employees (1970s and 1980s).
3 The contribution of American strategists (1980s to 1990s).
4 The company-wide rejuvenation era (1990s to date).

Each stage of evolution has added new dimensions and themes that define modern TQM and its continued relevance to businesses of all shapes and sizes, services or production, charities, governments and the emergency services. There is not a single business that can ignore TQM and its benefits.

TQM and the aftermath of the Second World War

The period of the early 1900s witnessed the rise of the large-scale industrial organization and the establishment of the 'quality department'. From the 1920s onwards, the quality movement was dominated by checking that the work designs of engineers were being adhered to by workers and that QC routines were used to measure the work. Not much happened in terms of management thinking from the 1920s until the 'shock' of the Second World War meant that factories needed to be converted to support different war efforts.

The post-war period of rebuilding was a landmark period in quality thinking. When the United States joined the war, the homeland factories became devoid of the male workers that were dominant in the factory systems, and the war supply chains, making tanks, planes and munitions, were short of qualified labour. Importantly, ship building was used as a proving ground for better training of novice workers using a government-led initiative called the Training Within Industry (TWI) programme – a programme to help equip new workers to become skilled to produce munitions and equipment in factories converted to make wartime products.

The TWI programme trains workers to build quality working into daily routines. It was so successful that it can be no surprise that companies still use the approach today. Even though after the war the US government failed to sustain TWI, they did export it to Japan during the reconstruction of that country after the devastation of the war. The TWI approach is used widely by world-class businesses to ensure workers are competent, and even today someone somewhere will be having training using this approach.

The rebuilding of Japan under General McArthur crystallized quality thinking in Japan and proved fertile ground for TQM to develop. Japanese industry had been stripped of its labour, machinery had been removed, and former trading groups of manufacturers had been disbanded. The country was in desperate need to make the most of every material and every second of human effort it could. Before the war, Japanese industry had struggled and had been 'closed' to the world, with limited international trade; the reconstruction was led by many notable Americans, who shaped early TQM thinking.

The key figures in the first phase of TQM were Americans, but the irony is that they gained fame for their efforts with Japanese companies. These individuals were known as the 'Early Americans' and were all tutored by the statistician Walter Shewhart. Shewhart's thinking and his 'science' of improvement were taught to others he worked with and mentored – and these individuals were to become the most influential TQM figures the world has ever seen: Dr William Edwards Deming and Dr Joseph Juran.

Although Deming gets a great deal more attention in the academic literature (and reverence from Japanese business), Juran has an equally interesting and effective approach to managing quality. Why Deming would receive greater accolades than Juran was once explained by the US operations management guru Doc Hall, who proposed that Deming was heralded (by the Japanese) as a saviour of industrial performance and it was, as Doc Hall explained in his inimitable Texan accent, quite simply that 'Deming was the first off the plane in Japan!'

W Edwards Deming

W Edwards Deming was a physically imposing character with a dry sense of humour and a sarcastic twist to his words. It was also patently obvious that he did not tolerate fools gladly (most YouTube videos will confirm his sharp tongue).

Deming was a statistician – just like his mentor and his good friend Juran – but he offered the world a lot more than a firm belief in data and statistically measuring processes; if this was his only contribution, he would be a renowned QA expert only! But he was actually a devotee of understanding, managing, and acting upon process variation. Rather than look at the historical development of Deming's thoughts it is probably better to provide a story that unites his thinking. The story is actually very interesting. Deming was a character who believed in *going to the workplace* (this is known as going to the 'gemba' in Japan[15]) and as such he did not actually publish his thinking until the mid-1980s, even though he had been influencing practice and training Japanese managers since the end of the Second World War. His work is very much worth the writing and today his books remain very relevant. The Deming Prize, based on his principles of TQM and his philosophy, is still the most revered Quality Award in Japan and cherished by those who hold it in its different forms.

To understand Deming as a quality guru, you must first understand his 14 points of management and his fundamental beliefs. He believed wholeheartedly in the company-wide integration of quality in strategy as well as daily activities of all workers, a respect for all individuals, continuous improvement and a keen attention to the psychology of managing change, the managerial-level understanding of variation, and a systems approach to business. In fact, Deming epitomizes the eight principles of TQM we discussed earlier. Whilst he promoted his 14 points of management that would lead to a TQM organization, the company management teams that he has taught have, over the generations, remained faithful to his principles and have handed the challenge from one generation of business leaders to the next.[16]

The paraphrased 14 points of management:

1. Create constancy of purpose for your business and build a 'quality first' priority for everything the business does.
2. Adopt a philosophy of prevention rather than spending time sorting out problems or spending money on excessive forms of inspection.
3. Cease mass inspection and move away from condemning batches of production.
4. Select a few suppliers based on quality (quality supplies are better than cheap materials that have a lower standard of quality assurance).
5. Constantly improve systems and workers on a daily basis and in line with the direction set by the organization and its customers.

6 Institute worker training in Statistical Process Control (SPC) so variation is monitored and will prompt a speedy reaction to prevent the production of defects.

7 Instil leadership among supervisors – and give empowerment to those who are closest in controlling any process.

8 Eliminate fear among employees so that they will feel comfortable to report (rather than hide) mistakes or under-performance

9 Eliminate barriers between departments because processes are more important than departments – processes deliver customer value and require departmental staff to collaborate to deliver this form of value.

10 Eliminate slogans: posters that try to urge people to think about quality are not as powerful as behaving and reinforcing quality by actions and good leadership. Posters on walls rarely win 'hearts and minds' or lead to meaningful change.

11 Remove numerical quotas: prioritizing the quantity produced in a shift or a day leads to sacrifices of quality in order to 'make the numbers'.

12 Enhance worker pride so that staff feel a positive glow when they achieve even modest improvements.

13 Institute a vigorous quality improvement education programme so that staff are constantly reminded that quality is important and are trained/equipped in the methods and logic to enact better quality.

14 Implement these 13 points without delay (Just do it!) and when you think you have 'done them' please go back and do them all again.

The 14 points are very big statements of profound insights into organizational management. But Deming did not stop there; he added more ideas for managers. The next one is known by many names but most popularly as the Deming Cycle or the PDCA cycle. The logic is very simple – managers must follow a process for systematic improvement:

1 Plan (P)

2 Do (D)

3 Check (C)

4 Act (A)

The PDCA cycle is associated with a process of innovation and standardization; the new working practice is documented, working procedures are changed and the innovation is sustained. Often, the PDCA cycle is taught and depicted as a ball gradually working its way uphill. At each rotation of the ball (the resolution of a workplace error and problem), improved quality, productivity and efficiency would result. The standardized solution is then introduced and is often depicted as a wedge that prevents the ball from rolling back – this is the essence of the PDCA cycle. The team must then find the next issue and start the ball rolling again.

The PDCA cycle and improvement

So, Deming provided the first systematic (and unending) process of improvement driven from the identification and resolution of variance in manufacturing and management processes of the organization. In effect, Deming had started to generate a manufacturing learning organization. Using the PDCA, teams of staff with mixed skills, many drawn from any role directly impacted by the problem, would:

- **Plan:** The team identify a goal or purpose of improvement. They reflect on the problem and its impact and formulate a theory of what is happening. The planning phase also includes the definition of measures of success by the team. Armed with these 'success measures' – of what good looks like – it is possible to establish a plan of action to achieve these goals and measures of a good project. Throughout this process, facts and information are collected and reviewed by the team. An example would be the plan to reduce working accidents and incidents in a certain area of an organization.
- **Do:** The team (and always the team – not individuals as this weakens ownership of the improvement solution and adherence to the new improvement standard) organize themselves to implement the component parts of the plan, sometimes but not always against a timeline or project chart. The team could – for example – begin a new layout of an office or production space as a result of the planning process and the key measure of accidents and near-miss reports as a result of a dirty, dark and dangerous workspace.
- **Check:** The check stage involves looking at the outcomes of the improvement process and the stages of changing – in our case – the layout and processes of safety in the physical area concerned. The team are looking to test the quality of their thinking in the planning stage and to look for signs and measures of progress. This is a learning stage and all team members need to be involved to see whether the improvements have made a difference, made things worse, or that nothing has changed in

measured performance. The team can then reason as to why the outcome has been the one achieved. This will lead to new identification of problem issues; perhaps the outcome measure of underachievement is less to do with the physical environment and more to do with unsafe behaviours at this point or unsafe equipment. This is the phase of any project that, even today, most businesses are bad at: reflecting and learning and going back to our initial assumptions and measures. If we do not do this activity, then how will our teams ever learn or really engage with meaningful improvement?

- **Act:** The team must now reflect on their learning and challenge themselves to find other parts of the organization that could benefit from their knowledge. This starts a process that is one of company-wide standardization (the SDCA process). So perhaps they identify that the reception area of the organization is equally cluttered and potentially hazardous to staff – they would then go to the teams in that area and explain what they had done so that the solutions (such as the use of floor-standing document holders, wall charts, colour-coded inventory etc) could be shared with the reception team, who may either take the ideas and implement them or – more robustly – begin their own PDCA cycle.

The PDCA cycle is repeated continuously and at all levels of, and beyond, the organization, to include customers, suppliers and external stakeholders. In truth, all parts of any organization cannot practise PDCA often enough. Deming was not only a fan and advocate – he would severely chastise managers for not using it to learn and solve their own problems. Deming loved using facts and numbers to provide a convincing argument for change, and that a convincing argument showing the improvement of a process had occurred. To some extent, Deming would see poor PDCA as poor management, and approaching him to ask for answers to problems would anger him as he saw this as the team role and disrespectful to him. He did not work in the area, he did not know how many accidents happened and where they took place, and he didn't invent solutions – that was the team's role. A harsh but fair approach – he was a firm believer in the involvement of all staff and breaking down departmental barriers as you will see.

Deming's deadly diseases

Deming was never one to 'run away' from controversy so he also offered the world his deadly diseases of what does not make a TQM business. Many of these ideas – despite their age – were prophesies well before their time.

The Deming deadly diseases:

- Lack of constancy of purpose resulting from senior management constantly switching priorities, giving the perception that the organization lacks a commitment to quality (workers see managers as jumping to whichever 'flavour of the month' they care to emphasize). Deming expected a constant commitment to 'the quality case' for better business. In the 1980s this constant copying of 'best practices' (that usually failed) was a great example of this lack of constancy!
- Emphasis on short-term profits so as to avoid and neglect long-range planning (setting the direction for quality improvement).
- Performance evaluations, such as individualistic setting of objectives through mechanical processes of Management by Objectives (MBO). For those unfamiliar with MBO, this is a 1950s concept of taking the goals of an organization – such as to improve customer satisfaction – then decomposing them to the next level in the organization below the directors. Sadly this method forgets the business is a series of processes and treats individual managers as responsible for or capable of understanding what needs to be done. So directors may say we need to improve customer satisfaction – the senior manager may say that customers want online access to product catalogues. Each senior manager would then look at the people who report to them and demand, 'You need to implement a website product catalogue' and would measure the subordinate as they did so. In a year, a formal review would take place where the subordinate would be tested to see if they had implemented the solution. Guess what? You may find they do not want electronic product catalogues at all and a physical print-out could be supplied with any product. The system is wrong and managers should not determine the answers. A good manager will get their team to do the research and come back with solutions or teams will not learn and will always go back to the manager to do this for them! Bizarre… no learning and frustrated management, and that's without the possibility that the subordinate actually didn't implement the change needed, so you had lost a year without finding that underperformance out!
- Executive mobility, where senior directors frequently leave the business and new leaders take over only to change the organization's direction and commitment to quality.
- Emphasis of visible figures alone and insufficient attention to growing cultural skills, improvement skills and investments in trust and collaboration.

- Excessive medical costs from workers who repeat simple tasks over and over again (resulting in repetitive strains and injuries) rather than multi-skilled workers who are flexible enough to conduct a number of tasks within a single shift.
- Excessive warranty costs as customers feel comfortable to request recompense for faulty goods.

The deadly diseases also included references to the unfounded belief that automation would transform a manufacturing business. However, if the best technology in the world is operated by unskilled workers it will result in suboptimal performance. Deming was quick to condemn managers who believed their organization's problems were unique and somehow different to those of other organizations. He was quick to criticize the over-reliance of businesses on quality control departments and audits as well as managers being slaves to computers rather than testing data themselves so that they could determine the facts and sequence of events that led to defects and poor quality. He also criticized schools for failing to equip young adults with quality and problem-solving skills. He reserved particular criticism for organizational managers who – through poor planning and execution as well as poor thinking – allowed quality practices to experience 'false starts' whereby great practice is implemented without the necessary understanding, supporting structures and worker conditioning needed to make it a success. These criticisms – as you will see – are shared with his colleague Dr Juran.

And naturally, as previously stated, Deming was a fervent believer in applying statistical methods to visualize process variation and when the process has moved into a zone whereby the lower or the upper control limit specification has been or is likely to be compromised and the point at which the process would need to be stopped and corrected. To Deming, TQM had a high level of quality assurance of the process using statistics and these facts help managers to make better decisions with their teams. A belief in statistical policing of key control items and key process indicators was shared by Dr Joseph Juran.

Dr Joseph Juran

Juran holds many of the answers to the problems facing today's manufacturing leaders. Like Deming, Juran's ideas were promoted by the Japanese Union of Scientists and Engineers (JUSE) but his ideas were at slight variance to Deming's. Juran favoured a much more management-led approach.

The first learning that Juran gave to the world was to stop thinking of customers as purely external to the organization – internal customers exist too! So, he promoted his idea that internal customers exist and are, in many ways, as important as the person who finally pays for goods and services. This concept is like Deming's view that departmental boundaries should be broken down so that teams can focus on process quality within and beyond a team. The customer concept is very powerful and is fundamental to business today – in effect every person has a supplier and a customer within the organization and when you recognize that you are part of a process, quality improvement becomes so much easier and more meaningful. That's because people understand the needs of the next person in the process.

Every business has scarce resources and another of Juran's contributions was to establish a quality council to guide and focus the improvement process of allocating improvement efforts and coordinating activities on a company-wide basis. Whilst Deming writes advice *for* managers, Juran takes a very managerial approach to top-down quality and stresses that all management teams must remain focused. The main mechanism for remaining focused and goal setting for the organization is the establishment of a quality council. And this brings us to his next point – a quality council should be familiar with and well practised in what he calls The Quality Trilogy.[17]

The Quality Trilogy is a high-level learning triangle of activities:[18]

1 **The process of quality planning** (step one), during which stage managers collect a lot of facts and information about the business and its range of issues (customer facing, internal, supplier related and such like). The most important issues are those of business competitiveness, profitability, costs, wastes and improving cash flow. So, you may be thinking this is quite like Deming; Juran agrees with him in principle, but wants a formalized and regular process to be conducted by managers and senior managers in parallel to other improvement activities. He states this process must focus on profitable customer satisfaction. He also was not a person who tolerated talk without action and was stern with managers who did this – he regarded it as keeping the *status quo* and that was not good for businesses in a modern and dynamic world. To avoid random change, Juran proposed managers must adopt the Pareto principle.[19] This is a fantastic method and is a lot of fun too. He wanted managers to focus on the vital few breakthrough business improvements that would generate the most returns; after all, most businesses cannot do everything so his view is you do the most important thing for your business. The Pareto principle states that 20 per cent of the total number of projects you would want to do will solve 80 per cent of the issues you face when your

organization is attempting to deliver great customer satisfaction or patient excellence.[20] These are the vital few projects managers need to promote (a prioritization process to provide a logical assignment of scarce staff and resources).

2 **Quality improvement** (doing the improvement) focused on key organizational issues often known as quality 'showstoppers', permanently fixes chronic organizational issues (not trivial ones). The improvement process is like the Deming cycle stage of **Do** – and once done and reflection has occurred, Juran demanded the final stage of **Control**.

3 **Quality control** is the stage that involves creating standards and measures (especially statistical process control charts) so that the issue can be monitored to see if it re-occurs. If thc issue is solved, then – after more rounds of quality planning – the team can move on to more important business issues.

Understandably, Juran required the senior management of an organization to go back and do it again ready for the next round of key challenges and breakthroughs. Juran was very much a management-focused author and his ideas were provided to promote quality at this level in the business. Again (like Deming) he disliked departmental management and management by objectives – which were a legacy of the mass-production factory and task-based organizations that were ignorant of processes.

Although Juran does not use the PDCA cycle of Deming, he does offer his own view, which is relatively similar in focus and process, but Juran sees the improvement cycle as a means of moving from symptoms to finding a cause and ideally providing a cost of that loss. The Juran improvement cycle is:

1 getting staff together to systematically focus on a problem and challenge their thinking and analyses to go from **Symptom** to **Cause**;

2 then switching from problem solving to finding solutions to go from **Cause** to **Remedy**.

His view was that all employees should engage with quality and that quality should go well beyond the workplace into every office as well as to the organizations that we now know as the supply chain. In his view, 'Big Quality' includes all business stakeholders and a much wider definition of the term 'customer'. His words are particularly relevant to patients of healthcare systems and the variety of different patients that exist. Juran would expect and demand that we understand their needs and their families in order to build products and services that are fit for purpose.

Juran's journey junctions

Juran offers an interesting insight into how TQM organizations evolve and how customer-centric organizations build businesses that are focused on excellence and customer satisfaction and start with product and service designs. The process is very interesting and starts by working out the value a product or service offers and getting the delivery of that product or service right before it is made for the first time and for an actual customer order:

Juran's nine journey junctions:

1. Identify the customer – this is the primary activity of leaders, managers and teams (especially involving engineers, product designers and process teams at this stage of 'awareness').
2. Determine needs – so that an appropriate solution of value to the customer can be designed and offered. Thinking about solutions prevents businesses and organizations from drifting into the comfort zone of just making a better and slightly improved product. Think of the mobile or cell phone and its evolution – it has solved many more customer needs than just talking to someone.
3. Translate customer needs into our language – the way in which customers speak (or do not speak) about quality and solutions is interesting. We rarely ask a car salesperson if the car is safe because we expect it. Customers will also tell you of their other expectations quite openly – such as 'I want peace of mind about the car's reliability and your quality processes' (which can be translated as 'I would expect to get a comprehensive multi-year warranty as standard'). It is interesting that Juran proposed the study and listening to the customer well before the organization makes the first product or service.
4. Develop the product/service to meet the needs of the customer only once these needs are expressly known and assess how the product/service will optimize these in the offering to customers.
5. Optimize product features using a systematic approach to engineering and design and use these features to determine the most appropriate way of making the product or service. This latter point is highly relevant to healthcare processes and equipment design.
6. Develop a capable process that can produce the product or service to the required standards and within specifications.

7. Optimize the process so that there is no waste or potential for quality losses to occur and so that customers get the best experience of the organization.[21]
8. Prove the process using tests and analyses to determine the robustness of the process and satisfy the internal commissioning quality checks that should be conducted. Finally,
9. Transfer the process to an operational status where it is now ready to satisfy customers and help generate money and customer satisfaction for profit-motivated organizations.

To many observers, Juran offers us a similar perspective on quality as Deming. This is unsurprising really, given they trained together, but on more careful inspection, there are differences between these two influential figures and elements of both approaches are to be found in modern 'best practices'.

Juran's big hopes

The benefit of a historical account of TQM and its evolution is that the reader can see how these early ideas have shaped modern business and have either succeeded or failed to be realized. Juran proposed that quality would become devolved to process managers and this would change the role and the type of quality manager needed (and in a way he and Deming allocated quality responsibilities to the staff that did each task within each process). He saw widespread management promotion of quality, which has also manifested as international prizes and awards in operation. He also predicted that professional examinations would become widespread for managers; this too has happened. He even saw national institutions adopting a TQM approach and these organizations adopting and promoting quality. He identified the legal system and local and national governments as embracing quality and this movement has also begun.

He also proposed that the average person would engage with the quality agenda and saw key quality words entering our daily speech and language. We talk about root causes, excellence, and from this we like to know that what we are buying is of good quality. Continuous improvement is expected and discussed in most organizations and by their customers.

The two of Juran's predictions that have yet to be fulfilled are the development of national indexes to measure quality (which has yet to make meaningful progress as governments still prefer crude measures of productivity and gross value added) and the teaching of quality schools. Certainly, the education system has engaged with this activity, but it is far less widespread than Juran would have hoped. The interesting discussion to have is what the world would look like if the very youngest students were 'quality aware' and could have a voice in designing the services they use.[22]

In summary

The first phase of TQM was therefore led by American thinkers who were working with eager-to-learn Japanese managers. These ideas were readily accepted by Japanese academics and professional bodies (JUSE) and adopted by industrialists as a means of driving business and productivity improvements. The first phase of TQM is critical and Deming and Juran's contribution of the management principles has shaped modern thinking. As a broad summary, these Early Americans were writing advice for managers on how to design organizational systems that support high quality and TQM. This level of any business is one of the most difficult to work with and the reason is simple – directors tend to show where a business should head and operational teams deliver the products and services that satisfy customers, but managers have to work together to change systems and get processes right.[23] It is the management grade of staff that determines the rate of change for an organization and often these managers find change quite difficult to deal with. But great processes do not work without a good and collaborative middle management team.

The next phase of TQM development will take a slightly different route and focus on the teams and management levels of a business.[24]

The popularization of TQM by the Japanese – TQM for the masses

Unlike today, when most management ideas are claimed to be a 'best practice' and implemented by organizational managers without a second thought, the Japanese spent a lot of time reflecting on the meaning of quality, how to engender a sense of pride in work, and which methods should be vigorously promoted to employees.[25] The second era of TQM was characterized by the development of tools and techniques that could be used by all employees to engage with the TQM agenda. A number of key figures emerged during this time and they will now be discussed. Interestingly, these figures have only added small methods to the toolbox of quality improvement in practice, but their impact has been profound as these methods have been successfully exported around the world!

Dr Kauro Ishikawa

Dr Ishikawa is known as the champion of tools for quality for all employees. He compiled a collection of QC tools and his view was that these tools would solve most of the problems encountered in the modern workplace – and he is yet to be proved wrong! He argued that the tools could be used by different levels and grades of staff in a business, from management to specialists (such as engineers, supply chain specialists and quality specialists) to teams operating processes.

The Ishikawa toolbox

The tools that were compiled by Ishikawa[26] represent a portfolio of techniques that individually provide some insights into a problem that requires to be solved – but collectively and used as a process to help find root cause solutions that can radically transform performance and improve it.

The Ishikawa Seven Old Tools (Adapted from Ishikawa, 1991[27]):

1. **Fishbone diagram** – so named because it looks like a fish but is a means of structuring the issues and potential root causes associated with a process problem or general issue. So the effect could be poor-quality products arriving at a customer organization. The fishbone is usually broken down into themes such as methods, machinery, materials, measures, management, manpower (more appropriately expressed as 'people') and Mother Nature (which actually means issues with the workplace and operating environment). Please see Figure 2.2 on page 46, but basically the effect of the problem (poor quality arriving with the customer) is written in the box by the fish head. The potential reasons (causes) of this effect are assigned to a theme and then presented on the diagram so a damage in transit could be due to poor loading of the vehicle (a methods issue), poor packing at assembly (a method issue), or by an item of equipment (machinery related or others).
2. **Tally chart** – a means of counting the frequency of an event or many different forms of event. The purpose is to take an issue – such as a loading issue, a packaging issue, etc – and count each time it has occurred. The addition of numbers to each failure means the vital few can be detected more easily. So managers and teams can spend time on the more important issues that happen most frequently.

3 **The histogram** – the histogram shows the data from the tally chart in terms of cause and the number of times it was observed or recorded. The graph shows a distribution of events. This is more meaningful than just reading a tally chart but not yet sufficient for effective allocation of resources to solve the issue.

4 **The Pareto chart** reorders the histogram from highest frequency of cause to lowest. There is a belief in management thinking that 80 per cent of all the times a failure happens (poor quality at the customer) result from only 20 per cent of the number of causes – so most problems are caused by poor loading and not the lower-frequency issue of poor packaging. Thus the Pareto tells the team what to concentrate on – say there are 10 identified causes of problems, the rule says that two of them should account for 80 per cent of the times a failure happens. So if there are 200 failures then the top two causes – say loading and packing – should account for 160 out of the 200. When you regard problems as biased towards just a few major causes then this makes problem solving more focused and productive. Solve the top 20 per cent of possible causes and you will release huge amounts of benefit! Solving something that happens very rarely may well be good and you should do it, but if you have limited resources then go for the frequent ones!

5 **The XY chart** is used to test hypotheses – such as loading errors increase as the number of pallets on a vehicle increase. This can be shown to be true or not. The XY chart is really useful, especially when looking at failures over capacity of the process, defects and factory temperature – it can be used to test most issues.

6 **The statistical or process control chart** shows variation over time and whether the variation is in control or not. Variation is to be expected but wild variation or a gradual creep towards instability or a known calibration which makes the product a defect must be controlled and it is good to use quality assurance and process management to visualize it using this chart.

7 **The flow chart** is a visual aid that helps staff to write a procedure to control a process. The chart will have boxes for activities and questions that allow the user to work towards the correct solution.

There is logic to the use of the tools which goes from a basic refining of the problem to identifying a cause, then the collection of data that can be developed into information of use when refining the problem, and then solving or monitoring it. The best way to use the Ishikawa tools is (Figure 2.2):

Figure 2.2 Working through the Seven Old Tools of Ishikawa

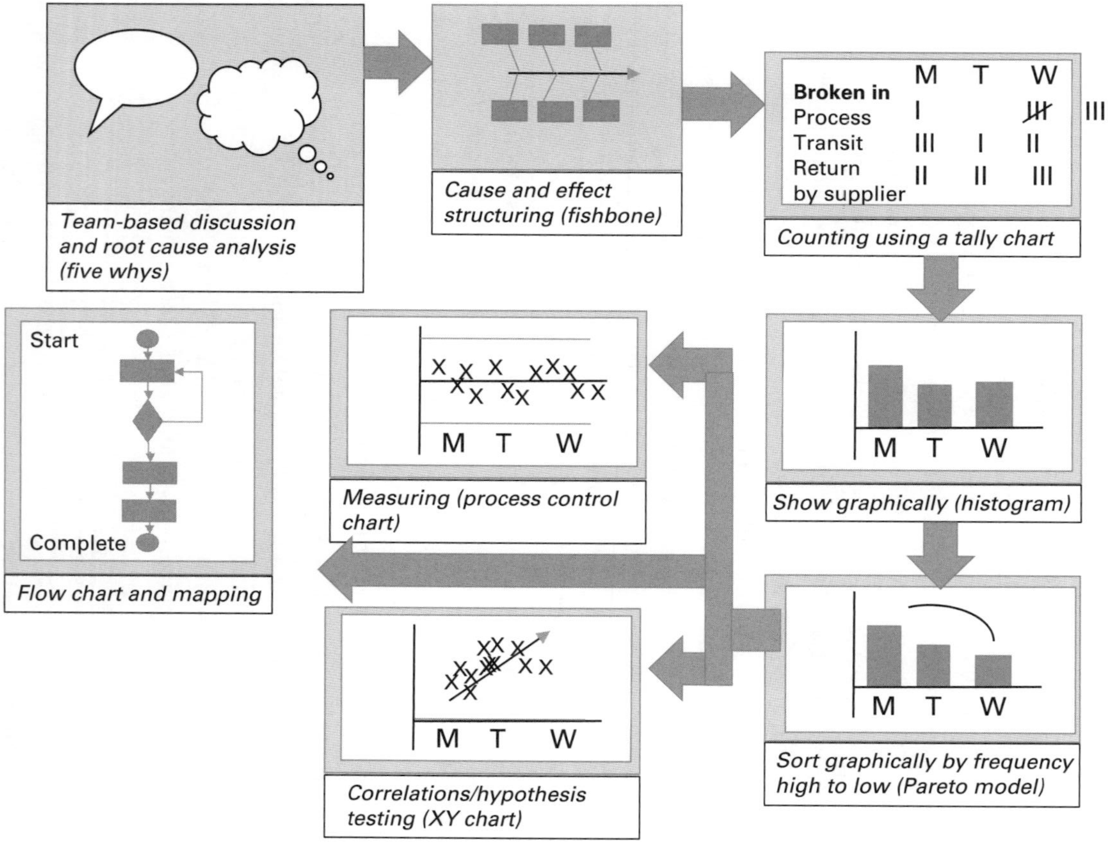

1 Brainstorm and use a 'five why' approach to identify root causes and use the Ishikawa tool known as the **fishbone** or cause and effect chart to structure these potential root causes into themes and causes, noting them on the spines of the fish):

   - The five why approach implies asking 'why?' up to five times when presented with a problem (it is Socratic reasoning). This is designed to move from the description of the symptom of a problem to the real cause. For instance, the symptom could be presented as 'I am always late for work':

     - Why? 1... I get to work late.
     - Why? 2... I don't set off on time.
     - Why? 3... I get up too late.
     - Why? 4... I don't leave enough time to get ready.
     - Why? 5... I don't set my alarm early enough to get ready on time.

     Hence the root cause of being late to work is not setting the alarm on time. This logic can be applied to most problems within a factory setting and the exercise will be conducted multiple times to ensure that all root causes are identified (it could be that the alarm needs the battery replacing more frequently, for example). Once the root causes have been identified the issues can be quantified and a robust solution put in place as a result of Ishikawa's set of improvement tools.

2 Select a theme and create a **tally chart**. Use this with the relevant teams, who should be close to the problem and capable of counting occurrences.

3 Convert the tally chart into a **histogram**.

4 Convert the histogram into a **Pareto** chart.

5 Focus on the vital few root causes and solve them (even when solved please consider the next step because you may want to still measure the process/root cause and ensure it is controlled).

6 If you cannot solve them then you can:

   a. continue to collect data and hypotheses about the root causes and use **XY charts/correlation charts**;

   b. monitor the process statistically to detect variation in performance and variation beyond acceptable standards and levels using **Statistical Process control charts**;

   c. develop a **flow chart** for decision making to control a problem.

These are the basic tools and they are very powerful; Ishikawa gave every Japanese worker the tools to engage with improvement.[28] His contribution is important – Deming and Juran created management awareness and Ishikawa gave operations staff the means to engage with TQM and improve their working lives as well as the prosperity of the business that employed them.

Dr Shigeo Shingo

Shigeo Shingo, who now has a revered international lean quality award named after him, expanded upon Deming's demand for prevention of quality defects. As an engineer, Shingo marvelled at the divorce of engineering knowledge from improvement and the tendency for non-engineers not to come up with preventative solutions.[29] Shingo, however, promoted error-proofing. He believed that engineers could identify sources of product failure and permanently prevent them using engineering-based solutions. So, Shingo advocated tools such as:

- Fixed-quantity solutions where a fixed number of products are needed and no more. The egg box that safely carries six eggs is an example of this form of mistake proofing as you cannot put seven eggs in the box and it is easy to see when you have one missing.
- The inability to perform an incorrect function – such as devices used in stationery filing cabinets that prevent the cabinet from falling on a user. Cabinets will fall if the centre of balance is disturbed and the filing cabinet will fall forward if all the drawers of the cabinet are opened – so modern cabinets have locking systems that allow only one drawer to be open at a time to compensate for this. Another example is the USB stick which can only be inserted into a computer one way around! Shingo's view was to 'engineer out' the problem.

Shingo contributed a lot to quality and his view – solve the problem permanently and use good science to prevent it – is highly important today and is built into the design of vehicles; the car won't start unless the clutch pedal is depressed fully, alarms sound when you leave your lights on etc.

Dr Masaaki Imai

Imai took Deming's principle of constant improvement and promoted 'kaizen' to Japanese industry. His approach was to combine the PDCA cycle with the SDCA (Standardize–Do–Check–Act) approach so that improvement would be continuous and not what was seen in the West, where continuous improvement did not happen and engineers would instead radically transform processes by buying the latest technology every five or ten years. The terms *kai* and *zen* can be seen to represent circle and improvement so Imai proposes that the journey of improvement is constant and small steps are needed to get better today. He added more detail to the standardization of improvement so that it was embedded into new working practices and standard operating procedures.[30]

He supported engaging people and talking about quality then enacting the two cycles of solving workplace issues and standardizing them. Sustaining improvement, for Imai, involved engaging everyone in improvement and drafting new standard working practices so that these standards allowed the next generation of improvement to be based on documented standards that were followed by staff members.

Dr Noriaka Kano

Dr Kano contributed to the 'designing in' of quality into products and services so as to focus on the customer. His idea is quite easy to illustrate – he contends there are three dimensions of quality: 'basic features', 'performance features' and 'excitement features'.[31] If we take the example of a hotel then the basic features concern the cleanliness of the room. Such a basic feature means that if it is absent or compromised then it will bring instant dissatisfaction. Once a basic feature is satisfied then doing more of it rarely brings high levels of customer satisfaction. The performance feature could be that the room is double glazed for a good night's sleep and has free WiFi available. If this is absent, then it is a means of comparing competitors and will result in the customer selecting the hotel that offers the most of these features. An excitement factor is a differentiator such as free in-room sport channels or box office movies, or a free chocolate/fruit in the room, or a free spa treatment. Interestingly, Kano's work applies to businesses that seek to achieve ISO standards – when the customer expects a supplier to hold to a certain standard (or a combination of them) then they will walk away if this criterion is unmet.

If the supplier has the standards and can show how they are effectively managed, continuously improved and audited with few non-conformances, then the potential customer has faith in choosing the best supplier and the excitement factors are likely to include what the supplier can do for the customer, such a daily deliveries of guaranteed great quality direct to the exact location in the customer's facility where the products will be used. Dr Kano therefore helps modern managers understand how the design aspects of systems support customer satisfaction.

The Japanese era, which commenced with the influence of the Early American school, was a vibrant period in TQM history. It balanced the Early Americans' advice for managers with the tools needed to make TQM a reality for the staff employed at an organization. During this period in history, two pieces of the jigsaw of TQM were in place – the features and principles for good management and the tools that staff needed to meaningfully engage with TQM. The third evolution of thinking returned to the strategic integration of TQM with business strategy and the characteristics of the quality features needed in the mid-1980s. The good leadership and good methods of phases 1 and 2 of TQM underpin all ISO standards and are visible in the best factories today and wherever a company has gained the relevant ISO standard.

The American strategists: the third evolution

The third era of TQM was spearheaded by influential and charismatic Americans and is typified by an attempt to awaken US industry to the strategic importance of quality. This period, in the 1980s, witnessed many new Japanese factories being built in America and the debunking of myths, mainly that Japanese lean systems could not work outside of Japan and that automation was their key competitive weapon. It wasn't – it was great attention to TQM. As the Japanese began to dominate key market sectors, such as electronics, motorcycles, cars, cameras and such like, US industry could no longer try to fend off the Japanese and hide behind their protection of domestic markets. Key and influential quality figures including Phil Crosby, Professor David Garvin and Senator Malcolm Baldrige saw the need to promote the 'Quality First' strategy for the nation and deliberately sought to raise the profile of TQM for US businesses under the Ronald Regan presidency. Baldrige also developed his Malcolm Baldrige National Quality Award framework[32] which was launched and patriotically developed after his untimely death during a rodeo accident.

Phil Crosby

Phil Crosby[33] was an enigmatic and charismatic individual who – it is alleged – had a smile that could light up a room. He was a natural showman and could captivate US audiences in the same way that the 'rather serious' Deming captivated Japanese managers, scientists and engineers.

Phil Crosby learned his trade as a quality engineer at US factories and soon gained a reputation for reducing defects and saving significant amounts of money. He was a firm believer in the concept of 'zero defects' and made this his 'strap line' together with the fact he believed that reaching the levels of quality systems design needed to achieve the performance level of zero defects would mean that improvement would pay for itself and 'quality was free' (it is less expensive to do things right than correct mistakes and defects). He proposed that all organizations should DIRFT, or Do It Right First Time, based on practices that supported a system of preventing defects, where quality was defined as conformance to product standards requirements and the requirements of the customer. For Crosby, a key measure was therefore the price of non-conformance to these established standards. He proposed that the savings made from quality improvement will more than pay for the costs of running the quality management systems in place.

His other major contributions included The Crosby quality vaccine that could be employed to support perfect-quality performance and included the sub-features of:

- integrity and the absolute belief of all grades of employee in the role of quality for the business now and in its competitive future;
- systems and using effective organizational processes to support quality education, customer satisfaction reviews, costs-of-production reviews and other measures of improvement trends;
- communication and the use of 'softer' organizational practices to listen to those in the job and learn from them as well as learning from customers; communication is also important for gaining agreement on standards of performance and opportunities for improvement within the factory;
- operations and operational processes should be developed to reach a level of capability/reliability and continuous improvement should be built into them;
- clear policies to create a constancy of purpose for all staff.

Crosby also offered his 14 steps to improvement:

1. Management must be committed and reinforce the importance of quality.
2. Quality improvement teams should be formed using representatives from each department to increase process thinking and inter-departmental collaboration.
3. Measures should be introduced to control key processes.
4. The cost of quality should be used to quantify poor performance and target improvements within the organization.
5. Awareness of the strategic importance of quality, for all staff, should be regularly communicated.

6. Problems in the organization should be identified using cost analysis and teamwork.
7. Monitors of the improvement process performance should be introduced.
8. Organizational and departmental supervisors should be trained to engage and lead quality improvement efforts.
9. The organization should promote and hold a Zero Defect (ZD) day to celebrate and reflect on progress towards the goal of perfect production.
10. To get to zero defects, the leadership of the organization should establish improvement goals.
11. The leadership, at all levels, should remove fear from all staff and encourage them to promote issues and barriers to progress towards zero defects.
12. The leaders of the organization should recognize and celebrate employees who participate (regardless of their achievements).
13. The organization should establish Quality Councils to promote and communicate quality improvement to staff.
14. Just like Deming, Crosby's last feature of a great business was to do it repeatedly – keep mastering the control of quality and its assurance.

Crosby also conveniently summarized the journey to TQM by depicting several organizational stages:

1. *Uncertainty* and confusion at the leadership and operational staff levels of the business. Quality issues are just treated as 'normal'.
2. *Awakening*, where knowledge of errors and defects is recognized and there is a motivation to stop these activities from threatening the customer service and financial performance of the business.
3. *Enlightenment*, where there is growing awareness of the extent of the problems and what needs to be sorted out to gain control. This stage also includes greater levels of education in quality methods for staff.
4. *Wisdom* and the point where business staff can identify and solve problems in the organization. The staff have the mastery needed to identify, solve, eliminate and sustain quality improvement.
5. *Certainty*, where the business at all levels and all departments (including suppliers and customers) can design products, plan production, fulfil orders and conduct all business activities and staff development with absolute certainty that quality is managed throughout the organization.

Crosby's contribution is an interesting one and his timing was perfect in terms of adding a renewed and strategic importance to ideas that originated and evolved from the application of US thinking with Japanese businesses. He and others of his time 'Americanized' and gave new legitimacy to quality and Total Quality Management for a nation that was highly patriotic and could never truly admit that it had lagged behind and its industry was not as good as the Japanese businesses that had inwardly invested in America in the 1980s. His work and charisma made Crosby world famous, yet many have criticized his contribution.

Cynics would argue that Crosby did little more than repackage old ideas (especially those of Deming and Juran) and give them a modern spin, but in Crosby's defence – it worked! And a failing US industrial base found it better to learn from him than to ask the Japanese for help. The significance of the fear held by Americans in terms of their competitive disadvantage was witnessed throughout this time period, including the Ford Motor Corporation's 'AJ' campaign, with AJ standing for the plan to catch up with the Japanese: the letters literally stood for 'After Japan'.[34] He was certainly a man of his time and he admitted that he wished he had not offered the world a list of 14 points because, he argued, managers forgot to think about quality and blindly followed these basic design principles. Overall, though, he can rightfully claim his recognition as a quality guru.

Professor David Garvin

The contribution of Harvard Business School's Professor David Garvin to the world of TQM was definitional and highly useful for today's manufacturing and service businesses because his work elaborates on the dimensions of quality that must be provided by a product or service in order to generate customer satisfaction. Many authors had talked previously in general terms about the concept of quality whereas Garvin added features and dimensions of quality that were useful to leaders, operational staff and designers of products and services.

Garvin's characteristics of a great-quality product

The work of Garvin[35] adds to the quality principles and approach designed by Kano.[36] Garvin proposed eight dimensions of product quality:

1 **Performance:** how well a product conducts and delivers its primary operating characteristics (the value it gives to a consumer – safety and miles per gallon for a vehicle for instance).

2 **Features:** the additional aspects of the product that add to the consumer/customer's experience of the product. These are often the secondary aspects such as layout of interior, colour scheme, ease when using the controls etc.

3 **Reliability:** the very low probability of a product malfunctioning and failing.

4 **Conformance:** the degree to which the product satisfies established standards, such as a Kitemark for a product or an ISO standard.

5 **Durability:** the economic and technical useful lifetime (length of value adding) for the consumer.

6 **Serviceability:** the ease of servicing and the service experience (cost, treatment of the customer etc).

7 **Aesthetics:** the subjective view of the look and feel of the product.

8 **Perceived quality:** the quality bestowed by owning the brand of product or the prestige factor and what it says about the owner.

These dimensions are very important and help organizational managers to interpret their own and competitors' products/customers and their choices. Service quality characteristics are also relevant to the modern manufacturer, as most businesses now offer a support service as part of the product offering. These classifications help but do not tell managers exactly what to excel in and whether all eight dimensions must be present; however, it is a highly useful approach. Garvin's characteristics have been developed by other authors (eg the RATER model)[37] for services and these include five dimensions of:

1 **Reliability:** completing customer requirements to a good standard every time.

2 **Assurance:** ensuring the customer has confidence in the organization, its products and services.

3 **Tangibles:** the presentation, equipment and graphics used that convinces the customer that the organization is competent and the best.

4 **Empathy:** services focus on what customers need and understand service provision from the eyes of the customer – opening hours, personalization of service, contact media, etc.

5 **Responsiveness:** the ability to get through to the organization and for the organization to execute customer needs promptly and within an acceptable time for the customer.

These approaches to definitional quality allow businesses to strategically compare themselves with others and position themselves.

Malcolm Baldrige

Senator Malcolm Baldrige's National Quality Award is highly revered in the United States and rivals other behavioural TQM prizes across the world, including the Deming Prize, The EFQM model in Europe and the Shingo Prize.[38] It is awarded by the President of the United States of America to companies that can prove they are high performing across a number of key indicators and after being examined by a team of scrutineers. The award is managed by the National Institute of Standards and Technology (NIST).[39] NIST has a systematic approach to the application and achievement of the award and it demands that a business scores highly (as a result of self and expert audits) on a range of factors but most importantly a whole series of measures of performance (the results of what a business does in terms of profits, customer service, employee data and such like). The main audit areas of the award include:

- Cluster of strategic considerations:
  - leadership;
  - strategic planning;
  - customer and market focus.
- Demonstrated organizational competence and capability:
  - measurement, analysis and knowledge management (encompassing the strategic and operational clusters).
- Cluster of operational fulfilment:
  - workforce management;
  - process management;
  - results.

The combination of the audit factors is a tough test of the organization's capability, leadership and delivery of value. Baldrige added these organizational features while Garvin and Crosby were promoting strategic quality management in the United States and therefore it has been added in this section. It should be noted that the other behavioural TQM quality prizes in the world (Deming Prize, Shingo Prize, EFQM) test similar characteristics of world-class organizations.

The global phenomena and company-wide rejuvenation era

The 1990s and into the 2000s saw a rise in global competition and new conditions for trading. The internet was a commercial reality and company managers sought to harness the new ideas of lean and Six Sigma quality systems and the performance addition these innovations were heralded as providing in the pursuit of competitive advantage. These new approaches to high-performance manufacturing and highly reliable production systems are all founded on the basic tenets of TQM. Indeed, many of these relatively new ideas would not have been developed had the principles of TQM not been evolved. The reader will notice that the three phases of TQM development and evolution have given the world and industrialists:

1. the management principles needed to run an effective business (phase 1);
2. the tools and techniques needed to make quality improvement real (phase 2);
3. the strategic importance of quality (phase 3).

These phases also mirror and complement the basic ingredients of an international standard and businesses that intend to achieve and conform to an international standard must show demonstrated evidence of these three levels being in place, operational and effective. Modern standards are structured using the High-Level Structure (HLS) approach, which provides a coherent logic and framework for the operation of international standards by focusing on and emphasizing the following conformance requirements:

- context of the organization (and the value it offers its stakeholders);
- leadership (engagement and competence);
- planning and support (for quality in every process and activity of the business);
- operation (including the processes, tools and techniques to control and assure quality);
- performance evaluation (knowing how the business is performing);
- improvement (learning and getting closer to perfect quality performance).

The features of a modern standard – HLS – will be covered multiple times in this book but these areas of conformance requirement assist leaders and managers to design effective systems and processes that embed total quality thinking into all standards, from quality management systems to information security. The HLS will be used to structure all subsequent revisions and standards in the future.

In summary

The principles of TQM remain relevant today – no organization has ever held TQM status for anything more than a brief period, but it remains aspirational for all businesses as a journey to excellence. Even those businesses that have managed to gain near-certainty in their internal operational control of quality still need to help customers and suppliers get better in a world where new manufactured products are being developed and entering the market together with new technological opportunities to revolutionize the way in which products are manufactured. It is quite possible that a few generations of great managers are needed to really achieve TQM and optimize performance, but the journey is so worthwhile. Deming once argued that business survival is not guaranteed unless you are working (each day) to achieve TQM and using great people to operate great processes to offer great products, as Toyota has demonstrated.

For employees, the continued commitment to TQM brings benefits too – TQM is a continued pledge to invest in employee skills in return for a lifetime of problem solving and innovation. For specialist staff, TQM brings meaningful and customer-focused projects that stretch the brain and make the day pass quickly. For wider business stakeholders – including the local community, trade unions, business financiers and such like – working to international standards that are based on a TQM logic also brings benefits as businesses waste less, engage more with stakeholders, and minimize risks.

This chapter was designed to explore TQM and equip the reader with its structure, logic and history and how it has aided the following:

- understanding and relevance of international standards to a business;
- embedding this understanding and use of standards in the TQM world and literature;
- recognizing that TQM and international standards flow from policies and strategies into processes and methods for greater control and performance;
- showing that modern standards are best on the latest knowledge and best practice in a specific area (such as ISO 9001 and the 9000 series for quality management systems).

The remainder of the chapters will delve deeper into the organization that controls international standards – the ISO – and the structures of the key standards that most industrialists will employ.

Seminar topics and examination questions

A chapter on TQM and its logic is a rich subject for the development of questions to reflect upon:

- Why strive to achieve TQM status when product life cycles are measured in months?
- How can one manager deciding to ignore quality management systems and principles cause problems for other managers?
- Should the human resource departments of businesses recruit new staff based on skills or the person's attitude towards quality at work?
- Is TQM just a clever way of getting employees to work harder by working smarter?
- If a business must cease placing orders with unreliable yet cheap suppliers, how can it assess if a supplier is a good-quality one?
- Are Dr Deming and Dr Juran's approaches to management compatible?
- Should the introduction of any international standard begin only after the directors of a business have been educated in the basic behaviours needed for TQM to be successful?
- How could a business educate its suppliers in TQM and the need for standards? Can the same education be beneficial in educating customers?
- Is it possible to implement all of Deming's 14 points? If so, is there a logical sequence when it comes to implementing them?
- How can TQM be both top-down from the business's directors and bottom-up from employees engaged in managing processes?
- Will companies eventually exhaust all problems in a business and stop improving?
- At some point, doesn't it become too expensive to keep seeking perfect products, services and business processes?
- Why are employees the number one asset in the pursuit of competitive advantage?
- Should customers be encouraged to complain?

- Does the root cause of every problem stem from something that a person did wrong?
- Quality is only relevant to expensive products or personalized services. Discuss.
- Can TQM be applied to a hospital? Are hospitals too complex to effectively implement an international standard?

Further reading

There are many great references and websites that will help with this subject area. Internet search words should include:

- the Deming Institute;
- EFQM model;
- MBNQA;
- the lean enterprise;
- the Seven Old Tools of quality management;
- Total Quality Management and synonyms.

Notes

1 ASQ (2013) *TQM: Introduction and overview of total quality management*, ASQ Quality Press (Kindle Edition)
2 Toyota Motor Corporation (1988) *Toyota: The first 50 years*, Toyota Motor Corporation, Nagoya, Japan
3 Tasler, N (2017) Stop using the excuse that 'change is hard', *Harvard Business Review*, Summer
4 Womack, D, Jones, D and Roos, D (1990) *The* Machine *That Changed the World*, Simon and Schuster, New York
5 Winslow-Taylor, F (1967) *The Principles of Scientific Management*, WC Norton & Company Press, New York
6 Blake, R and Mouton, J (1964) *The Managerial Grid*, Gulf Publishing, Houston
7 Hammer, M and Champy, J (2001) *Re-Engineering the Corporation*, Harper Collins, New York

8 Moss Kanter, R (1984) *The Change Masters: Innovation and entrepreneurship in the American corporation*, Simon and Schuster, New York
9 Senge, P (2006) *The Fifth Discipline: The art and practice of the learning organization,* 2nd ed, Random House, New York
10 Monden, Y (2011) *Toyota Production System: Beyond large-scale production*, 4th ed, Productivity Press, Portland, OR
11 Andersen Consulting (1993) *In Search of World Class Manufacturing Practice*, Andersen Consulting, London
12 Braungart, M and McDonough, W (2009) *Cradle to Cradle: Remaking the way we make things*, Vintage Publishing
13 Snowden, D and Stanbridge, J (2004) The landscape of management: creating the context for understanding social complexity, *E:CO* Special Double Issue, 6 (1–2), pp 140–48
14 Slack, N, Brandon-Jones, A and Johnson, R (2019) *Operations Management*, 8th ed, Pearson, London
15 Bremer, M S (2016) *How to Do a Gemba Walk: Take a gemba walk to improve your leadership skills*, 2nd ed, CreateSpace Independent Publishing Platform
16 Deming, W E (1986) *Out of the Crisis*, MIT Press, Massachusetts
17 Juran, J (1995) *Managerial Breakthrough: The classic book on improving management performance*, McGraw-Hill, London
18 Juran, J (1989) *On Quality for Leadership*, Jossey Bass, New York
19 Koch, R (2017) *The 80/20 Principle: The secret of achieving more with less: updated 20th anniversary edition of the productivity and business classic*, 3rd ed, Nicholas Brealey Publishing
20 Ibid
21 Monden, *Toyota Production System*
22 Defeo, J (2014) *Juran's Quality Essentials*, McGraw-Hill Education, New York
23 Mizuno, S and Akao, Y (1994) *QFD: Customer-Driven Approach: The customer-driven approach to quality planning and deployment*, Productivity Press, Portland, OR
24 Bicheno, J and Holweg, M (2016) *The Lean Toolbox*, 5th ed, Picsie Books, Buckingham, UK
25 Liker, J (2004) *The Toyota Way: 14 management principles from the world's greatest manufacturer*, McGraw-Hill Education, London
26 Ishikawa, K (1991) *A Guide to Quality Control*, Asian Productivity Organization, Tokyo
27 Ibid
28 50minutes.com (2015) *The Ishikawa Diagram: Identify problems and take action*, 50minutes.com
29 Shingo, S (1986) *Zero Quality Control: Source inspection and the Poka-Yoke system*, Routledge, London

30 Imai, M (2012) *Gemba Kaizen: A common sense approach to a continuous improvement strategy*, McGraw-Hill Education, London

31 Coleman Snr, L B (2015) *The Customer-Driven Organization*, Routledge, London

32 Bou-Llusar, J C et al (2008) An empirical assessment of the EFQM Excellence Model: evaluation as a TQM framework relative to the MBNQA Model, *Journal of Operations Management*, doi:10.1016/j.jom.2008.04.001

33 Crosby, P B (1987) *Quality is Free: The art of making quality certain*, Penguin Books, London

34 Axson, D A J (2010) *The Management Mythbuster*, Wiley, New Jersey

35 Garvin, D A (1984) What does product quality really mean? *Sloan Management Review*, Fall

36 Behzion, H and Baghishani, M (2014) *Criteria and Measures of Customer satisfactions: SERVPREF, SERVQUAL, customer satisfaction, service quality, total quality management, Kano's Model*, Lambert Academic Publishers

37 Zeithaml, V, Parasuraman, A and Berry, L L (1990) *Delivering Service Quality: Balancing customer perceptions and expectations*, The Free Press, New York

38 Lee, S M, Zuckweiler, K M and Trimi, S (2006) Modernization of the Malcolm Baldrige National Quality Award, *International Journal of Production Research*, **44** (23), pp. 5089–5106, DOI: 10.1080/00207540500161043

39 www.nist.gov (archived at https://perma.cc/68MT-S55Y)

Introduction to management system standards 03

If you look at many company websites (or the reception areas of factories you may visit) you will often see a logo that has the typical blue (or sometimes red) letters 'ISO' and a number on them. This is typically the printed certificate awarded to a business that has achieved (by conforming to) an established standard of the International Standards Organization and has been certified by an independent company as conforming to that exact standard.[1]

The certificate states the requirements standard, and the number underneath the logo will tell you which standard it's conforming to along with its revision date, which indicates whether the company is working to the latest standard of best practice. These are badges of honour for most businesses and reflect a lot of hours of exerted effort by many members of staff to gain the award and prove that the business operates all the processes necessary to be deemed fit to hold it.[2] The organization that has been proven to meet the requirements of a standard has successfully convinced an independent organization (known as a third party) that it is competent and worthy of 'the certificate'. The third-party organization conducting the assessment has no interests in the business concerned but is an expert in that standard. The independent 'third party' business is also not the ISO itself – a common mistake made by many. The ISO develops, manages, maintains and revises internationally accepted standards only. It does not do anything else – it is the global 'go to' organization for management standards.

This chapter will provide answers to questions such as:

- What is the ISO?
- Where did it come from?

- Why does it exist?
- What does it do and how does it do it?

LEARNING OBJECTIVES

At the end of this chapter, you should be able to:

- describe the role and purpose of the International Standards Organization;
- explain how national bodies and technical committees are involved with standards development and acceptance;
- describe the global 'democratic' and equitable approach of the ISO;
- explain the basic terminology (and Annex SL) of modern standards and the portfolio of documents that support an agreed conformance standard;
- explain the process of standard conception through to standard revision and the issues of managing a cross-country and multilingual organization;
- understand the criticisms levelled at the International Standards community.

ISO – what's in a name?

The term ISO is a shorthand way of saying the International Standards Organization but many know the organization by its correct title which is the **International Organization for Standardization**. ISO, as we will term it, is a 'not for profit' non-governmental organization located in Geneva (headquarters) and the number of staff working there is quite small (they are known as 'the Secretariat'). The Secretariat supports the setting of international standards and the members of the ISO. The membership of ISO includes national standards bodies which represent the interests of their economies and industries. Members also vary in their chosen level of engagement with ISO, with various levels of membership existing, each offering certain rights and benefits. For example, the national body that promotes the interests of the United Kingdom is the British Standards Institution (BSI) and for Germany it is Deutsches Institut für Normung (DIN). So, each participating country will have only one representative national body that coordinates the use of standards in their country. In this way, ISO can be likened to a federal network of collaborating partners. With such a membership, ISO is actually 'global' in its influence, and currently engaged with over 163 member countries. Through engagement with the ISO, even the smallest country can propose, shape, and refine a standard that applies to all businesses around the world.

IOS or ISO?

> The International Organization for Standardization could be abbreviated to IOS, but to ensure it is recognized the world over, it has adopted the acronym ISO. *Isos* in Greek – as many commentators point out – means equal and 'the same' which is a fitting description of the way in which the ISO works.

ISO was founded in February 1947 to set standards and promote worldwide proprietary industrial and commercial standards to break down barriers to trade. It is a voluntary organization and no country is forced to join nor to leave. The ISO therefore uses voluntary collaboration to ensure that every national body supports international standards. An ISO international standard is essentially a document that sets out guidance for requirements so that an organization can make products and services that are safe, of high quality, supported by effective management processes, based on good practice and can be audited and assessed by first, second or third parties.

At this point we should differentiate between 'a guide' document (also termed a standard) and a requirements standard to which conformity must be assured – the former is a document that helps managers and businesses understand how best to exploit a given requirements standard. Essentially, they help managers to 'read around' and explore issues that will enhance the effective implementation of a conformance standard. A requirements standard for a management system is a document that sets out all the practices and processes that an organization must operate effectively in order to self-certify or become certified by a third-party assessor. The use of requirements standards is a significant distinguishing feature of high-performing and highly reliable manufacturing businesses.

But what does this mean?

Well, they help to strategically guide and practically support the development of organizational working practices to allow the effective and efficient exploitation of a standard. The standards therefore represent best known practice; they eliminate issues of trying to best guess what should be implemented by providing guidelines and a conformance standard. The use of standards has been proven, by research, to support superior performance, reduce waste, reduce costs, and create a system of continuous improvement.

In the words of the ISO – 'We're ISO – the international organization for standardization. We develop and publish International Standards.' Well that is a pretty good description but there is a lot more to that simple statement:

- The ISO is an independent charity founded in 1947 that develops and publishes standards.
- The organization has a membership of over 163 countries worldwide. Each country is represented by a single national standards body.
- The headquarters is in Geneva Switzerland, where a small and dedicated staff (secretariat) support the processes of development and publishing.
- The organization relies on voluntary membership and inter-country collaboration to enact new and revise existing standards that are relevant to modern businesses.
- National bodies make up the membership of the ISO and supply experts to support the processes of development and publishing. These unpaid national experts work within technical committees or work groups that support a portfolio of standards within a single area of focus or context. Some international standards are also modified and renamed for industry-specific settings, such as the automotive, aerospace and defence sectors.
- There are currently over 22,000 active international standards (and related support documents). These documented standards and guidelines cover almost every technology and industry sector.
- A standard is a document that sets out requirements, specifications, guidelines or characteristics that can be used consistently by an organization to ensure that its materials, products, processes, services, policies, and other organizational working practices support 'best practice' for that standard's sphere of influence or subject.
- A standard is denoted by the letters ISO and a number that relates to the exact standard or guideline and these form portfolios of commonly themed standards/guides for sale and use.
- Standards (the documents) are available for purchase directly from the ISO.

- The most popular standards include the ISO 9000 series (quality management systems), of which ISO 9001 is the conformance standard. The other documents are guidelines and assist businesses when implementing and operating ISO 9001.
- ISO standards are audited by third-party independent businesses that are skilled in identifying gaps in the logic and working practices of companies seeking to achieve or maintain an existing standard (such as ISO 9001).

So, to reiterate, a standard is just a document.[3] But the document can be a guide which either defines the terminology and gives guidance on specific topics within a critical area of a standard such as customer satisfaction, project management, defining competence etc, or helps guide the implementation of a requirement standard (the latter is the standard to which a business wishes to be certified and details the requirements to gain conformity). A requirement is an area of management practice for which there must be proof that a company wanting the standard conforms to. A conformance standard states how a business 'shall' operate in order to conform to the clauses (requirements) of a given and dated standard.

At this point it is prudent to explore a few of the words that have been used. To many readers these will be quite different to words used in everyday management or student life.

Table 3.1 Table of terms

Term used	What it means and why it is important
An international standard	A document that provides rules, guidelines or requirements placed on a company that wants to achieve a standard. The standards document sets out what is needed to achieve the best management system for a given context. Standards cover product standards, codes of practice documents, guidelines, and international management standards (the latter is the subject of this book).
International management standards	These are documents that describe, support or represent conformance to documented standards. The conformance standard is the most important as this contains the requirements (often termed clauses and sub-clauses) that an organization must demonstrate that it has implemented and is operating effectively. The conformance standard is used by auditors to assess the level of conformance achieved by a business.

(continued)

Table 3.1 *(Continued)*

Term used	What it means and why it is important
A guideline	This is a document that helps the management and leadership of a business understand which practices could be used to support an effective implementation and conformance of the business with the conformance standard or best practice.
Conformance standard	The one standard in a portfolio that states the broad 'theme' of activities and the detailed tasks/procedures that must be in place and managed correctly if the company is to reach a level of conformance and achieve or retain the conformance standard. The theme could be the supporting practices that make a business confident that its processes are controlled. Within this form of control and support is **the onus of the business to demonstrate** that adequate support processes are in place. One such theme is **'support'** to daily operations management, meaning that the **staff employed are trained and assessed as competent** to operate the process and procedures. Another sub-clause for conformance is that **all documents that support production are formally controlled and revised periodically** (numbered) whilst ensuring that they can be audited and regularly reviewed for improvements and new revisions issued and training conducted to ensure the staff meet the new standard operating procedures.
A requirement or clause	This is **a management practice or procedure that must be operated by a business** so it is deemed **to conform to a standard and its clauses**. Evidence must be provided that conformance is widely promoted, formalized, measured and the leadership of the organization is engaged in active ways to enforce conformance.
Conformance	An **audited set of processes that provide evidence that the product, service or organizational system meets the requirements of a standard** (as expressed by its clauses). The auditors can be internal (staff) or external (customers or independent third-party organization).
Certification	The investigation, assessment and provision, by an independent third-party organization (that is competent to conduct such assessments) that a product, service or management system meets the specific requirements of a conformance standard. The successful conformance of a business with a particular standard results in a formal written assurance that the business conforms and the issuance of a certificate to prove this (hence the term certification). Certification is known as registration.

(continued)

Table 3.1 *(Continued)*

Term used	What it means and why it is important
Third-party certifying organization	A business that specializes in auditing certification must be capable of, and hold the ISO standard for conducting certification audits, namely ISO 19011. These auditors conduct an external and independent investigation and tests of an organization's systems (in place and active) against the requirements of a specific standard (such as the quality management system ISO 9001) and if the organization is deemed to meet the requirements of the specific standard the auditor will conduct certification (also known as registration) and award the ISO certificate as appropriate. The certification body is hired by the applicant organization. Auditors must themselves conform to very strict principles and behaviours and will fail businesses that have more work to do and practices to effectively operate in order to protect the high levels of management needed to demonstrate a business meets the requirements of a standard.

ISO facilitates the development of a standard using its members and international experts, then publishes it and will periodically revise it – this is the most rudimentary analysis of what the organization does. Local companies will then voluntarily select the standards that support their strategy and market demands and apply it to their working practices. For a company to conform and then be certified they must meet every requirement in the standard (everything that is written down must be achieved and evidenced). Then a business seeking certification must convince an independent business (that is not the ISO because the ISO does not conduct audits nor certify businesses) that it has met every requirement/clause within the standard. The independent certification body (CB), also known as a 'third party', will require significant evidence gathered from multiple audits of the management system before it will be satisfied that a business conforms to the features and proven application of the requirements within a given standard.

If, however, the business fails to achieve an acceptable level of control then the independent company will not certify, and the business will have an opportunity to then put right any non-conformities and start again. The auditor will tell the business (often in a detailed written report) exactly what needs to be improved and the business can re-apply for certification when it has made the corrections to its processes. This is how an agreed standard is then used in the market for certified businesses to exploit for greater effectiveness and business efficiency.

So, we now understand the outcome and use of a standard. This is relatively straightforward and is what most business managers will see and experience, but the journey from an initial idea to the publishing of a standard for use by the business community is a very complex process.

The role and structure of the ISO

The purpose of the ISO is to develop and publish standards of value to businesses and standards that facilitate international trade. The members represent the majority of countries in the world and they engage so that their industries can trade globally using the ISO certifications as endorsements of good practices. The members of the ISO are National Standards Bodies (NSB) (standards agencies that represent a country) with differing levels of membership. For ease of administration there is only one national body organization per country. There are three forms of membership:[4]

- full members;
- correspondent members;
- subscriber members.

Full members have four rights (see below) as well as statutory obligations to the ISO which are implemented within guidelines of good practice. All ISO members are bound by legal obligations to abide by and enforce international policies and regulations concerning competition, protection of personal data and use of copyrighted materials. The culture of ISO as an organization is collegiate, friendly and positive for mutual benefit based on mutual respect.

In return for active engagement, each country has the right to vote; a less well-known fact is that each country has only one vote, so sometimes there can be a little bit of inter-country lobbying to help shape a standard. Ironically, the largest economies like China (with a large population) and the smallest of countries, such as the beautiful island of Malta, both get just one vote. Voting is an important and fundamental aspect of approving international standards as we will see later. What differentiates the different sizes of economies (such as Malta and China) is the financial contribution of the country to the management of the ISO organization. This contribution is an obligation of ISO and each country is expected to pay its 'fair share'. The correspondent and subscriber members pay a fixed cost that is determined by the ISO Secretary General (or General Assembly) and full members abide by a calculation that equates to the economic prosperity of the country concerned. The calculation includes a formula which evaluates the gross national income as well as imports/exports of the country concerned. As such, the smaller economy of Malta would pay less than China if they both subscribed as full members. The national body can select which standards it wishes to join, and it will join the technical committee relevant to the standards they are interested in supporting.

The four rights of a full member are:

- participate in developing ISO international standards;
- sell ISO standards in their respective country and use the copyright and logo of the ISO;
- participate in developing ISO policy;
- participate in governing the ISO.

The levels of membership mean that correspondent members can engage in the same activities as the full members except governing the ISO itself. The subscriber member can only participate in the development of international standards. When developing ISO standards, a national body must:[5]

- vote on all draft standards, at the relevant stages of development, in the committees that it participates in as a P-member (participating member);
- organize consultations among its stakeholders to develop national positions on draft ISO standards and present them to the relevant ISO technical committees;
- respect the results of ISO consensus building;
- follow the ISO Code of Ethics and the ISO Code of Conduct;
- follow TMB rules and respect TMB decisions;
- when holding secretariats, act without bias and ensure you have the resources to perform your duties.

The technical committees and work groups

ISO standards are developed by over 3,000 technical bodies, which engage with over 100,000 experts from over 160 countries. These experts comprise:

- practising and expert managers from industry and commerce;
- policy and interested civil servants from government;
- consumers of products and services;

- labour organizations and trade unions;
- applied academics and research bodies;
- standards bodies;
- non-governmental organizations.

Technical committees are established to manage series of standards, such as the ISO 9000 series of guides and the ISO 9001 requirements standard. The ISO meetings (face-to-face and virtual meetings held anywhere in the world) develop standards, exchange ideas and collaborate with experts who know 'good practice' and build it into the standards they work on. Experts are unpaid and work to develop standards for the benefit of business and the competitive exploitation by certified organizations when the standard is published and available. The experts are structured into around 250 technical committees. Ironically, technical committee No.1 (TC 1) concerns screw thread standardization and TC 2 concerns fasteners – Whitworth, whom we discussed in Chapter 1, would have been delighted at this! The most important for the control of modern and popular management systems are TC 176 for quality management systems and TC 207 for environmental management systems. Others that cover business management processes include:

- ISO/TC 251 Asset Management.
- ISO/TC 260 Human Resource Management.
- ISO/TC 262 Risk Management.
- ISO/TC 283 Occupational Health and Safety.
- ISO/TC 279 Innovation Management.
- ISO/TC 323 Circular Economy.
- ISO/TC 301 Energy Management and Energy Savings.
- ISO/TC 184 Automation Systems and Integration.
- ISO/TC 199 Safety of Machinery.

These are just a few of the 250 technical committees that influence how the world functions!

ISO members select whether they want to be involved with a particular standard as well as their level of engagement with a technical committee which supervises the development, publishing and revision of a given standards portfolio. There are two levels of engagement – a member can be an observing member (an 'O' member) and offer comments and advice, or they

Figure 3.1 The ISO structure

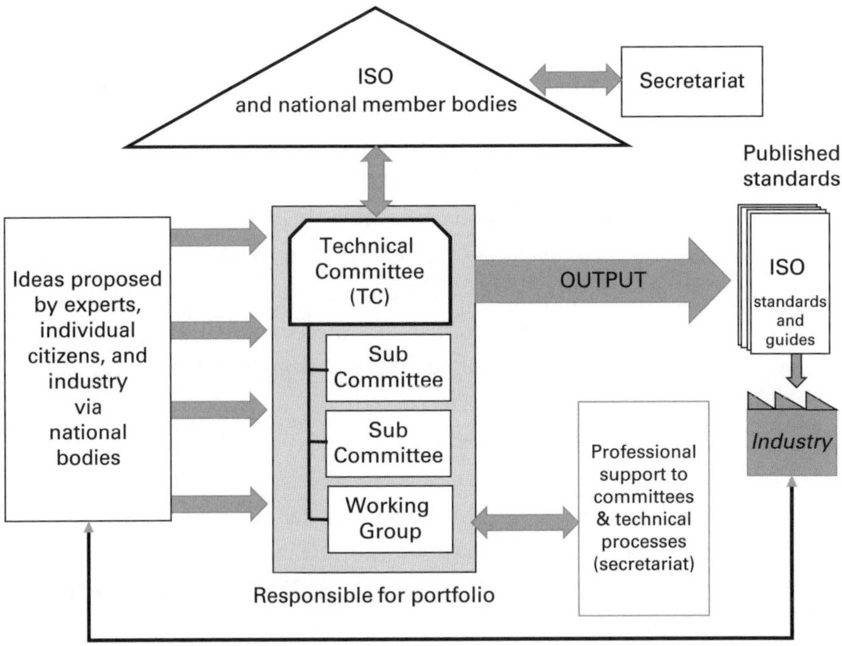

can participate directly as a P-member; this role carries voting rights at key stages of the standard development.

In summary, ISO has members (national member bodies) that engage with the processes of developing, publishing and using standards. They choose what technical committees to join and the level of commitment. As P-members they will vote at certain times in the standards development process and members also supply experts to support the development of standards that are appropriate. It should be noted that the central secretariat and other ISO boards/committees are there to support technical committees. An overview of the ISO structure is given in Figure 3.1.

The key support groups include:

- The Technical Management Board (TMB) which establishes technical committees, appoints chairs and monitors the progress of technical work undertaken by active technical committees (committees are active when they are developing or revising a standard/guideline and then go dormant when there is no work to be done). The TMB reports to the ISO council.

- The ISO Council, which is the key governance body of the ISO. It reports to the General Assembly and comprises representatives from 20 member bodies (rotated periodically), ISO officers, and chairs of other committees including:
  - representatives from the President's committee (adviser to the council);
  - representatives from the commercial policy and information technology advisory groups;
  - representatives from the conformity assessment team, the consumer issues team, and the developing countries team.

The process of making standards[6]

The lifecycle of a standard can be regarded as a process that has the following stages:

1. Ideas are put forward by citizens to their national standards body. These can be submitted online and will provide the basis on which a new standard is needed.
2. The national standards body (NSB) may review the proposal and support it or reject it.
3. A supported proposal will be sent to an established **Technical Committee (TC)** or a special group known as a project committee (PC) that will be formed to accommodate the proposal. The PC exists only for the development of a single standard. If multiple standards are needed, then this remains with the technical committee or one must be created. A PC will be closed down after it has published its standard.
4. The document that is sent to the technical committee is known as a **New Work Item Proposal (NWIP)** and will result in a work group being established to progress the concept to a full standard if approved.
5. The NWIP will be discussed and reviewed and expert input sought to form a working draft (WD) with the option of gaining consensus and progressing to a **Committee First Draft (First CD)**. The document may at this stage be issued as a **Publicly Available Specification (PAS)**, which is a published document that satisfies an urgent need in the market and will be published if deemed necessary by the experts of the working group or consensus provided by a group external to the ISO. These

documents are issued and published but have a lifecycle of six years, after which they must be converted into an international standard or deleted: PAS exit stage.

6. If the document is not exiting via a PAS option, then it will progress to the next stage, which is to gain consensus from the TC. The accepted draft will then become a **Draft International Standard (DIS)** or an ISO/TC technical specification. International management standards will become a DIS.
7. The DIS now needs greater input than just the TC staff and is sent for a broader input from members and other interested experts. The result is – through various iterations – a **Final Draft International Standard (FDIS)**. At the FDIS stage all the text used will be approved and will have been reviewed and scrutinized over many weeks and meetings.
8. The FDIS is then presented to the P-members for a formal vote. If voted for, the FDIS is also checked by the secretariat as a form of quality assurance. The final text is then approved, and the document will be sent for publishing.
9. Publication of the official ISO international standard. Potential for promotional launches and marketing activities to raise awareness amongst businesses in each member country may also be conducted.
10. After a period, the international standard will begin the process again for a **revision** conducted by the TC to ensure it remains a valid, legitimate and contemporary document of best practice. Typically, standards will be systematically reviewed every five years and will return to the technical committee for such a review and revision. A new date will be issued so that the standard moves from, say, a 2014 year issue of (fictitious) standard ISO 990001:2014 to a new one of ISO 990001:2019. Companies holding the 2014 standard (certified) will be expected to move to the requirements of the 2019 standard within a certain handover period if the standard has been revised. ISO 990001:2019 then becomes the new world standard. It must be noted that the review may not trigger any changes, or it may be withdrawn altogether. If a standard is updated, then the previous standard is withdrawn; the technical term for this is supersession of the standard.

The process illustrated in Figure 3.2 is a generic view of the transition of a standard from an initial idea to the formally published standard. It should be noted that to expeditiously bring a document to the international community (not a standard) then a series of International Workshop Agreements

Figure 3.2 The standards lifecycle schematic

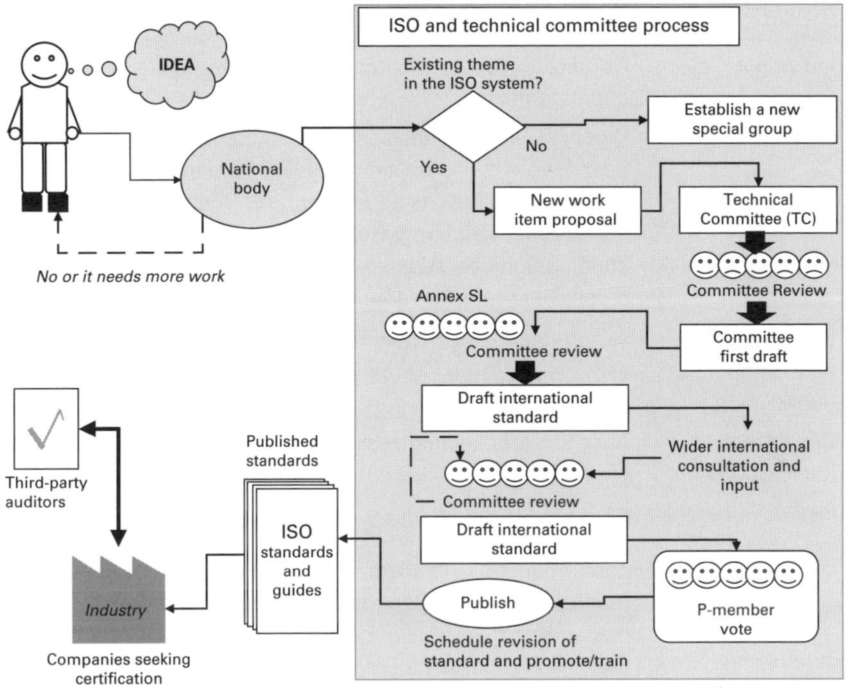

(IWAs) can be used. This route can be used to start the process that results in the full lifecycle of a standard as outlined in this section. It is a quick mode of generating interest with fewer rules than the overview presented here, which is the full route for a standard.

The 'basics' of ISO are now known to the reader, so the next section will answer the simple question of who the stakeholders in the ISO process are and why they support ISO standards. The purpose and value provided by ISO offers many benefits for stakeholders, as shown in Table 3.2.

The stakeholders and their interests are each very powerful influences, a business ecosystem if you like, and engaging stakeholders (individuals, businesses and economies) to improve performance using ISO standards is a very prudent strategy. Each individual standard will demand certain practices (these will be explored in future chapters) but each standard is the 'best known' practice for the effective management of a business and the value it provides to consumers and customers.

Table 3.2 Stakeholders and the ISO: the benefits[7]

Stakeholder	Benefits of ISO management standards
Individual manufacturing businesses	Certification and an assurance that systems are implemented. Use of ISO certification as a selling point. Engagement of best practices and financial savings from implementation. Improved profitability and fewer risks. A structure for management and a new operating model. Engagement of staff, customers, suppliers and other stakeholders in processes that must continuously improve.
Customers and consumers (the public)	Assurance that the manufacturing business has standards in place to assure high-quality products that are safe and well managed.
Customers (business-to-business trading)	A means of selecting certified businesses as trading partners because they operate standardized systems and have been certified as competent and capable of meeting the strict requirements of a standard (certification through conformance). A confidence that business risks are being managed properly. Confidence that the right type of management is leading the certified business. Confidence that the conformance process will have resulted in implemented 'best practices' and a good competitive price offered for parts supplied by the certified business.
National governments (mature economies)	Industries with businesses that meet international standards are likely to export more and generate tax incomes for the government. Employment levels are protected. Certified businesses will generate less waste and less resource depletion for better sustainability.
National governments (emerging economies)	Businesses with certified standards offer products with the same management competence as mature economies and can enter markets more easily to generate wealth and income for the government as well as rises in employment and other benefits.
Local communities	A new way of engaging with a manufacturing business that is better equipped to communicate and engage with the local community as a legitimate partner in the success of the business and a business that understands its commitment to the locality.

Taking and using a standard for better business

To complete the cycle of a standard, once it has been published, the country members (national bodies) that support the standard will delete and withdraw any country-specific standards that compete with the new one and promote the ISO standard for use with the relevant industry in the country. The ISO standard becomes the benchmark for that country and other standards that compete with it must be removed. At the same time, assessment and auditing companies will be accessing training in the new standard so they can start to sell their consulting services to help businesses gain certification. In addition, some businesses will be promoting the standard to their suppliers.

Once a standard has been published, a business leader can buy it online and use it to change their business practices. They can do this by themselves using a credit card if they choose and, at the end of implementing every requirement, they do not have to seek certification. There is a lot of expertise to master so the help of a consultant (which may be the company that will certify the business) can sometimes be useful – remember there is a requirements standard to use as well as various guides and other documents to read and understand (most requirements standards will have a family or portfolio of supporting guidelines to look through). For ISO 9001:2015 certification there is ISO 9000, ISO 9002, and ISO 9004 just to begin with, so it is understandable why businesses tend to:[8]

1. Seek outside independent help if needed at this point.
2. Gain awareness of the need for a new international management standard and its usefulness for the business (including visiting other companies and attending conferences).
3. Gather senior management and employee stakeholder commitment to the standard (gain consensus that this is good for business now and in the future).
4. Set up a pilot team to steer the implementation of the standards project.
5. Set up an implementation team to conduct the initial reviews.
6. Provide training to the steering and implementation teams (including added resources – staff and a budget):
    a. Review the exact standard and specification team with representatives from across the business.

   b. Visit others who are certified to the standard and 'go see' how to use the standard and what has been learned.

7. Conduct an audit of what is in place within the business against the requirements of the standard.
8. Document gaps and what can be done to close them. Prioritize those gaps with big payback to the business and which can be achieved immediately (quick wins). Remember to make systems easy to do right and difficult to do wrong. Train everyone in the new process and embed it:
   a. Document all processes and collect evidence that existing processes are being followed. If not, then review the process and amend or retrain staff.
   b. Collate all processes for the business against each clause and requirements.
9. Present the findings to the main leadership and wider business:
   a. Explore the good and the bad of what is currently practised.
10. Implement changes to adhere to the requirements and to meet conformance levels. Seek outside help if needed:
    a. Document processes and revisions (control all documents so that they are authorized and reviewed effectively, they are coded, and an archive is managed).
11. Management review and pre-assessment report (how well you meet the standard).
12. Screening for a third-party auditor:
    a. Shortlist third-party organizations that can help provide a consultancy report and select a reputable and effective provider.
13. Third-party audit and corrective actions:
    a. Learn from the pre-assessment audit and improve processes accordingly.
    b. Monitor and improve by yourself (update documentation where necessary).
14. Assessment:
    a. Fail decision – apply more effort in the areas of management that need to improve to conform.
    b. Pass:
       i. Improve any minor issues that have been detected.

15 Celebrate success internally.

16 Promote success with your local stakeholders and trading partners.

17 Establish reviews and use internal/external audits to identify opportunities for improvement.

Most businesses do not just use a single standard – such as the ISO 9001 quality standard – but instead use multiple standards. It is common to see ISO 14001 environmental management systems and ISO 9001 quality management systems used together along with occupational health and safety ISO 45001. In the past these standards, which govern different aspects of good management, looked slightly different. So in 2012, a project called Annex SL was introduced (following great amounts of work throughout the world) to harmonize the words and approach used so that all standards would look similar and allow certified businesses (and those seeking certification) to operate with less bureaucracy. The ISO had standardized standards! Annex SL was therefore the first high-level structure for any standard; its introduction was a major step forward that has helped businesses to harness more of their efforts for even more business benefit.

Annex SL – the standardization of standard formatting

Annex SL is a high-level structure (HLS) providing a common set of management standard themes and requirements, which has made standards writing and, for business, the use of multiple standards, much easier. The name Annex SL may well change over time and be replaced but the new approach to a high-level structure will be enduring as a means of systematically structuring standards. It is a generic and high-level structure that governs all standards regardless of whether they are a quality standard, an occupational health standard, or any other new or revised standard. The following are common sections, split into two parts for a reason:

1 scope;

2 normative references;

3 terms and definitions;

4 context of the organization;

5 leadership;

6 planning;

7 support;

8 operation;

9 performance evaluation;

10 improvement.

The first three sections therefore set out the administrative aspects of the standards document that is used for certification and conformance. Scope details what the standard will or will not do, normative references provide information on other documents that are considered vital to use with the standard being implemented, and the terms outline the technical definitions of key words and terms used by the standard.

Sections 4 to 10 form the main architecture of the processes needed to conform to the standard. These are what most employees would see as associated with the standard – they show a company what is needed and what must be in place and working effectively (it will be audited!).

The context of the organization explores the business and its stakeholders, the leadership section demands that a company shows its commitment to the standard, the planning section requires a business to declare how objectives and risks associated with the business practices of the standard are managed, and the support section probes the actions to exploit the opportunities, minimize the risks and use the standard to maximum effect. The support section demands evidence is provided that all processes and resources are identified, that they are capable and competent, there is high awareness, high levels of communication, and all processes are documented or recorded in a verifiable manner. These actions support the best use of resources to exploit business opportunities and reduce business risk. The operation element of the standard and its many clauses and requirements asks for evidence that all internal and subcontracted business activities are managed and controlled effectively. The performance evaluation section requires that monitoring, measurements, audits and reviews are all conducted. Finally, the improvement section requires that a company has processes that can deal with non-conforming practices and materials etc, as well as providing auditable evidence that the business is continuously improving. Annex SL therefore embodies all the principles we have seen during the initial chapters of this book.

Internal stakeholder benefits

The new approach and standards in general do help internal staff within a business and the benefits of that ISO blue logo and actual standard include those shown in Table 3.3.

Table 3.3 Internal stakeholder benefits

Stakeholder	Benefits
Business leaders and strategy processes	Knowing the business is organized and management around practices that are considered 'best practices'.
Marketing	Convincing new customers that the business has all the capabilities needed of a great company.
Sales	The implied value of a business that meets an international standard and the confidence that the business has all the management practices to offer great value. It offers customer confidence and a sales opportunity (as a differentiator).
Operations	Process controls and procedural improvements that make the workplace a great environment with an engaged workforce. Process efficiency improvement, operational certainty, competent workers and cost savings.
Finance	Less waste and more profit as well as processes to show measured improvements.
Supply chain	The ability to use the standard with suppliers and gain the same benefits.
Human resources	Training that meets the needs of the business and a workforce that is educated and loyal.
Information technology	Clear value from good information and data control.
New product development and introduction	Effective processes with engaged use and less time needed to bring a new product to market.

The benefits are significant to all employees and the fact that each standard requires that the certified business has an audit system and continuous improvement learning cycles (based on innovations and gaps identified by the audits) means these standards are living documents and adapt over time to offer even greater value to the business and its success.

Auditing

The audit process for any standard relies heavily on:

- **internal audits conducted by first-party staff** – these staff are employees and are trained to be competent in conducting audits on behalf of their employer;

- **external second-party audits** conducted by customers and trading partners;
- **external third-party audits** conducted annually by competent independent organizations (for an audit fee and as part of continued certification); a very deep audit is conducted every three years.

The outcomes of any audit, which should be greeted positively by managers and staff as these audits are a means of feedback and learning, include observations and areas where the auditor thinks you can improve: minor non-conformances that are system weaknesses, minor issues that could lead to a major failure in the management system if left uncorrected, and finally major non-conformances that are fundamental failures in implementation (eg missing processes or contradictory evidence that raises doubt about the competence of the management and integrity of the system). All such outcomes are learning opportunities, and some carry significant implications – especially poor conformance where the management of the business will be expected to correct issues quickly and effectively.

So, the ISO develops and publishes standards, but it does not conduct the audit processes. The audit process is personal to each business and is conducted by staff and paid third-party certifiers. We will return to a deeper analysis of auditing in a later chapter but it is important to note that the ISO revises and issues its new updated standards every five years or so and therefore every holder of a specific ISO standard must review their processes and 'come up' to the new standard when it is introduced. As such, the world of standards is changing and improving to help businesses improve and enact new best practices.

What are the most popular standards and why?

Naturally, with over 22,000 active standards available, some are more popular than others. The most popular standards do represent the bulk of users and certified companies in the world (see Table 3.4).

These standards dominate most of the activity for auditing and certification processes and are interoperable through the high-level structure approach (initially Annex SL). They give the reader a flavour of what is covered but ISO 9001 and 14001 dominate the world of standards and are – for most sectors – mandatory levels of certification in order to do business and be treated as a credible business.

Table 3.4 The most popular ISO standards

The standard	The focus of the standard
ISO 9000 series (ISO 9001 is the conformance standard)	Quality management systems for manufacturing and service organizations of any size and product/service range.
ISO 14000 series (ISO 14001 is the conformance standard)	Environmental management systems standards for the sustainability and opportunities and risks of environmental control.
ISO 45000 series (ISO 45001 is the conformance standard)	The management of occupational health and safety processes for protection of all staff and stakeholders.
ISO 27000 series (ISO 27001 is the conformance standard)	The management of the business for information security and control of digital information.
ISO 50000 series (ISO 50001 is the conformance standard)	The processes and systems needed for the effective management of energy for a business.

Critics of the international management standards community

The ISO and other organizations have been very quick to defend themselves against criticism. They believe what they do is for the betterment of society, national states and individual businesses. So, Table 3.5 will present both sides of the arguments that have been used as criticisms and conspiracy theories!

Unsurprisingly, at the heart of the standards process and industry is a concern to make businesses better and to help companies to survive and prosper. Standards are therefore associated with the key business needs of becoming world class, raising performance levels, understanding business risks, creating economic and environmental sustainability, and enhancing trade.

Table 3.5 Critics of the ISO and its processes

Critical theme	The critics' view	The standards community view
Exclusion of developing countries	ISO standards allow mature economies to set standards that developing countries lack the skills to conform with and businesses lack the financial resources needed to get certified.	Standards allow developing countries and businesses to trade with developed markets. The cost of buying a standard is low and so are the rates for auditors in developing countries.
Adding cost to doing business for companies that gain certification	ISO standards cost money to buy.	Standards are relatively inexpensive to buy. The strategic and operational performance benefits from the 'quick wins' alone will pay for the costs of a standard. Most certification businesses will also quantify the business benefits to be more than the implementation costs. Standards may also be viewed for free at many libraries on request. The costs of third-party auditing can be expensive.
Ignoring sector-specific practices and needs	The ISO management system standards are generic for all businesses so how can they help an individual business with unique challenges or specific sectors?	The standards represent 'good practice' and all business leaders need to implement such practices. The quality of implementation and solutions developed by the company are most important. There are sector-specific standards that translate ISO standards (such as ISO 9001) into sector standards (such as TS 16949 for automotive quality or AS 9100 for aerospace quality).
Politics and trade	The ISO is dominated by a few powerful countries.	Untrue! ISO members are all equal and fully engaged with the standardization agenda.
Too bureaucratic and costly	ISO inhibits effective change and slows adaptation.[9]	Untrue! The speed of issuing new work instructions post improvement and also in focusing improvement has been accelerated with Annex SL.

In summary

This chapter has presented a brief overview of the ISO and its main processes of developing and publishing new standards that benefit the world. The 'mechanics' and structure of the ISO are an interesting subject. The ISO is not an audit business though – these organizations are independent and serve as the certifying businesses within a country and there are often many of them per country. So the reader now knows more of the ISO and how it helps raise business performance. This chapter extends the thinking of the first chapter which laid out in no uncertain terms the importance of quality as a concept for getting things right and as a strategic direction for any manufacturing business. Chapter 2 went further to explain how the concept of TQM and its main principles are embedded in every international standard. Some may think that quality principles and TQM only impact on the quality management standard and guidelines of ISO 9001 (and supporting guide documents). This is untrue. ISO 9000 series is the most popular standard in use today and it has a natural affinity with TQM. But TQM means *Total Quality Management* and that means any standard that is operated and used by a business.

Seminar topics and examination questions

This chapter has broadly reviewed the ISO and its central purpose and there are many questions worth debating for students. These include:

- Does the international adoption of standards enable or prevent developing countries entering mature Western markets and selling products?
- Is it fair to have one vote per country no matter the size of the country, its industrial base or population?
- Why don't China or India or Russia just set up their own standards rather than support the ISO?
- Should the ISO do certification audits? After all, it develops the standards.
- Aren't standards so generic that they are meaningless? Surely the ISO 9001 standard of quality management is different when applied to a nuclear power plant than to a company making windows?

- Do international languages and cultural barriers cause confusion during ISO standards development meetings?
- Technical committees are more important than national bodies. Discuss.
- Why would a national body decide not to adopt a standard?

The next chapter will present and explore the most popular management standard – ISO 9001.

Further reading

There is a huge amount of information and useful data held on the ISO's main website and national body websites. Many authors tend to focus their books on specific standards rather than the ISO infrastructure, so it is best to look online.

Notes

1 Seear, D J (2014) *ISO 9001:2015 Back to the Future: A review of the new ISO Annex SL structure for certification standards using the draft ISO 9001:2015 to explain the changes*, Author House Publishing

2 ISO (2019) Certification [online] Available at: https://www.iso.org/certification.html (archived at https://perma.cc/Y7FD-4EY4) [accessed 24 April 2019]

3 Hoyle, D (2017) *ISO 9000 Quality Systems Handbook – updated for the ISO 9001:2015 standard: Increasing the Quality of an Organization's Outputs*, Taylor and Francis, London

4 Please use the internet to search for ISO_Membership_Manual

5 BSI (2012) *BSI Pocket Guide to Standards Development*, Chiswick, London. You can search the internet for a free copy.

6 Ibid.

7 ISO (2012) *Standards: What's the Bottom Line?*, ISO, Geneva

8 Hewitt, D and Ainslee, V (2019) *Quality Management Systems: A guide to ISO 9001:2015 implementation and problem solving*, revised 2nd ed, Purple Parrot Publishing

9 Seddon, J (1997) *In Pursuit of Quality: The case against ISO 9000*, Oak Tree Press

Quality management system standards

04

The 'Number One' competitive priority for any 'world class' business is to manage the corporate process of quality. The Total Quality approach has many principles and methods but, for many, it lacks a concrete set of methods and processes that establish and help to sustain the drive to perfect value and minimal waste through quality improvement.[1] ISO 9001 is the conformance standard of the 9000 series, which supports 'best practice' in quality management.[2] It has elements of the standard that ensure quality control, quality assurance and the capabilities needed to become a Total Quality Management (TQM) organization. It can be no surprise that this standard is the most popular and has the most certifications worldwide.

Put quite simply, a quality management system (QMS) is all the processes and activities that are carried out by an organization in order to satisfy the expectations of customers and other stakeholders in the market and context of the organization as well as all the organizational, leadership and management routines necessary to ensure that processes are operated optimally.

LEARNING OBJECTIVES

At the end of this chapter, you should be able to:

- understand the importance of quality process management as a competitive weapon;
- understand and define the main features of a quality management system (QMS);

- describe the historical evolution of QMS systems from the British standard BS 5750 to the latest revision of ISO 9001;
- understand the relationship between ISO 9001 and other guides in the ISO 9000 series portfolio;
- explain the importance of using Annex SL and why it brings simplicity to the implementation and ongoing management/improvement of quality processes within an organization;
- explain the major reasons why customers expect ISO 9001 certification and why businesses seek to conform to the standard;
- understand the key features and audit points of a QMS;
- describe the generic steps needed to effectively implement ISO 9001.

Introduction

It is a well-known saying that 'the customer is always right' and organizations that get customer service right are those that will prosper in today's highly competitive market.[3] Those organizations that do not offer high-quality products and services will face a more uncertain future. Organizations offering a product or service must ensure there is customer demand and that this demand can be satisfied profitably with minimal waste and cost. Businesses therefore need a robust and functional quality management system (QMS) to structure and guide the implementation of quality in every activity of the business. A QMS is a portfolio of activities and processes that consistently delivers what the customer wants/needs and is a strategic investment to align the organization's strategic direction (setting quality policies to meet the intended goals or outputs) with the structures needed to deliver customer quality and value. The ISO 9000 series of document standards enables the leadership of organizations of all sectors and sizes of business to implement and achieve consistent and sustainable quality processes to ensure products and services that customers want are delivered in the most effective and efficient way. It is no surprise that ISO 9001 is the most popular global standard with over 1.2 million certifications and rising.

Quality management systems

A robust quality management system is critical to organizations that must compete with others on a global scale and must prove they have the capabilities to deliver great products and services. A quality management system provides a framework and means by which business leaders can deploy strategic objectives in the form of policies, processes, procedures and continuous improvement activities. Maximizing the flow of materials from suppliers (inputs) into products that fulfil customer needs is critical and requires a quality management system framework to do so (Figure 4.1).

Figure 4.1 An integrated management system that coordinates the transformation of inputs into outputs

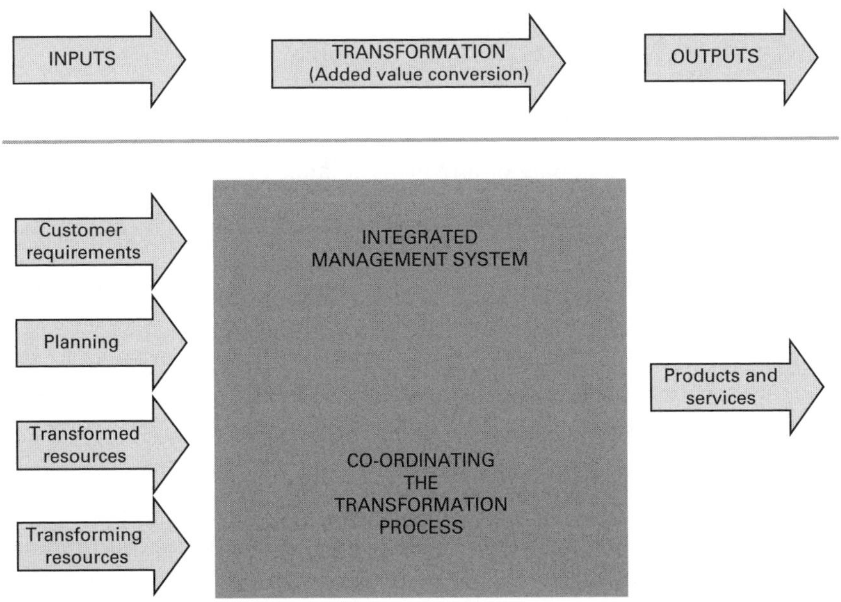

The ISO 9000 series offers a robust management system (with ISO 9001 as its conformance standard) that helps staff to deploy, guide, plan, focus, monitor and improve all aspects of organizational quality. Operating a business with effective quality management practices in place harnesses innovation, efficiency and effectiveness by developing processes that offer customers what they want, when they want it – with minimal costs. A QMS works at

Figure 4.2 QMS that takes into account other standards

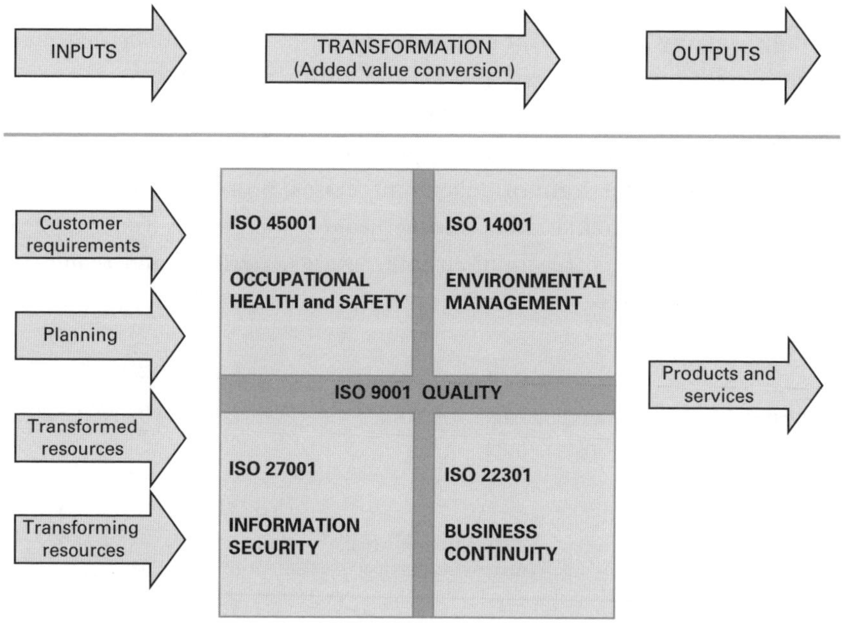

the heart of the value adding of any business and offers much greater control over inputs, the process, and customer outputs. With Annex SL in place, the ISO 9001 standard also provides the foundation upon which to add environmental management systems (ISO 14001) and occupational health and safety (ISO 45001) – see Figure 4.2.

ISO 9001 allows formalized control, repeatability, accountability of the processes and ongoing learning through measurements, audits and management reviews. The standard and its audits improve weak areas of the business such as areas for improvement and issues solved via non-conformance detection and resolution. A QMS relies on people, processes and technology to achieve best practice and to learn how to improve. This is only achievable with employee engagement at all levels, realized through staff training, communication and internally recognized and respected standards. Using the formalized processes through documentation, employee responsibilities are assigned to ensure staff within an organization are clear on what piece of the jigsaw they are that goes into achieving the quality objectives and policies.

ISO 9001 is focused on process management (Figure 4.3) rather than on departmental activities and responsibilities. Processes pass through departments and are critical to customers (quality and delivery of products are critical processes). No department can take sole responsibility for a customer process such as the quality of a product because product quality is as much the result of good supply chain and purchasing management as it is the operations or quality departments. Taking ownership of product quality is a team responsibility! If you stop and think about what it would mean to optimize the quality management of a business, you are likely to identify issues such as:

- A good strategy and plans that set the direction for quality improvement and business success.
- The whole leadership team must be engaged rather than passing quality responsibility to a single manager; how could one person ever be responsible for the quality of an entire organization?
- There should be measures to see how the business is trending or making advances towards its goals. It should also be mindful of business risks that may interrupt product flows and profitability.
- Processes should be documented and staff trained. The business should use capable machinery operated by trained and observant staff.
- Tasks should be formalized so that staff can be trained and these documents used to write up new improvements that can then be used to train others in a cycle of continuous improvement.
- Everyone should be attentive to the customer; management should review the business often and everyone should exploit the advice of auditors who are there to help a business get better and better.
- Finally, it is important to celebrate success when objectives are achieved and to find ways of reinforcing the quality priority for all staff and suppliers.

This is the basis of a QMS that uses quality policy and the objectives of an organization to determine and improve the processes which are required to achieve those objectives having considered the needs and expectations of the customers and interested parties (along with any regulations that need to be adhered to). Those responsible for carrying out activities (leadership, operational and review) must be identified and adequate resources provided for each of the processes in the system. For an organization to maintain and continually improve their QMS, measuring the effectiveness and efficiency of each of the processes must be established to ensure that each process is robust and capable of delivering a high-quality output regardless of what activity it takes place in and what process step it is.

There are many quality management models available to business leaders and most can be combined. Hence the ISO 9001 standard can be used not only to drive and support the application of lean business principles (just-in-time production), it can also support the statistical power and discipline of the Six Sigma approach, and can assist businesses to achieve quality prizes

Figure 4.3 Process approach within a quality management system

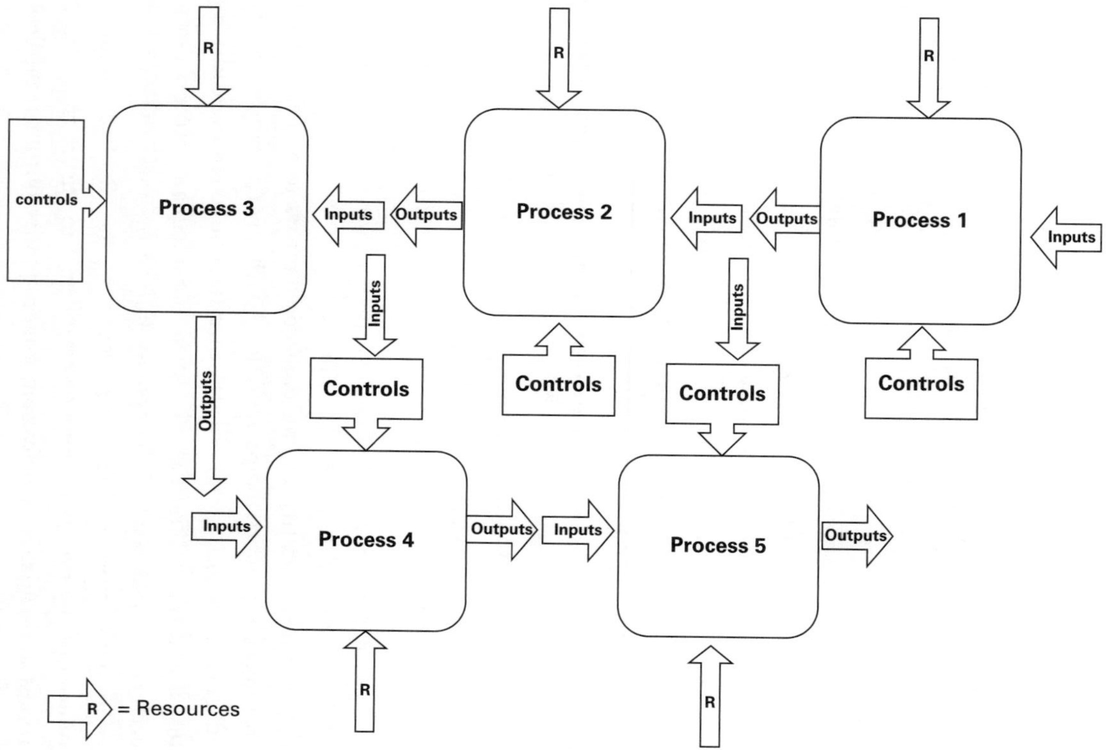

such as the EFQM Awards (European Foundation for Quality Management) and excellence model. Overall, ISO 9001 and its guide documents help a business to progress towards TQM. Whichever approach is used with ISO 9001, the unifying goal is to ensure that production (the output) is of high quality and produced with minimal waste. Satisfying customers profitably and ahead of the competition is key! And effective process management with an engaged and thinking workforce is essential.

ISO 9000 family

The evolution of quality management dates back a long way to the early 1900s, where quality was managed by inspection only; products either met specification at the end of the process or they failed. If products failed quality control, they would either be reworked until they were good for sale or scrapped as defects at a cost to the business and a loss of production time that could never be recovered. The Japanese nation, inspired by the early quality gurus, moved from control to quality assurance – managing reliable and capable processes resulting in good outputs at each stage of the process. By the 1950s (the inception of Japanese TQM), industrialists could control and assure processes; they then expanded to become 'total' in their approach to business and making a profit. In 1959, the US Department of Defence developed a standardized system of quality assurance that established procedures to manage processes that could affect the outcome of a manufactured product (known as standard MIL-Q-9858) but little of this form of assured control migrated to general manufacturing. By 1969, NATO AQAP (Allied Quality Assurance Publications) revised this standard (again this was further revised in 1974 by the BSI) and interest grew in how a military form of production control could be used for general products. The BSI then formalized the BS 5179 series of guidance standards for quality and further revised these documents to form BS 5750. BS 5750 is very much what we would perceive as a quality management standard that went beyond product and process specifications to include policies and a range of managerial activities necessary to support competent production. The standard was submitted to the ISO and adapted to become ISO 9001 (plus guides), the most popular standard of all time.

To assist organizations in the implementation, maintenance and improvement of a QMS, the ISO conceived a set of international standards known as ISO 9000 series that can be applied to any organization, regardless of size or industry. Within ISO 9000 series there are four critical documents, namely:

1. ISO 9001:2015 (Quality management systems – requirements and conformance standard);
2. ISO 9000:2015 (Quality management systems – fundamentals and vocabulary including definitions);
3. ISO 9002:2016 (Quality management systems – guidelines for the application of ISO 9001:2015);
4. ISO 9004:2009 (Quality management systems – quality of an organization – guidance to achieve sustained success).

An independent but related standard is also ISO 19011:2018 (Guidelines for auditing management systems).

From this list it can be seen that the ISO 9000 family covers everything that is needed to establish a robust quality management system. It is interesting to note that when a standard is referred to or stated, it is presented with the letters ISO along with its exact standard/guide number and date – such as ISO 9001:2015. The date expresses the latest time the standard was updated, which is the standard that businesses are expected to conform with. All businesses must remain up to date with a new conformance standard (say in year 2021 the new standard is released to be presented as ISO 9001:2021) and will be given a fixed time to transition from an existing ISO standard to the new revised one. Failure to transition will mean the business fails to conform to the newest standard. In the year 2019, ISO 9001:2015, ISO 9000:2015, ISO 9004:2018 and ISO 19011:2018 were the latest updates. ISO 9000 will always deal with the terminology and definitions used for clarity when implementing a QMS and it is crucial that professional managers understand the fundamental wisdom and concepts of this document; it is a 'must read' for anyone working with the requirements standard ISO 9001. ISO 9001:2015 details the conformance requirements for efficiently and effectively operating a QMS; ISO 9004:2018 will always provide management guidance for attaining sustained success and how to meet the expectations of all interested parties focusing on continual improvement for customer/stakeholder satisfaction. It is also important to remember ISO 19011, which is not strictly part of the 9000 series but is a very important document as it sets out the key auditing principles along with clear guidance on how to conduct audits and evaluation of the audit process itself. It is quite ironic that you hear the term 'ISO 9000' from many people in presentations and at conferences when they are really talking about the conformance standard ISO 9001.

Learning point

There are many important documents in the 9000 series – not just one! ISO 9001 is the most important from a certification perspective – it is the conformance model. It has a date of latest issue and it is the structure of the modern business.

History of ISO 9001

The quality principles that have been discussed in previous chapters are implicit within the QMS and learning and continuous improvement processes of ISO 9001. They include customer focus, leadership, engagement of people, process approach, continuous improvement, evidence-based decision making and relationship management to name a few. ISO 9001 is a true systems approach, and through revision of the standard, it is a constantly evolving document that ensures businesses are directed to build robust processes that use quality principles to create real processes of value to customers.

Readers are reminded that any business can buy the ISO 9001 standard and implement it. It is not mandatory for a business that has implemented all the features of ISO 9001 to be certified by a third party. Uncertified implemented ISO 9001 QMS systems do deliver benefits and help meet the requirements of customers along with regulatory requirements for effective business and continuous improvement, so they are still highly valuable. Equally, a poor approach and attitude to exploiting ISO 9001 will result in a business that has a basic form of conformance but will fail to get the real benefits of the system and its rewards. It is also interesting to note that a QMS influences management practice and permeates the organization from there – it should also positively influence the design of products themselves, so the business offers great products to delighted customers. However, having the ISO 9001 certification is not a product 'guarantee' but it does provide confidence and assurance that all the essential and implemented features of an effective quality system are in place.

So how did ISO 9001 come about? ISO 9001 was derived from the British standard BS 5750 that was first published by the British Standards Institution in 1979 and was the first civilian quality system standard. The standard promoted the use of a quality policy and a series of documented and auditable procedures. The procedures also had to be controlled with tracking identification so that they could be updated, and a new procedure issued. The main criticism of the BS 5750 approach was that it was bureaucratic and used for conformity rather than as a means of leading and managing quality for an organization. The ISO technical committee 176 (TC 176) was established in 1979 with the specific responsibility of developing a series of international standards for quality management. The development of a published international standard was intended to assist cross-border and global trade. In effect, the standard would work as an international 'trade passport'.

TC 176 published the first edition of ISO 9001 in 1987 as a mirror image of the BS 5750 structure for conformance with documented procedures. This was the start of many subsequent revisions as the standard was reviewed by TC 176 and new 'best practices' were introduced to make the standard more meaningful and relevant to business (Figure 4.4). Technical committee revisions are mandatory and will typically result in a new standard every five years or more. Such revisions are important, and the world does not operate with paper-based systems and documents as it did when ISO 9001 was first released. New lean ways of working have become popular and markets/regulations have changed to increase complexity for managers and leaders.

The revision process affects every ISO 9000 series document and guide. Today process management is very important and this was first recognized in the terminology changes to ISO 9000:2005. A process is defined as a set of interrelated activities that transform inputs into outputs. A procedure was specified to carry out the activities of a process (how to). The modern ISO 9001:2015 revision embodies both an intention to make QMS systems easier to manage and less bureaucratic, and the goal of enhancing the flexibility and adaptability of the standards in practice. Hence the use of Annex SL as a higher-level structure for all standards (not just the 9000 series). It is likely that

Figure 4.4 ISO 9001 history

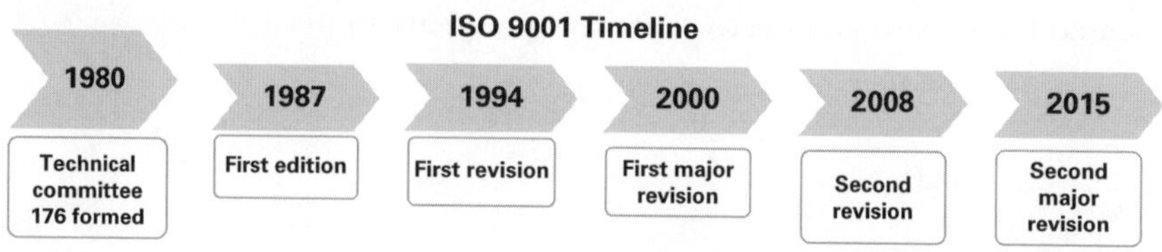

revisions will extend to around every 10 years with a three-year 'grace period' for organizations updating from an older version to the new published QMS.

Annex SL[4] evolved from ISO Guide 83 (2011), a publication defining a common management system. For the first time, this guide formalized a consistent structure, terminology and framework for all the ISO management systems to adhere to. Annex SL (Figure 4.5) has two more clauses than used in the ISO 9001:2008 version. Of these high-level structured clauses, 4 to 10 have sub-clauses. These sub-clauses demand that the management and leadership of an organization must introduce procedures and processes to control of these activities and provide evidence of control and auditing. As previously explained, the first three clauses are specific to the discipline or industry. Clause 1 sets out the scope of an organization's management system that aligns with the organization's context (clause 4); clause 2 relates the standard to other relevant references, and clause 3 sets out the terms and definitions required to understand and implement the specific standard – in this case the current version of ISO 9001:2015.[5]

The first three sections of clauses of ISO 9001:2015 QMS demand that organizational leaders specify and scope out what an organization must provide to satisfy the market (customers and regulators) and ensure that employees understand the need for high quality, improvement and conformance to the standard. The term 'normative reference' can be thought of as a signposting of the leadership and staff to other helpful documents in the portfolio and series. Finally, terms and definitions help add greater clarity to the words that will be used within the standard and these can all be found in ISO 9000. These initial sections may appear somewhat bureaucratic to some people, but they are highly important and the ISO process and TC 176 are made up of many members with many different languages – so getting words and meaning right is very important as a means of helping leaders/managers to implement effective processes.

Figure 4.5 Annex SL structure

The remaining clauses (4 to 10) are areas that are auditable and require conformance. Annex SL uses 45 statements that use the term 'shall' – these are embedded in the clauses and result in a total of 84 requirements where the company 'shall' do and evidence something to be able to conform to the standard.[6] These are not optional or negotiable. They are also the mechanics of getting ISO 9001 to work effectively, to drive greater business efficiencies and to start the learning process that will take the business closer to full TQM.

The main operational clauses and their implications include sections 4 to 10. Section 4 of the standard is very much an attempt to get senior leaders and those who set the direction and strategy of the business to see the business as a 'living system' and recognize the wider environment that can impact on the growth or risks to a business (see Table 4.1). Section 5 outlines the key responsibilities of the business leaders so that staff 'follow' the quality direction of the business and see the QMS as the means to achieve the goals of the business and a brighter future.

Table 4.1 Working sections of the ISO 9001:2015 standard 4–5

Section	Clauses	Implications for ISO 9001 implementation
4 Context of the organization	Understanding the organization and its context	Organizational leaders must understand the meaning, context and environment of the business and why the organization exists. The business must understand its dependencies and need for internal alignment of goals/objectives.
	Needs and expectations of interested parties	Leaders need to understand the external and internal issues that are relevant to the business and its quality management system.
	Determining the scope of the management system	Businesses must understand the needs and expectations of customers/interested parties and the scope of the QMS and its processes.
	The management system	

(continued)

Table 4.1 *(Continued)*

Section	Clauses	Implications for ISO 9001 implementation
5 Leadership	Leadership and commitment	The role of organizational leaders is to set an example, communicate effectively with staff throughout the organization and engage employees with the quality priority. Leadership should also delegate and empower staff to drive, learn from and proactively manage the QMS. Senior leaders must show commitment to the QMS and its policies, and dedicate management to the products, customers, planning and review of business activities and the QMS.
	Policy	Employees should be aware and engaged – knowing their role, responsibility and contribution to the business and its QMS. Leaders and managers must assure active self and employee engagement with the QMS as a means to achieve its set objectives/targets. Accountability of staff is key to embedding ownership of the QMS.
	Organizational roles, responsibilities and authorities	Leaders must critically assess the risks or threats that exist to the organization in its context and the opportunities that exist to exploit the QMS too. Requires management's commitment to the QMS and to developing appropriate policies.
		Management must be dedicated to the organization's products, customers and planning and review processes.

Table 4.2 Working sections of the ISO 9001:2015 standard 6–9

Section	Clauses	Implications for ISO 9001 implementation
6 Planning	Actions to address risks and opportunities	Senior leaders must identify and address risks and opportunities to the business by establishing quality objectives and how to achieve them, including the relevant business functions involved, organizational levels and business processes.
	QMS objectives and plans to achieve them	Senior leaders and managers must create processes and procedures for planning changes to the QMS.
7 Support	Resources	Ensuring that the organization determines and provides appropriate resources for the operation of the QMS.
	Competence	Evidencing that the human resources are competent and that an infrastructure exists to operationalize the QMS.
	Awareness	Improved awareness and communication of the need to change and how to change.
	Communication	Provision of adequate work environment for the implementation, maintenance and continual improvement of the QMS.
	Documented information	
	Resources	
8 Operation	Operational planning and control	This section covers operational planning and control (eg of the processes), design, development and requirements of products/ services along with product realization.

(*continued*)

Table 4.2 (*Continued*)

Section	Clauses	Implications for ISO 9001 implementation
9 Performance evaluation	Monitoring, measurement, analysis and evaluation Internal audit Management review	Ensuring the effective measures of QMS performance and improvement are established. The creation of routines to analyse and improve the QMS. The setting of routines to perform periodical internal audits. Creating a means of monitoring customer satisfaction. Development of data analyses to monitor, measure, analyse and evaluate performance. The establishment of a QMS management review process (conducted at planned intervals) to ensure the continuing suitability, adequacy, effectiveness and alignment of the QMS with the strategic direction of the organization.

Section 6 (see Table 4.2) moves from leadership to technical quality management system alignment and the setting of objectives. These objectives represent future aspirational goals rather than gaps and weaknesses. They are challenges to staff and require innovation and engagement of staff to achieve. Section 6 also demands that senior managers and leaders invest in process development, most notably the development of planning processes that allow goals to be set and plans introduced to ensure the business is improving.

Section 7 represents another level of detail and requires that business leaders can demonstrate that the QMS is capable and that staff are trained and competent, supported by routines and documented tasks and activities so that the correct standard of performance is formally available to staff. The majority of the management system requirements stem from clause 8 (operation) as it covers control, planning and management of both internal and outsourced processes. These requirements will vary from discipline to discipline. But clause 8 is critical for the management of day-to-day tasks that an organization must control along with planning for unforeseen issues. Clause 8 can only be enacted when clauses 4 to 7 have been reviewed and implemented.

So clauses 4 to 6 effectively cover the areas of organizational context, commitment and planning and it is only after carrying out this initial work and understanding that an organization will have a clearer idea of what their goals and objectives are and what support (ie internal and external resources) they might need to meet their targets. All of this is covered in clause 7 (support). For an organization to continually seek to improve (clause 10), there must be some form of performance assessment that is evaluated to give meaningful data from which to make corrective actions; this evaluation is covered in clause 9. An organization is continually seeking ways to improve their operating QMS, be it through their processes or adjustments that are required to their products or services whilst constantly keeping their customers' needs and expectations in mind. Linking this back to clause 8 (operations), if innovation is required in the development of the product/service to come up with new solutions, 'communicating' with the customer (or future customer) is covered in this earlier clause.

As a result of Annex SL, clause 8 has been expanded significantly; this is the element of the standard that most employees will experience on a daily basis. Clause 8 has many sub-clauses which include evidence that management have processes and controls for operational planning and control, and the determination of requirements for products and services leading to effective design and development of products and services process. The clause also demands that management shall control externally provided products and services (by suppliers at the beginning input stage and mid-process) as well as procedures that govern production and service provision and the release of products and services that are at an acceptable standard for purchase by a customer/consumer. Finally, clause 8 also demands that an organization shall control its nonconforming process outputs, products and services. The latter means that any process or product that is discovered to be defective must be the subject of a process that quarantines, isolates, and corrects the failure. The process is designed to prevent issues and failures from leaving the company and getting to the hands of a customer.

ISO 9001 QMS clause 9 focuses on the development of business measurement, analysis and auditing routines. These processes and procedures support greater feedback and the ability of managers to intervene to correct variations in performance and also to review trends to ensure the QMS is enabling business improvement. Measures are necessary to track actual business performance against the leadership goals and to promote learning for staff. Measurement and regular reviews of individual processes and the quality system ensure it remains effective and scrutinized.

Section 10 (see Table 4.3) demands that all the processes in the organization must be covered by a set of procedures that are monitored to ensure their effectiveness, and to achieve this it is important that appropriate documentation is used and adequate records are kept. When defects are detected, appropriate and corrective action must be carried out, so that nonconforming process interactions are controlled and interventions to improve can be measured to show actual evidenced improvement. Preventative action is encouraged and implemented to ensure that errors or defects do not reoccur. Internal auditing provides the key role of policing a QMS to ensure it is robust and remains fit for purpose. This all starts from product inception (design) through to product realization and delivery, managing resources along the way.

Within each clause, just like the layers of an onion or a Russian doll, there are sub-clauses which detail the exact requirements of the standard. The ISO publishes and sells standards and therefore the entire series of sub-clauses cannot and will not be investigated here; business leaders should buy a copy of the relevant standard. It is not the intention of this book to go into details of the sub-clauses but to illustrate the language and type of 'shall' that is

Table 4.3 Working sections of the ISO 9001:2015 standard 10

Section	Clauses	Implications for ISO 9001 implementation
10 Improvement	General improvement	Controlling non-conformity in products/services (including any arising from complaints) through corrective action.
	Non-conformity and corrective action	Taking corrective and preventative action having considered the results of the analysis and evaluation.
	Continual improvement	Continual improvement by assessing the suitability, adequacy and effectiveness of the QMS.
		Assessing the management review to determine needs or opportunities for improvement.

expected by the ISO and its national body with responsibility for the country concerned. Copies of the latest standards can be easily obtained and at a reasonable cost.

QMS documentation: old and new

The ISO 9000 series of standards has been simplified over its many revisions to enable easy use by organizations of all sizes and to remain relevant to modern managers.[7] Documentation was often considered a chore in the early days because the ISO 9001 standard was perceived to need:

- every task documented and printed out;
- every process documented and printed out;
- a manual of everything printed out;
- the skills of the workers and training records printed out;
- all production documents to be signed;
- all quality inspection activities to be printed out;
- any change to any task, activity or process or policy to be printed out for every single manual everywhere in the factory.

So, in the late 1980s and early 1990s, ISO 9001 was considered to be a bureaucratic system that was almost destined to have issues because it required a lot of administration to make sure everything was up to date after the first documents were written. Not just that – every updated document needed a revision number and to pass through a committee which would check the update to make sure it was safe and scrutinized as effective and appropriate. Critics of the early standards highlighted this aspect of standards management, but it is interesting to note that many critics did not offer an alternative to managing in this way and most did not actually criticize the improvements that resulted from this approach to quality management. Interestingly enough, the documentation now required has a more modern approach and evidence that is relevant means it does not have to be a paper-based system entirely. According to the ISO, 'It is stressed that ISO 9001 requires (and always has required) a "Documented quality management system" and not a "system of documents".'[8]

So, electronic documents and other forms of evidence are acceptable to an auditor and for running a business subject to the process of 'control'. Relevant documentation is key and such evidence must be controlled via a process that maintains the integrity and assurance of being the latest version, and has been subject to controlled and authorized revisions. This is a major clause and one that many applicant businesses do not invest enough time in when managing and preparing for audit/certification. Up-to-date work instructions and other documents must be controlled and available for workers, or else they will not conduct a task, activity or process to a quality-assured and safe level of performance. Auditors will observe workers conducting activities and demand that evidence is substantiated – especially asking how the worker knows they are working to the latest approved revision. Standard operating procedures these days are typically available to workers on a digital tablet, making their life a lot easier when maintaining and changing controlled documents.[9] In the past, life was not so convenient and business managers would have to physically go and replace paper documents throughout the organization.

A diagram that shows the complexity of documented processes (Figure 4.6) shows how high-level organizational leadership and strategic direction of the QMS requires policies and documented vision (often displayed in the factory as a guide for workers) through various levels of operationalizing processes and procedures, activities and work instructions as well as additional records. The ISO 9001 system therefore covers all documents that form part of a 'living' and effective quality management system that is constantly improving. Although this is an older figure, it remains very useful for students and managers as it reinforces the discipline needed to certify to ISO 9001 and even the simplest business will operate a lot of key processes.[10] ISO 9001 applies to large and small businesses alike and is used for florists as well as manufacturers of aircraft and hospital equipment.

In documentation terms, the quality manual acts as a directory for the documents and procedures below and highlights the organization's commitment to quality. It is from this manual that operational procedures can be set for the management to control the system. That is, how the commitment to quality will be applied to the organization's operations, so the 'who', 'when' and 'where'. Developing these procedures entails reviewing and analysing current practice from which to develop draft procedures which can then be released for comment before being reviewed, revised and ultimately accepted, ready for approval and issued for use. All of these activities and routines are continually monitored and reviewed and where necessary adjusted and upgraded. ISO 9001 sets out many mandatory quality procedures in this second tier, from which six tasks are required, namely control of documents, control of records, internal audit, control of nonconforming product, corrective action, and preventive action.

Figure 4.6 QMS document pyramid

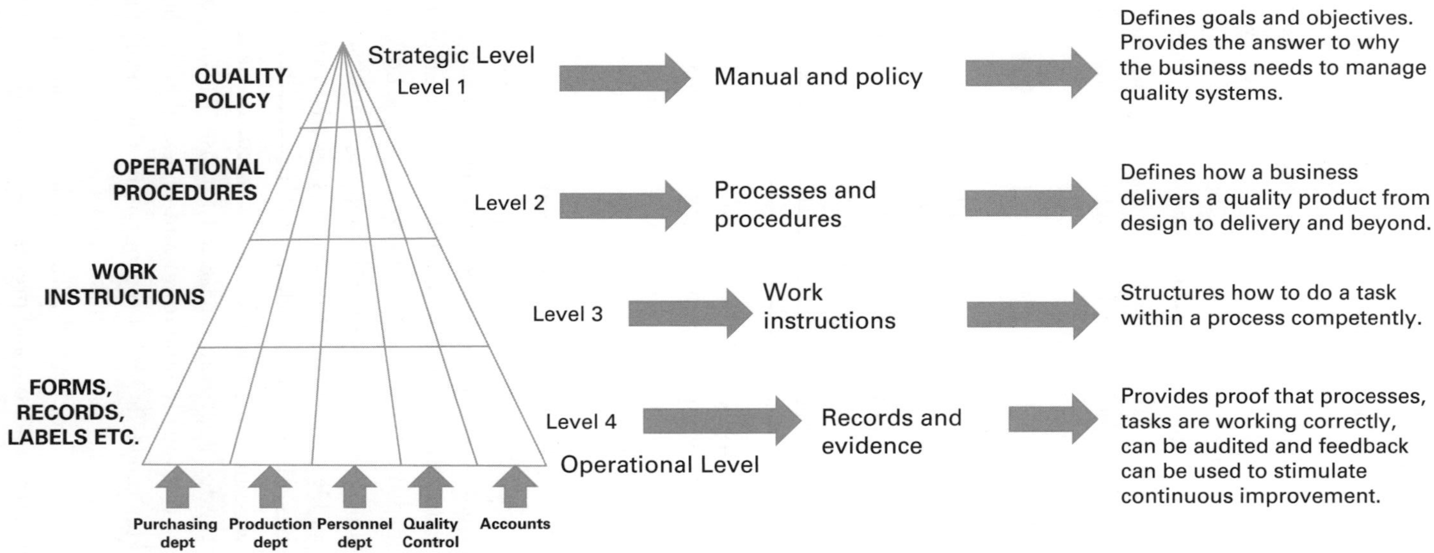

It is worth stopping for a moment and thinking through the role of 'evidenced proof of conformity' and control of documents. The best way to think about this subject is to adopt the view of a certifier and auditor. Section 7 and others of the Annex SL approach state that businesses shall demonstrate that processes are capable. So let us think about how we can provide evidence to satisfy an auditor. Well, we can show how the capability of a machine is controlled and show statistics and graphs of machine variation. How do we know we are using the machine in the right way? Well, there are standard and controlled instructions. Okay, but what about people? How do we know that 'Jo' is competent – well she would have been trained to use the machine. Okay, but how do we know that? She has a training record. Okay, in that case can we see it please? When was the employee training record last updated? By whom was it updated? This is the sort of evidence needed but more important is the discipline that all this requires, which is needed to run a world-class manufacturing organization.

Having set out the operational procedures, the third tier of the pyramid can be addressed and that is 'how' these procedures will be carried out. This breaks down the procedures into documented work instructions giving details of the day-to-day operating instructions. This can be both written and spoken direction to staff to ensure that each employee knows what is to be done, by whom and when. A work instruction is basically a mandatory task that must be carried out which is subordinate to a procedure and gives increased focus and detail on a particular task that is not set out in the procedures.

It is a must to keep adequate records or supporting documents; this is the base tier of the pyramid, which is used to support the other pyramid levels through evidence captured.[11] The management of this data system is essential for audit purposes and when it comes to analysing areas of weakness and strength within the system or if products need to be traced and recalled. Hence the varying departments within the organization must adhere to this documentation structure. This final tier could be anything: forms, documents, records, labels, tickets, job cards, purchase orders, stamps of approval, signed and dated documents, routing sheets, goods inwards notes, registers etc, each of which provide traceability of actions that are carried out in the day-to-day running of the organization.

Whilst it is essential that detailed procedures are documented to define a system, this does not mean that ISO 9001 standard's requirements are now satisfied. It is also not the case that the more an organization documents its each and every element and function the greater the control and accountability.

Documentation must be relevant and is dependent on the context, culture and operating environment of the organization in question. ISO 9001:2015 defines documented information as meaningful data that is required to be controlled and maintained by the organization and the medium on which it is contained. ISO 9001's documenting process is simply a way of creating control of documents that enable an organization to improve and be accountable. Controlling documents can be tricky, hence it is typical for a master list of documents to be prepared and safely saved, from which easy cross-referencing can be carried out if required. ISO 9001 does not prescribe how documents should be titled or how they should be controlled. The standard doesn't even state that a scope, purpose, reference documents section, or any other type of format is required. It is at the discretion of the organization in question to make their own judgement on this, hence they could document a procedure using a simple flow chart or a one-page instruction sheet, whilst another organization may see fit to create a 20-page detailed document. Most importantly, the documents must be fit for purpose of use. The whole premise of the documentation system of an ISO 9001 QMS is threefold: to document what you do in an appropriate form for auditing; to do what is outlined in your document by working to the procedures that have been established and written down; and finally to use evidence to prove that you conform (to the standard requirements) whilst reviewing procedures which can be used to continuously improve.

The importance of quality policy and objectives for a QMS

Quality policy is not just a manual for top-level managers. Employees at all levels of the organization must get to grips with this manual, be it through training or communication by managers, as auditors will test staff on their understanding of it. Under clause 5 (leadership) of ISO 9001:2015, there is sub-clause 5.2 entitled 'quality policy' under which there are two other relevant sub-sub-clauses concerning 'establishing the quality policy' (5.2.1) and 'communicating the quality policy' (5.2.2). The former sub-sub-clause sets out the requirements placed on top managers to ensure the effective application of the quality policy, linking back to the organizational quality objectives and appropriately reflected in the process design along with effective monitoring and measurement of data. The latter requires the organization to ensure that the policy is communicated to all interested parties. The 2008 version of this standard only required the policy to be relevant to an organization's purpose, whereas the 2015 standard has this additional requirement. The quality policy is as such not just for internal consumption and application, it must be made available to appropriate interested parties as well.

Sometimes things do not meet their quality mark and an effective quality policy can act as a reference point on how to deal with such issues. Staff must be motivated and understand where and how they fit into achieving, maintaining and improving on the quality of the product or service that is being delivered to customers.

Pause for thought

So let us stop and review our knowledge so far. ISO 9001 is the **most popular standard** in the world for quality management systems. It is just a **document** that can be bought online within five minutes. The document sets out what must be in place for an effective QMS (ISO 9001) and is supported by other documents in the 9000 series. It is **relevant to all businesses, regardless of size or product.** The latter often confuses people – how can a QMS have the same elements for making spectacles as for making air conditioning products? Well they have the same **organizational processes!** We have to design, make and ship products. We use competent people and capable technology. We have leaders who must exploit quality for competitive advantage and profits. So it doesn't matter what the product is – the processes are similar. What is different is the size of the business, which will influence how much effort is needed to get certified and to maintain good audits. We also know that **ISO 9001 is audited** and that we must show – with evidence – **conformance to the standard** and its many clauses (and sub-clauses). Failure to conform with a clause/requirement/sub-clause will be picked up by an **internal or external auditor** and a '**non-conformance notice**' will be issued which implies the company must fix the gap in its practices in order to restore the effectiveness of the QMS. We also know that **measures and improvement processes** (clauses of the standard) inform better management and the whole QMS will evolve over time. We also know that **quality is the 'Number One' competitive priority** for all businesses.

So, evidence and documented conformity is critical for business and a serious business will ensure that meaningful data and relevant information is identified, controlled and managed effectively – after all these are the very documents that are needed by all employees to do a quality job! Formalized control of this information and how it is used in a process is essential. The way in which this information is collected, where it is collected, how often it is collected and reviewed etc is a management decision. At the end of the day the QMS has to be fit for purpose and when it is it will greatly assist every engaged employee. But as Annex SL shows, ISO 9001 is not just a series of documents. It is a thinking and improving system that involves people, technology, processes and proof that should result in profitable production and very satisfied stakeholders.

Leadership, communication and staff engagement are all clauses and are features of the best companies in the world. So documents such as the highest-level quality strategy, quality policy, objectives and the quality manual for an organization are documents that a quality business would expect to get right. The development of the 'right' organizational culture is important to dispel any traditional belief that ISO 9001 is just about lots of pieces of paper. Annex SL certainly returns all attention back to the organization in its context, using quality to improve the future of the business and a much greater purpose for the QMS. The culture, levels of engagement and commitment of staff will differentiate the effective exploitation of the QMS and will have a much different bearing on how the QMS is implemented and what it means for all employees. In this manner, two competitors could have the same ISO 9001 intention to certify or maintain the standard but a business that has embedded a good culture using Annex SL to structure the approach to people will find the system much more effective and efficient than one that spends much less time engaging staff and embedding working practices.

Learning point

A top-down bureaucratic 'command and control' style of implementation will result in demanding conformance with the ISO 9001 standard, whereas a democratic, facilitated and learning approach will allow staff to see the importance of a QMS and how they can shape it to collect data and control tasks so that jobs are easier to do right and difficult to do wrong. It will also ensure that ISO 9001 is less demanding on people's time by embedding into daily working – such as auditing during the day or conducting problem solving using proper data that helps make jobs easier and assures better quality for the consumer who wants a great product.

ISO 9001 and the 'PDCA' improvement cycle

Clauses 4 to 10 of the high-level structure (Annex SL) form the plan–do–check–act (PDCA) cycle of Deming (Figure 4.7) so that a business can improve on its weaknesses and ensure it meets the needs and expectations of consumers. Achieving these two outcomes also assists a business to deliver its intended outcomes within its context – profitability and products that are in demand as a result of excellent organizational quality.

Using the high-level structure Annex SL, ISO 9001:2015 has been shaped so that the same ten clauses are present. However, some additional sub-clauses have been added to clause 6 (planning) and clause 8 (operation), which is helpful in the field of quality management. For clause 6, there is only one additional sub-clause, and that is planning of changes.

ISO 9001 clearly focuses on processes and also the product design process (the actual product may also have a specific product standard or Kitemark too). Product design is enhanced by the introduction of ISO 9001 as designers have access to customer needs (the business context) and feedback from customers in terms of issues with products and other valuable insights. The standardization of documents for designers is also a major benefit so that an audit trail of what was specified can be maintained and

Figure 4.7 Clauses 4–10 of Annex SL and how they fit into the PDCA cycle

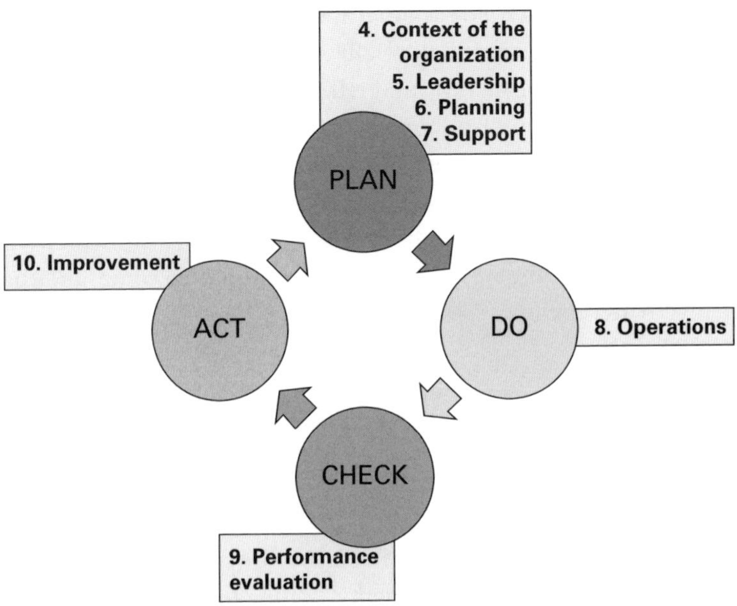

cannot be 'bypassed'. Designers who wish to champion strategies such as 'voice of the customer' programmes (using design methods such as Quality Function Deployment – see Hauser and Clausing, 1988[12], Design For Manufacturing (DFM) or Design For Assembly (DFA) and many of the Six Sigma design methods) will be able to exploit the procedures demanded of ISO 9001 conformance. The approach brings a new level of discipline to the control of processes and also when seeking to improve processes in a controlled and systematic manner. The benefits are significant for product designers and offer many new opportunities to enhance the strategic importance of getting products right 'by design'.

The modern differences (ISO 9001:2008 to ISO 9001:2015 onwards)

Several key changes were made to ISO 9001:2015 compared with ISO 9001:2008. Namely, more emphasis was placed on leadership with a focus on encouraging risk and opportunity management. The PDCA cycle became more explicit, with greater emphasis on aligned and market-driven objectives, measurement and change with communication, awareness and involvement of people within the organization at all levels. There became fewer prescriptive requirements and procedures to allow more organizational innovation and flexibility in the face of increasing market, customer and regulator complexity. The standard also recognizes, very importantly, that technology has advanced, especially information technology (IT). The early BS 5750[13] was bureaucratic and relied heavily on paperwork; modern technology has self-monitoring and other forms of audited control which are now accepted as legitimate sources of evidence for audit purposes. Future generations of ISO 9001 will probably not be as bold as the transition to the 2015 standard but will probably continue to allow new capital and informational technology evidence to be submitted to an auditor and potentially greater remote access by auditors.

Auditing: from gaining to maintaining certification[14]

For an organization to gain the ISO 9001 conformance standard and maintain it, auditing of the QMS must occur. Auditing means comparing what is observed and recorded against the clauses of the standard. The purpose of auditing is to learn and improve. The process is a form of policing but it is a means of showing where weaknesses exist and where to improve the QMS. Businesses and leaders who really get the principles of TQM will see auditing as a very valuable insight into business performance and the cultural embedding of the ISO way of working. There are three forms of ISO auditing that the organization must subject itself to. In **first-party audits**, competent and trained employees of a firm self-audit processes and procedures and any aspect of the ISO 9001 standard.[15] Often employees will go to another area of the business, select a process and investigate it to see whether staff follow a procedure that they have been trained in, that the procedure is available, and that the staff member knows why they are performing the actions they are. The **second-party audit** is conducted in the main by a customer of the organization (potentially a supplier can audit a customer). Such audits tend to take place much less often than the daily audits conducted by staff doing periodic and planned internal checks and random audits. Second-party audits tend to be annual events and last a few days. Finally, a **third-party audit** must be conducted by an independent organization. The latter is performed at least annually by a 'qualified' and competent organization that has achieved and conforms to the standard that is applied to such auditor organizations. These organizations conduct certification audits (termed registration in some countries) and surveillance audits (annual audits and deep audits every three years). Third-party auditors are powerful and can determine what they want to audit so as to verify whether or not an organization conforms to the requirements specified in the standard.

If an organization is successful in its certification application process, they can then say that they are 'ISO 9001:2015 certified'. It is not correct for them to say they are 'ISO certified' as this is meaningless in the context of ISO standards. Authorized third-party auditors will issue a certificate to a successful applicant organization clearly outlining the scope of their certification to a standard. Again, auditing is the subject of another chapter but there is some confusion about the terms 'certification' and 'accreditation'. To make life simpler, certification is the award of a certificate by a third party which proves an applicant organization meets the requirements of a given standard. Accreditation may be viewed as the formal recognition by an accreditation body that a third-party certification organization operates to international standards. Implementation and certification to ISO 9001:2015 is typically good for business and may be a contractual, regulatory or market requirement, so working with a third-party certifier and third-party auditor (certification body) should be regarded as a positive activity and the auditor should be treated as if they were an extension of the factory teams. Auditors see many businesses and have great skills so it makes sense to use them and get as much from them as possible.

Does ISO 9001 deliver?

The historical testing of the standard has provided significant evidence that 9001 certification is regarded as a positive signalling device (organizations use certification as a signal of quality and an offer of confidence to customers). ISO 9001 supports a positive image for an organization's brand, increases a company's reputation and differentiates the business from its competitors in the market. ISO 9001 certification thus gives consumers confidence that the company in question is operating to certain verifiable and tested standards. The BSI Excellerator (2011)[16] data demonstrated that ISO 9001-certified companies benefited greatly from its implementation. These benefits included:

- 75 per cent of businesses had improved their levels of customer satisfaction and loyalty;
- 75 per cent of businesses had improved operational performance;
- 71 per cent of businesses had acquired new customers and retained existing ones;
- 55 per cent of business had achieved cost savings.

Demonstrating internal and external (customer and other stakeholder) benefits is part of the ISO 9001 requirements. Monitoring customer (and interested party) satisfaction requires the evaluation of their perception using available information/data and forms part of the review process as well as reinforcing the concept of customer needs and expectations in everything that the organization undertakes. A profitable and improving business is good for staff, customers, investors and all stakeholders. Improving quality positively impacts on an organization's return on investment through continuous improvement of operational processes and results (cutting waste), with increased profits and market share. Within the organization, employees feel more motivated with better working conditions (such as health and safety) and understand that their valuable input within the organization leads to greater job satisfaction – after all, every cog in the system counts. This impacts on customers as the products meet a quality standard and are thus more dependable and reliable. The benefits to society may not seem so obvious but with improved health and safety in the workplace along with a happier more motivated workforce, sick leave decreases, which feeds into less waste in terms of time off and shift covering, ultimately leading to increased security for families where one is an employee.

In summary

This chapter has set out the main features and considerations of the ISO 9001 standard – the most popular standard of all the ISO standards. The standards help businesses to meet customer expectations, enhance their own brand and reputation and continually improve. The process of certification will require commitment from all staff, a vision, goals and objectives. Processes will need to be examined, documented and controlled. New stakeholder engagements will mean that an ISO 9001 business will support suppliers and customers as well as other interested parties but most of all it will support the innovative power of the business's 'Number One' asset – its people. An effective system will reduce costs, improve productivity, reduce defects, generate new sales leads and allow the retention of existing customers. It is most importantly a mechanism that translates a vision of TQM into the ability to exploit operational excellence.

Helpful link: ISO (2019) *ISO 9001 Quality Management* [online] Available at: https://www.iso.org/iso-9001-quality-management.html [Accessed 24 April 2019]

Seminar topics and examination questions

- Why is ISO 9001 so important to the modern manufacturer?
- If you worked for a local hospital as a buyer of products and equipment, would you buy from a business that did not have ISO 9001?
- What steps would you take if you were introducing ISO 9001 into an established magazine printing business?
- What are the major elements of the Annex SL higher-level structure?
- What are the responsibilities of the leaders of a certified ISO 9001 business?
- What is meant by the term certification and why does it have benefits for a modern manufacturing business?

- If you were developing a new version of ISO 9001, what aspects of organizational quality management would you add?
- Which auditor is the most important, first party, second party or third party?

Key terms

Just to help the learning process – here are a few terms that have been introduced during this chapter.

Table 4.4 Key terms

Word or term	Importance
Annex SL	A high-level structure that allows a standardization with the way in which standards are written and presented to business.
Audit	The process of checking to see if what has been documented as practised is as practised and whether such practice meets the clauses and requirements of the ISO 9001 standard.
Certification	The process of conforming to the latest version of the ISO 9001 standard.
Clause	A requirement within the Annex SL structure for ISO 9001 to which a business must conform.
Conformity	The process of ensuring that all clauses of the ISO 9001 standard are met and with evidence.
Management responsibility	All the actions, roles and processes involving management. The focus on management (which is tactical) has been overtaken in the 2015 ISO 9001 revision and leadership is now preferred (strategic and requires all staff to engage).
Technical committee	Technical committee TC 176 is the standard reviewing, developing and publishing team who take a standard or guideline from conception to a lifecycle of revisions to include latest best practices.

Notes

1 Edgeman, R (2019) *Complex Management Systems and the Shingo Model: Foundations of operational excellence and supporting tools* (The Shingo Model Series), Productivity Press

2 Gillet, J, Simpson, P and Clark, S (2015) *Implementing ISO9001:2015: Thrill your customers and transform your cost base with the new gold standard for business management*, Infinite Ideas Limited

3 Osterwalder, A et al (2014) *Value Proposition Design: How to create products and services customers want*, John Wiley & Sons

4 Remember SL is just part of ISO's numbering scheme and not an initialism

5 Hazel, J (2016) *The Memory Jogger ISO 9001:2015: What is it? How do I do it? Tools and techniques to achieve it*, Goal QPC, New York

6 Asbury, S (2014) *Health and Safety, Environment and Quality Audits: A risk-based approach*, 2nd ed, Routledge Publishers

7 Cochran, C (2015) *ISO 9001:2015 in Plain English*, Paton Professional

8 ISO: Guidance on the requirements for Documented Information of ISO 9001:2015 [online] Available at: https://www.iso.org/files/live/sites/isoorg/files/archive/pdf/en/documented_information.pdf (archived at https://perma.cc/8CR4-G4UQ)

9 A controlled document may be regarded as any digital or hard-copy paper entity which is required by a company and ISO standard (or regulator). It is subject to a systematic and tightly controlled process of writing and revision so that its integrity is maintained. In addition, it ensures everyone in the factory is working to the latest and agreed way of conducting an activity.

10 Dobb, F (2018) *The ISO 9001, 14001 or 18001(45001) Certification Audit: Make it painless, eliminate auditors' invalid nonconformities: Volume 8 (ISO-Quality)*, Brodsworth & Woods

11 Tricker, R (2017) *ISO9001:2015 Audit Procedures*, Routledge, London

12 Hauser, J R and Clausing, D (1988) The House of Quality, *Harvard Business Review*, May–June

13 Munro-Faure, L and Munro-Faure, M (1993) *Achieving Quality Standards: Step-by-step guide to BS5750/ISO 9000 (Institute of Management)*, Financial Times Prentice Hall, London

14 Tricker, R (2017) *ISO9001:2015 Audit Procedures*, Routledge, London

15 Cochran, C (2017) *Internal Auditing in Plain English: A simple guide to super effective ISO audits*, Paton Professional

16 BSI Group: Making Excellence a Habit [online] Available at: https://www.bsigroup.com/Documents/about-bsi/making-excellence-a-habit-brochure.pdf (archived at https://perma.cc/CA6R-928R)

Operational excellence (OpEx) 05

The world of manufacturing has many different terms that seem to mean the same thing and probably the most confusing of all the manufacturing discussions concerns the development of highly performing manufacturing businesses[1] or highly reliable manufacturing business.[2] It often seems like you must commit to being lean[3] or being Six Sigma[4] (6σ) or being agile[5] or something else. It can often feel that there are massive dividing lines between these ideas too. In reality there are differences in the focus of the approaches but many of the tools and techniques are the same. Essentially operational excellence is an approach to designing an organization so that it uses its manufacturing (and support activities) in such a way that it can compete in markets that have demanding customers, increasing expectations for product quality and reducing times from order placement to actual delivery – and meet all of these challenges and still make a good profit and return for the owners of the business.

The main objective for a manufacturing business is to make money and manage its cash flow. Improving the quality procedures of an organization via a quality management system (QMS) is an excellent step on the journey to improvement and ultimately total quality management status. Many businesses also state that they intend to become 'world class' or be the 'best in class' – what they are really saying is they will delight customers through collaborative 'win-win' relationships and teamwork to provide the best products and services that are continuously improving. The latter is operational excellence. The debate is therefore more about what route a company takes to achieve excellence; as we have seen in earlier chapters, the quality route is the most sustainable and involves the least trade-offs.

LEARNING OBJECTIVES

At the end of this chapter, you will be able to:

- understand what is meant by the term operational excellence;
- differentiate between the different (and often competing) approaches to operational excellence, especially the main approaches of Lean, Six Sigma, Agility and the Internet of Things;
- appreciate how ISO standards support leaders and managers of businesses to achieve a level of competence and operational excellence.

Introduction

Even a charity must make money. Many businesses fail even though they have great products and are profitable because they forget they must manage their cash flow. Cash flow is the cycle of money whereby customers pay for products and the money is invested in materials that are converted into new products and sales which then generate more money. When businesses get the flow of money wrong or it takes longer to get the money from customers than it takes to pay suppliers, some companies will enter negative cash flow and money will leave the business before it comes in. Making money is about the best use of time – the quicker a product can be made the better in general, and so time management is a very important aspect of modern management.

The art is to add value to materials by making products that customers want to buy and getting paid for them as soon as you can[6] – ideally you get paid before you make the product! Dell computers operate in this manner, as you specify a computer online and then place your order with your payment and your laptop is assembled to your exact specification. For some other businesses things are a bit more complicated and manufacturers do not actually sell their products – they lease them and get a smaller amount of money each month (most cars are sold in this manner and use a lease over a number of years). Operational excellence simply means that a business is seeking to be the best it can in terms of offering great products, in very short amounts of time, to the highest level of quality and at minimal cost. Operational excellence minimizes costs and maximizes revenues – it is challenging but is an ideal approach to exploit a QMS as well as other ISO standards that give customers a reason to buy.[7]

Operational excellence is a means of generating a competitive advantage over business rivals and it is also a challenge to the entire staff of a business to improve and improve at a rate faster than the competition. A key issue for any business owner or leader is just what to do to achieve operational excellence and get all the benefits that being a high-performing business brings. The choice and options available to a business leader can be greatly supported by ISO standards and using these creates a platform and systematic approach to implementing and sustaining good practices. So, there are obvious linkages to ISO standards and every approach to operational excellence tends to rely on ISO 9001 as a minimum system feature.

The modern world

The modern world is quite harsh and unforgiving. Business leaders that lack vision, the drive to improve performance and are unable to engage staff to deliver improvements face an uncertain future. It is similar to the biological world – if you cannot evolve then you won't survive; even the quality guru W Edwards Deming stated that 'You don't have to change. Survival is not mandatory!' (paraphrased). Industrial history is littered with individual businesses and entire industries that didn't change. For example, industrial museums are full of American and British cars made by businesses that most people have never heard of. Customers, sadly, are unforgiving too. Nostalgia is not often cited as a reason why they buy from a business. Businesses have to earn sales and work hard to protect their customers from rivals. In addition, there are very few monopolies in the world, so every sector has some form of competition. To earn an advantage over competitors, businesses must improve and seek operational excellence.

Usually when a presenter is asked what they mean by their use of the term 'operational excellence' there is a brief pause and a series of short statements about being 'world class' or 'the best'. In essence, operational excellence is the delivery of superior customer value through the execution of a challenging business strategy and based upon the use of production and manufacturing as a competitive weapon. It involves the engagement of all staff, the principles of TQM and a systems approach to optimized performance. It is also the relentless pursuit of ways to improve and enhance the profitability and reputation of a business. As markets change and customers demand more, operational excellence is a journey too. The core of operational excellence, OpEx for short, is the management of quality, time and adaptability of the business.[8]

Manufacturing: the options

The different forms of manufacturing can be broken down into three basic types:

- The **make to stock** organization makes products against a forecast and puts them into final storage awaiting orders. The company will often manufacture products in large batches and push products to the final store.
- The **make to order** or 'make on demand' organization holds much less stock and uses actual orders (not forecasts) to trigger production. The company will make one item at a time or will produce in the smallest batch size possible – ideally one item.
- The **hybrid organization** makes some of the production process in a batch and some they will make one at a time. So a company making cars may paint 10 in blue then 10 in red and 10 in green etc, but will take just one car at a time (when a customer order comes in) and assemble it to the exact customer specification (such as sat nav, leather seats, tinted windows, air conditioning etc). Or it could be a soft drink or milk products company that fills products into different sizes and packaging.

ISO 9001 can be used by each of the three forms of business and improve them all. The approaches to achieving operational excellence for each form will vary slightly though, as will the company approach to making money.

Modern approaches to manufacturing operational excellence (OpEx)

Since the 1990s, mass production of a small variety of products in very large quantities has not fitted the modern market needs for product variety, personalized production and less waste. Very large batches of products that are invested in storage warehouses (which cost money to operate) consume cash and cash flow is a process that needs to be strictly managed if businesses are to succeed. The general trend for manufacturers is to reduce batch sizes and increase the variety of products that are available to customers without holding too much stock. Without much stock to instantly satisfy customers, the modern producer must be flexible and compress time from the receipt of an order to the delivery of the product and the fulfilment of that order.[9] The main OpEx approaches that have emerged since the 1990s include:

- the lean movement inspired by the Toyota Motor Corporation's just-in-time approach and Toyota Production System (TPS);[10]
- the Six Sigma (6σ)[11] approach inspired by US businesses such as Motorola and General Electric (GE);
- the agile/quick response manufacturing (QRM) School[12] which seeks to compress time and was applied widely in sectors such as textiles and manufacturing in general;
- the Internet of Things (IoT) and a modern approach that exploits advantages in new technology and digital internet information systems.[13]

The lean movement

The lean approach,[14] also referred to by many as just-in-time (JIT), is one of elimination of waste; also known as Kaizen, it was designed by Taiichi Ohno of the Toyota Motor Corporation.[15] It was diametrically opposed to the dominant tradition of mass production (ie producing large batches regardless of the demand) and instead used synchronized manufacturing process that produced goods based on real customer orders. It was deemed to be lean because it used less stock, less time, less space and less effort to make products using a lean method rather than the traditional approach of mass production. From a cash flow perspective, making products to order and only when they were ordered meant there was less need for stock or large batches (making large batches of products 'just in case' an order is placed actually consumes vital business cash and putting goods into stock for long periods is an investment of business cash in something that is not selling).

Mass production with large batch sizes *pushes* stockpiles (against a best-guess forecast) into large warehouses. Lean focuses on continuous problem solving, seeking to cut waste and become as lean as possible to give customers what they want, when they want it. Lean effectively makes an operation more efficient, improving its quality and making it faster whilst operating at a cost that is as low as possible.

Planning and control is a critical element of a lean approach, with operations managers overseeing the production line and linking in with the supply chain to cut waste and find areas to improve. Hence there has to be a synchronicity of flow to the lean production line that eliminates waste such as excess stock or too little stock. Staff are considered an organization's assets and essential to being successful at implementing a lean approach within an organization. Therefore, production and delivery of products are smoothed or levelled (Heijunka)[16] to ensure that there are no bottlenecks in the system to create stress on employee or machine.

The term 'lean' was used to describe the way in which the Toyota Motor Corporation could build a car in half the time needed to make an equivalent car by a mass producer in the West. The Toyota Production System (TPS) was termed lean because it used less of everything – less time, less space, fewer defects and people, with much less stress.[17] The lean production approach is based on the manufacturing of products just in time (JIT) for customers and all improvements are based on reducing process waste. For lean producers, waste is defined as any activity that adds no value to the customer and for which the customer would not want to pay. Value, on the other hand, is anything that converts a material into a final product that can be sold to a customer. Lean relies on a steady demand and flow of goods between trading partners that work together closely and try to smooth the demand for products. So, a level form of demand and improvement processes (where every employee is focused on finding waste and removing it) combine to allow products to flow without delay or any form of excess cost. Unlike mass production, which sought ways to make workers labour faster, the lean approach will only make a product when one is sold.

Quality management must be at the heart of any business and hence it is one of the central pillars of this house of lean (see Figure 5.1: the Toyota Production System used the term 'Jidoka' to refer to built-in quality[18]) whilst still recognizing the importance of a JIT approach with the central belief of waste reduction/elimination (ie muda). This waste could be anything from excess inventory, time-wasting activities, space layout or anything that does not add value to the process and hence the customer. Waste is also anything that adds no value to a customer and adds unnecessary costs to a business by poor design of its operations.

Figure 5.1 House of lean for a quality management system

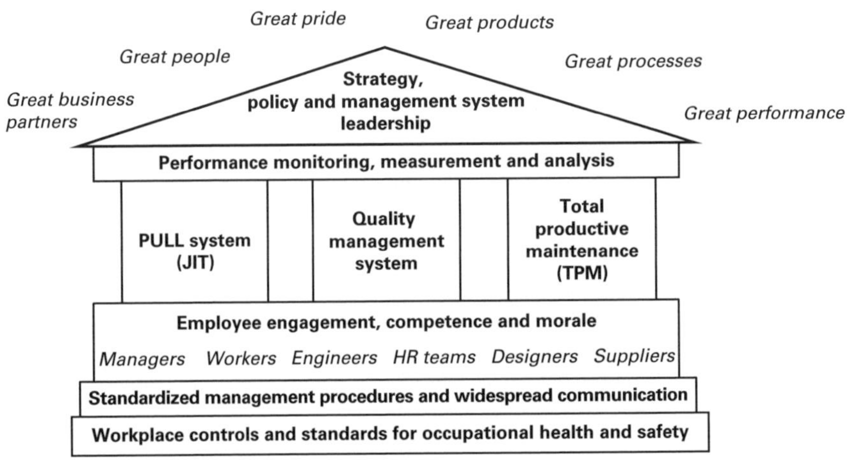

Employee engagement should always be considered an important part of the day-to-day running[19] and ultimately overall success of an organization, hence it is essential that employees are considered valuable organizational assets who can contribute ideas, be it innovation or anything that contributes to continuous improvement. Employees can make or break an organization and as such are critical in stabilizing the house of lean if engaged with and motivated appropriately. Machines also must be looked after and maintained and are a stabilizing pillar within the house of lean.

The lean approach uses a set of people-based and technical innovations and production system features to satisfy customers instantly and with minimal waste. These features of the lean system are shown in Table 5.1. The main intention of a lean business is to prevent mistakes or to make them instantly obvious so that flow of work does not stop. Staff are highly skilled and empowered to make autonomous decisions in the interest of the business.

Table 5.1 Main features of the lean approach

Feature	Purpose
Cellular production[20]	The organization of the production process into self-contained cells producing a limited range of outputs using dedicated staff and small-sized equipment.
Standard work[21]	A series of standardized operating procedures (SOPs) that are controlled and used to show workers what to do (similar ISO 9001 requirements).
Andon	A 'traffic light' mechanism which is suspended from the factory ceiling where lights show working cells (green), cells with quality issues (amber) and on stop (red).
Level demand	Smoothing of all demand between a customer and supplier so that sold stock is replenished in a controlled fashion. Where this is impossible then a small amount of finished goods is introduced to allow any demand variation to be absorbed or in-process stock is introduced to allow orders to be finished to order.
Takt time	The demand rate for a product converted into time – if 80 products are needed in an eight-hour shift, the rate is 10 products per hour. The measure is used to ensure the production facility is keeping pace with the rate at which customers are taking product away.
Kanban pull	The use of small amounts of stock in process. When stock is taken by a customer cell then a reorder is pulled from the internal supplier production cell. This is known as a pull system. The logic is to sell a product, order a replenishment of the same product and make a product of that specification (sell one – order one – make one).

(continued)

Table 5.1 *(Continued)*

Feature	Purpose
Heijunka levelling	The spreading of orders (for shipment to customers) throughout the working day so a little product is taken often and regularly rather than large amounts of product being taken in one go.
Quick changeover	The quick changeover from one variant of product to the next so a wide variety of products can be made in a day (similar method to racing car pit stop).
Mistake proofing	The use of devices in the workplace that prevent or make it difficult to make mistakes. Includes the use of alarms and physical devices that prevent mistakes from being made, such as only being able to place a product in a holder in the correct way.
Visual management	The use of colour coding and simple devices to allow easy management of the workplace and to know the status of items (such as stock levels etc).
The 5 S	A five-stage approach to maintaining a clear, arranged, neat, disciplined and continuously improved workplace.
Total productive maintenance[22]	A systematic approach to maintaining equipment so that it does not fail because of a catastrophic failure. For a business with very little stock this would cause major problems for all customers.
Policy deployment	A multi-year and annual challenge to all employees of a business to improve by setting challenges – such as to improve quality by 10 per cent in the next 12 months against the quality performance in this current year. Also known as Hoshin Kanri.
Teamwork	The use of a team-based organizational structure to manage and produce goods rather than a departmental approach. Used to speed up decision making and locate all staff needed for production and administration at the point of production.
Problem solving	Teams engaged in finding waste and eliminating it using problem-solving methods and root cause analysis.
Common uniform	All employees wearing a common uniform to reduce demarcation between teams and to reinforce the identity of the company and its staff.
Supplier association	A team of some or all suppliers to a business that meet regularly to share strategy and understand the performance of the business so suppliers can support their customer to improve and share innovations that are good for both businesses (a win-win relationship).

Lean and ISO standards

Working to make products to actual customer demand means that a lean business system must be very precise and make the most of all the production time available. Many lean businesses ('make to order') support business customers as well as direct consumers; typically in an 'assemble to order' form. Lean businesses rely heavily on ISO 9001 as well as other standards, especially ISO 14001 environmental standard and ISO 45001 for occupational health and safety. Lean businesses also like doing business with ISO 9001-certified suppliers and will often state this standard is a precursor to even doing business together.

Within the production organization, the ISO 9001 discipline suits the requirements of a lean business. The 'fit' is very good and offers the mechanisms to control even a very complex business and formally improve it. The setting of QMS objectives supports the policy deployment challenge process and the planning through to ensure continuous improvement clauses are fully compatible with a lean business seeking to become a total quality management business. But quality is just one aspect of the design of a business and many lean businesses use multiple standards to manage occupational health and safety and the environment to name two.

The Six Sigma (6σ) approach

Six Sigma is a statistical and disciplined approach to improve production processes. Whilst the plan–do–check–act cycle is an integral part of ISO 9001 when it comes to seeking improvement, there is another never-ending improvement cycle known as DMAIC (define–measure–analyse–improve–control) or the Six Sigma cycle. Both implement a cycle of questioning and re-questioning to improve. Both are based on incremental improvement that is continuous small-stepped operational performance improvement. The DMAIC cycle is a tool used in Six Sigma that is driven by data to assess and optimize operational processes and product/service design. Even though DMAIC arose out of Six Sigma, some organizations use this improvement cycle without implementing a 6σ approach.

The 6σ approach originated in America as a direct response to the internationalization of Japanese industry and the threats posed to the electronics, car and other sectors. It has fewer defined organizational and business management features than lean but is very strong in terms of the methods for determining the capability of processes and technology as well as the improvement of process management.

Six Sigma was developed in 1986 by Motorola (CEO Bill Smith is credited with its creation) after company engineers realized that their current quality measurements were not adequate. This realization came at a time of risk for Motorola when overseas competition had started to threaten their market position. Six Sigma was conceived to improve processes and hence quality with an ambitious aim of improving quality by a factor of 10 within a two-year period by measuring defects and improving quality. Motorola came up with the slogan of 'Total Customer Satisfaction' and what impact this would have on their operations processes. The company wanted to emphasize a constant focus on their customers and ensuring that every process would add value to them. To achieve this, they deduced that to achieve such satisfaction for their product users they needed to ensure that their product was reliable with no defects or early-life failures whilst at the same time being delivered when promised to the customer. By adopting the 6σ approach, Motorola have claimed that by the year 2000 they had saved $5 billion and by 2006 they had saved $17 billion.[23] Since its birth, 6σ has been adopted by many other well-known companies such as General Electric, Bank of America, Caterpillar, 3M, Whirlpool and Boeing to name but a few.

Six Sigma's key aim is to design and implement processes that are 99.999996 per cent defect free. The seriousness of any defects in the aviation industry is obvious, hence the importance placed on becoming defect free. The focus must be on the design specifications of a product/service and its processes to identify and eliminate current defects and prevent any future ones from occurring. Becoming 99.999996 per cent defect free (see Table 5.2) would just about ensure that latent and undetected defects do not surface or come to light only at the point when the product is in the hands of the customer. To achieve this, Six Sigma uses statistical methods to reduce variation in processes by utilizing the data measured to solve issues and eliminate defects.[24] Therefore, the approach is one of continuous improvement with the emphasis on customer satisfaction; having viewed the three key elements of quality (products, processes and employees/inputs) from the perspective of a customer, does the product achieve a quality standard that customers will be satisfied with?

Six Sigma is therefore an approach which involves a range of methods; it is a statistical concept and a hard measure as well. It equates to 3.4 defects per million items produced (which is for all intents and purposes 'perfect production' levels) and is an aspirational goal and objective for a business. Whereas lean originated in Japan and has spread to the rest of the world, the Six Sigma approach originated in the United States and has also spread globally. It is very much a process-focused approach.

Table 5.2 Defects and Six Sigma

If the organization's quality yield is	Defect percentage	Defects per million opportunities (DPMO) or rejects in parts per million (PP) is	The actual sigma level
30.9%	69	691,462	1
69.1%	31	308,538	2
93.33%	6.7	66,807	3
99.38%	0.62	6,210	4
99.977	0.023	233	5
99.99966%	0.00034	3.4	6

Six Sigma and variation[25]

Variation is present in every process; it's known as 'white noise' and is typically quantifiable and usual. There are a number of typical causes of variation in processes, some of which are controllable and some of which are not. Common cause variation refers to the fluctuation within the process that is not totally controllable, such as fluctuations that stem from unknown factors. The best a process can be is also constrained by equipment that creates present technological limitations, issues and, at times, challenges. Common cause variation in a process is also known as natural patterns and was the thinking behind quality gurus such as Deming and Shewhart. Hence the need arose to measure variation and understand possible assignable causes of variation such as issues with tools, environmental instability, outside influences, 'black noise' and how the process is actually performing over time (its stability or not), at all times looking for ways to improve the process issues or variance.

SIPOC (suppliers, inputs, process, outputs, customers)

SIPOC is a high-level view of a process that effectively summarizes the inputs and outputs in the processes and is utilized in 6σ to identify areas for improvement. In a nutshell, it is a form of process mapping (see Figure 5.2). It acts as a visual for the processes in question that can aid employees to see at a glance what is happening. This diagram ensures everyone is on the same page, that there are no misunderstandings with leadership being able to use it to communicate to all those involved in the process, and that all can see the exact element of a process that is being discussed. It can also enable quick and easy identification of issues and problem areas that do not add value to the customer.

Figure 5.2 SIPOC – supplier/input/process/output/customer

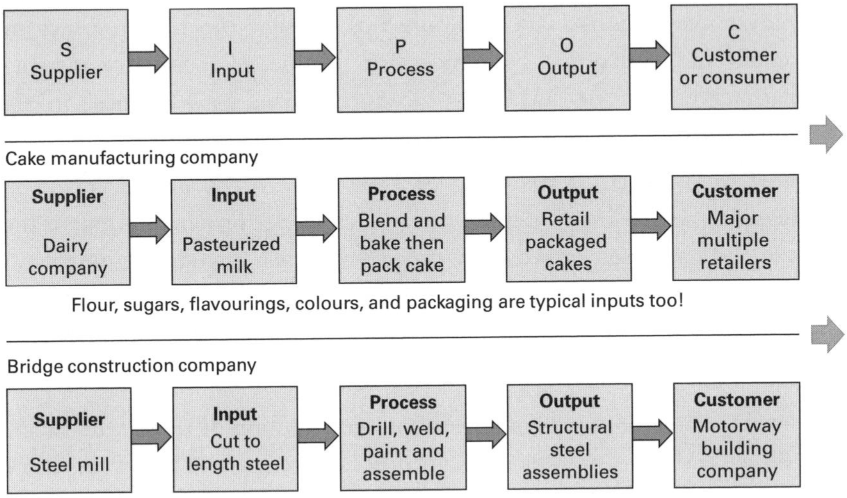

The SIPOC tool is not just exclusive to Six Sigma; it dates to the late 1980s when it was used in total quality management and has subsequently been used in other management improvement approaches such as lean and business process management. In 6σ, SIPOC is often used in the 'define' stage of the DMAIC cycle and for lean management and kaizen events. Some in the field coin it COPIS (as they feel that the customer should always be put first) but most use the acronym SIPOC. Whichever one is used, the acronym stands for:

- **Supplier:** an individual or company that inputs into a process.
- **Input:** a supplier will add a resource to a process.
- **Process:** where inputs are converted into an output.
- **Output:** a resource generated from a process (set of steps).
- **Customer:** an individual or company that receives the output (product/service).

The 6σ methodology draws on the most extensive range of techniques including basic root cause methods that were popularized by gurus such as Ishikawa and highly sophisticated experimental statistics, designs of experiments and hypothesis testing. It is a very technical approach – often with issues of elitism and a language that is very technical and beyond most factory staff – and 6σ companies use a variant of the plan–do–check–act process. The 6σ version of the Deming cycle of plan–do–check–act applies to new products and existing processes:[26]

- The **DMADV cycle** means to **Define** the goals of a process or product, **Measure** the key characteristics and variables against customer needs, **Analyse** the variables and relationships, **Design** the new product or process and **Verify** that the process or product is capable of meeting customer needs. The DMADV procedure is used for 'designing in Six Sigma' for new products and processes.
- The **DMAIC cycle** is made up of **Define** the needs of the customer, **Measure** the process to determine its current performance, **Analyse** the issue and its causes, **Improve** the process and then introduce **Controls** so that the performance of the process is measured and controlled and ideally the cause of the problem is prevented from reoccurring. DMAIC is used for existing product and production issues.

The 6σ approach does have a rather unique definition of those who facilitate, direct and oversee/govern the 6σ process operation. The management of the 6σ process is likened to that of the expertise gained by martial arts fighters, particularly karate belts awarded to those who are experienced, well practised and can use that skill to instruct others. The 6σ skill levels vary between companies but tend to include:

- **Yellow belts** are newly introduced to the 6σ system and have a basic awareness of it, its methods and application. Yellow- and green-belt staff are the most numerous in an organization.
- **Green belts** experiment and use 6σ to discover root causes and solve problems using the DMAIC stages. These staff report to black belt specialists.
- **Black belts** are project leaders who are well versed in the application of the methods and processes of Six Sigma. They manage green-belt staff and use them to complete the DMAIC process. They are knowledgeable and skilled with an ability to apply their knowledge to almost any issue. The staff work autonomously on business-critical projects and work with/seek the guidance of master black belts. There is usually a black-belt specialist per every 100 employees.
- **Master black belts (MBB)** are very few and are those capable of training others in the technicalities and process management needed for a disciplined implementation of 6σ.

Table 5.3 outlines the simplified features of the 6σ approach. It should be noted that many lean features – especially related to quality – are also 6σ features.

Table 5.3 Simplified features of the Six Sigma approach

Feature	Purpose
Hypothesis testing	The use of process and product data so that – through specialist knowledge and process understanding – relationships can be tested, such as defects will rise when the heat generated by an item of equipment increases.
Critical to customer	Any task or measure of an activity that must be controlled because variability will lead to defects and customer dissatisfaction.
Critical to quality	Any variable that – if allowed to vary – will create defects. Such a process, task or variable must be controlled with high precision.
Control charts	Statistical analyses of variation presented as a line graph with limits to show when a process has moved from normal variation to abnormal conditions.
Gage R&R	The application of Six Sigma methods to instrumentation, calibration and setting devices.
Process capability	The mathematical understanding of the capability of an item of equipment and its ability to meet product specifications.
Root cause analysis	Extensive use – by all staff – of basic problem-solving tools. See the Seven Old Tools of Ishikawa.
Statistical tests of goodness	A series of established and accepted statistical tests that ensure data is valid, correct and can be used for decision making by managers and specialists. Includes visualization and control of processes with statistical process controls, control charts and such like.
Design of experiments	A mathematical approach to product design which focuses on critical variables and reduces the complexity of all inter-relationships of variable.
QFD	Quality Function Deployment – a systematic approach to understanding the voice of the customer and translating it into ever more detailed working specifications. The process takes vague customer ideas, converts them into requirements and quantifies them. Many iterations of the approach make it possible to specify product design features, then specify process controls that support good quality; subsequent iterations can actually specify the equipment settings needed to control the process, which ends up with a perfect customer product.
Taguchi loss function	The concept and methodology for design which states that there is a significant loss for every small movement away from a specified target value.

Unlike other approaches, 6σ can be quite elite and not every staff member will be comfortable when using statistics. Lean and 6σ businesses share the use of root cause analysis tools but 6σ goes further so that full control is exercised to understand the causes of variation and to reduce variation that is 'abnormal'. In a utopian manufacturing world, 6σ would be used to measure all critical processes and action would be taken to ensure every input and process is controlled.

Six Sigma and ISO standards

Six Sigma, just like the lean approach (and the two are often combined), works very effectively with the ISO 9001 standard. The intention of Six Sigma organizations is to find and manage variation in production processes. The ISO and high-level structure (eg Annex SL) approach supports such activities by controlling the inputs to and the processes within a factory and gleaning significant customer feedback. Reducing variation is also served by the ISO 'shalls' related to the production of goods, the management of competence and the effectiveness of measures and improvement processes. Six Sigma organizations recognize the importance of ISO controls to manage inputs (and thereby limit variation). Variation in staff skills is controlled through the maintenance of staff training records and competence. Variation in technology is measured, as these measures are critical to quality and critical to the customer. Improvement is undertaken in a controlled manner and promoted by Section 10 of the high-level structure. In short, ISO and the use of Six Sigma are highly compatible.

Six Sigma can be utilized within a QMS to help an organization meet ISO 9001 requirements. The ISO recognized the need to develop standards to assist organizations using Six Sigma, namely ISO 13053 and ISO 18404. The first covers important elements in the methodology of Six Sigma (ie DMAIC Cycle) and the latter standard covers the implementation and defines the competency levels to standardize them. Whilst 6σ companies make use of different levels of competencies, referred to as belts (white, yellow, green, black and master black belt (MBB)), each organization is different and hence the attainment of a belt level may vary from organization to organization.

Key points from ISO 13053 and ISO 18404 standards are outlined below:

1 **ISO 13053-1:2011 – 'Quantitative methods in process improvement – Six Sigma – Part 1: DMAIC methodology':**
   - the methodology covers the five DMAIC phases;
   - the standard looks at best practice for each of these five phases;

- the standard gives recommendations around the management of 6σ projects;
- the standard describes the roles, expertise and training of employees involved in 6σ projects;
- it is relevant for product, service or transactional processes;
- Part 2 of this standard covers the tools and techniques needed when adopting a Six Sigma approach; each phase of the DMAIC cycle is covered here;
- Part 1 of this standard is generic, enabling any organization in any sector to use it, hence Part 2 of the standard can be applied to any sector and size of organization.

2 **ISO 18404:2015 – 'Quantitative methods in process improvement – Six Sigma – Competencies for key personnel and their organizations in relation to Six Sigma and Lean implementation'.** This standard covers lean and Six Sigma implementation of competencies that help in creating a benchmark for practitioners that adopt either of these two approaches. Here are some key points that are relevant:

- Assists in constituting what 6σ certification level requirements should be:
  - Covers only three of the belts (green, black and MBB).
  - For each of these levels, ISO 18404 lists performance criteria and demonstrating evidence of understanding, applying, managing and training.
  - Lists 23 key competencies that are thought to be essential in the area of Six Sigma certification. This standard considers all of these competencies to be consistent across all the sigma certification levels.
- Assists in constituting what lean certification level requirements should be:
  - Covers lean practitioner, lean leader and lean expert.
  - Lists 18 key competencies that are thought to be essential when becoming certified in the field of lean management. The expectations of a lean expert will be more demanding than those of lower levels.
- Assists both lean and 6σ organizations in ensuring the practitioners being recruited (as a 6σ black belt or lean practitioner for example) in the field have the relevant experience and training. So this standard assists organizations in determining whether applicants have the relevant experience and quality that would be expected of such competency levels.

Agility and quick response manufacturing (QRM)[27]

The term agile implies a significant degree of responsiveness and flexibility of a production system and factory practice. The agile and quick response models share a common concern for time-based competition (or more simply – compressing time so that a business is more responsive). The most accepted definitions of the approaches include:

Agile manufacturers operate organizations that have tools, processes and human resource skills which enable the people and technology of the organization to respond quickly to market changes whilst retaining a high degree of control over the quality and costs of a business. The ability to respond (strategic flexibility but with high levels of control) is core to the agile manufacturer.

Quick-response manufacturers (**QRM**) focus on time-based competition and are intent on lead time reduction (administrative and production processes). The approach engages operational and support staff with a new material planning method (called POLCA) which is similar to the lean approach but better able to handle variable demand and variable production batch sizes and also uses cells like the lean business. Such businesses are fascinated by critical paths for new and existing product delivery and pay great attention to the dynamics of a modern production system.

Neither approach is simply activities of 'selling from finished goods stock' and using quick response logistics and transportation to deliver products to customers. These approaches compress time everywhere in the production as well as pre-production and post-production stages. The intention is to produce only small batches of products at a competitive cost. A quick and agile business will use flexible production layout and mobile cells to accommodate orders quickly and produce custom orders. These businesses rely on good data systems and very close working relationships between all members of staff. Some key features of agile QRM are highlighted in Table 5.4.

Agile/quick response and ISO standards

The ability to compress time in administrative and production processes also relies upon good standards such as those of a high-level structure (eg Annex SL) and ISO 9001. The ability to rapidly change production, create bespoke product routings and deploy skilled staff requires:

- standardized processes to plan production, assess and issue materials, and control processes in the manner described in each major clause of ISO 9001 in the high-level structure;

Table 5.4 Simplified agile QRM features

Feature	Purpose
Small batches	The use of process and product data so that – through specialist knowledge and process understanding – relationships can be tested such that defects will rise when the heat generated by an item of equipment increases.
Quick changeovers	The minimal amount of time to change a machine from one product to the next variant – see lean approach
Concurrent engineering	Engineering and other teams working to bring projects to market quickly by working in parallel rather than sequentially to avoid delays.
Concurrent working	Working together to compress time such that administration teams may be taking orders, checking credit ratings and other activities to plan production at the same time or using IT that allows this to happen. The purpose is to reduce administrative and operational production time.
Co-located teams	The location of all necessary staff in one place so that – through dynamic interaction – decision making is quicker and time is compressed.
Suppliers on site	The use of factory space by suppliers so that packaging materials and such like are made at the same time as production of the main product begins.

- up-to-date training records to show that staff are competent and trained to manage key business processes;
- rapidly configured customer specifications and drawings using existing processes;
- access to good machinery records;
- measurement of performance;
- improved processes for time compression.

All the above activities are covered by the ISO 9001 standard and therefore the standard can be employed to support this form of competitive advantage.

The Internet of Things

The Internet of Things (IoT) is a modern phenomenon which has been created by the convergence of new digital information services and new production technology. The business model is often called Industry 4.0 as it is heralded as the fourth industrial revolution. The first revolution brought mechanization and automation, the second in around 1910 brought mass production, and the third revolution saw computers and automation working together; the new fourth revolution has created the cyber-physical system[28] and even virtual supply chains.

The commercial world is highly connected and internet connectivity means devices such as laptops, smartphones and other appliances can be integrated with production and design systems. Research into connectivity dates back to 1982 when a coke machine on the campus of Carnegie Mellon University in Pittsburgh, United States, became the first appliance to be connected to the internet. A graduate student named David Nichols designed the system to use the internet to track the contents of the vending machine remotely, solving a problem of stock outs and lost sales. Later, machine-to-machine (M2M) communication was tested by others and embedded software and technology began to relay data and integrate with users to change business models and cash flow.

Many sectors now embrace this form of production, including healthcare, building smart cities (infrastructure management), energy management (smart meters fitted in our homes) and such like. The very cars we drive are also connecting us with the wider world using telematics. These devices, electronics and software programs are connecting us through a network known as the Internet of Things (IoT). It is this modern approach which offers a new route to operational excellence. All that is needed is an IP address for machines and things to access internet connectivity and for other internet-enabled devices to communicate with them. It is not just connectivity alone that drives the IoT; people and processes are a critical element.

CASE STUDY Taxi firm

Let us take a fleet of cars working for a local cab firm. The firm can tap into the telematics of each of the cars in the taxi fleet to track their exact location, giving them real-time data on their office computers. This assists in their customer satisfaction, ensuring greater efficiency by guiding the right taxi driver to arrive when and where promised. Whilst the devices are speaking with each other, it is the call handlers in the process that have to interpret this real-time data to make on-the-spot decisions.

IoT and operational efficiency

It is easy to see how the IoT can transform manufacturing and design processes to make them faster, based on real-time data. The harnessing of this disruptive technology is key to using it for competitive advantage and improved process efficiency. If seamlessly integrated with business processes, innovation will occur and productivity of the workforce/machinery will rise. The ability of machines to communicate also enables more effective problem solving and remote monitoring to find the sources of production issues, to cut down on waste, and be alerted (by the machine) to things that require maintenance or readjustment. Supply chain digitization also makes it easier to control the flow of goods, information and money around a global system.

Controls, sensors, monitors and alerts allow employees to increase their technical skills and the reducing size (and increasing capability) of new technology is transforming production through the IoT and data-driven optimized performance. Two major areas of management tend to typify the IoT approach – Industry 4.0, which is being led by the most advanced manufacturing nations in the world, and the benefits of a new production technology called 3D printing (and the many materials that can now be printed).[29, 30]

Industry 4.0[31]

Industry 4.0 is of tremendous significance to the way in which manufacturers operate, allowing a very bespoke and personalized process of making to order and even making a product to a custom design. The use of information technology means that production can happen almost anywhere in the world and batch sizes are very small – often just a single piece. Cloud computing and cyber-physical systems are now a reality and the applications of the approach appear almost endless.

3D printing

The advent of 3D printing and other low-scale technologies that allow personalized products to be printed has meant that certain industries can benefit from printing products to order. The technology works with a range of materials including plastics, with applications in most engineering sectors, prosthetics and Formula One race cars to name but a few. Other applications include the printing of gold jewellery, concrete buildings, chocolate shapes and many more. The ability of the technology to find new applications is tremendous and can have a transformational impact.

The combination of new technologies, the processing power/accessibility of cloud computing, and modern smartphone applications opens a new world of opportunities for designing and manufacturing bespoke and personalized products. However, even the most bespoke production requires processes associated with quality and delivery of products. So, ISO standards still cover the main processes – the context of the organization means it must develop the potential and capability to send quality assured digital information to an item of equipment with minimal manipulation. So many other ISO standards will be relevant, including data security.

The IoT and ISO standards

ISO Technical Committee 184 (TC 184) holds responsibility for inter-operability, integration and automation; it has been working for a long time on the issues of Industry 4.0 and will continue to manage this area of production management under its remit. The advent of Industry 4.0 and the IoT does not challenge the application of ISO 9001 – it actually makes it more important. Buying goods from people where there is no existing trading relationship or history of working together means ISO 9001 will provide assurance that the business processes that should be in place to ensure a product is managed correctly actually are.

The advent of the IoT has created a 'whirlwind of opportunities' and many untested potentials. McKinsey and company (2016) estimated the IoT market size in 2015 to be $900 million and was set to reach $3.7 billion by 2020.[32] ISO 9001 assists production managers when using the IoT but the ISO and its member countries have also identified opportunities to standardize a virtual world to make it safe and secure for users: **ISO/IEC 30141 standard**, which provides an 'IoT reference architecture'. It aims to address confusion of terms surrounding IoT (see Table 5.5) by standardizing vocabulary and sharing best practice used to minimize risks (such as online safety and security). The standard contains key operational sections focused on abbreviated terms, IoT reference architecture conformance, goals and objectives, characteristics of IoT systems, IoT Conceptual Model (CM), IoT Reference Model (RM), IoT Reference Architecture (RA) views and IoT trustworthiness. The standard adopts four lenses to review IoT systems (Functional view, System view, Networking view and Usage view). It is expected that this standard will be globally embraced by member nations to provide a standard baseline (from which to develop systems, structures and protocols) to those using IoT.

Table 5.5 Simplified features of the IoT approach

Feature	Purpose
IoT	The Internet of Things, which uses the internet to connect devices and production equipment so that they can interact and exchange information.
3D Printing	Technology that deposits materials in layers to build a product. Material is softened, laminated in a layer and solidified under computer control to create three-dimensional objects.
DM	Distributed manufacturing is a decentralized form of manufacturing using a network of enterprises (geographically dispersed) that are coordinated. Facilities are small in size and can be mobile.
Cyber physical systems	A form of manufacturing that is controlled and monitored by complicated computer algorithms and is integrated with users/consumers via the internet.

In summary

Using ISO standards in conjunction with good business logic to reduce variation and to give customers what they want in a fast and quality-assured manner is a good approach to operational excellence and it is good for cash flow too.

Customer expectations change and can be changed by businesses that deliver operational excellence. Businesses that aim for anything less than excellence will give away competitive advantage and potentially risk cash flow. So OpEx, whilst difficult to define, is 'a must' for modern manufacturers. A long history of manufacturing, being the first to achieve certain product breakthroughs, and winning historic awards count for very little today and history is no indicator that a company will succeed in the future. Holding an advantage with operational excellence will be fleeting unless the leaders and staff of a business are working to improve its processes and looking to where customer expectations and technology are going. Following an OpEx strategy is a means of driving change, using a QMS effectively to control improvement. Whether a business subscribes to being lean or another form of OpEx, it is a business decision and is dictated by what best suits the fit of the organization within its context. This chapter has reviewed the main forms of OpEx and demonstrated how ISO standards are integral to each approach – converting intent to compete with the means to do so with the high-level structure. As future chapters will show, there are a number of other ISO standards that can support these approaches to competitive advantage.

Programmes of operational excellence also offer significant opportunities for product designers. The best products are those that 'design out' quality defects and are flexible so that they can be customized (at greater levels of profitability) to order. Thousands of hours of problem solving can often be eliminated by a few design changes and the use of international standards allows designers to take a broader role across the entire lifecycle of the product. Using design as a competitive weapon is a major source of advantage to businesses and it exploits staff innovation and the tacit knowledge that competitors find hard to copy.

The purpose of this chapter was to pause and relate the discussions about international standards and business goals and objectives to the contexts that ISO 9001 is applied to (and many other ISO standards too). ISO 9001 is applicable to lean businesses and their relatively stable and closed ways of working with customers. It supports the processes that allow greater flexibility and agility and it supports the statistical mastery of the production process demanded by the Six Sigma approach. Finally, the unusual context of the IoT and Industry 4.0 creates a transformation and a disruptive technology information form of manufacturing where 'anything can be made for anyone and to anyone's product specification'. Once again, in this unusual context, ISO 9001 provides major business benefits. So the claim that ISO 9001 is applicable to all business regardless of size and the technical complexity of a product holds true.

The usefulness of ISO 9001 as a main foundation to any business is a common finding from the application of the QMS to any working environment. Approaches such as lean and Six Sigma fit nicely within a functional QMS and a standard to cover these two approaches has been developed: **ISO 18404:2015 – 'Quantitative methods in process improvement – Six Sigma – Competencies for key personnel and their organizations in relation to Six Sigma and Lean implementation'.**

Company leaders will be able to choose the scope of the implementation and standard but, due to the strategic importance of ISO 9001, it is likely to be company-wide, from design to recovery of products at the end of their economic lives. The ability to use electronic documentation has also marked a watershed in the use of the standard and many businesses (faced with the challenge of making a very wide variety of products) have automated their work instructions and other documents. The use of electronic documents, which are reviewed as a paper system would be, means that specific product instructions can be displayed in front of the operator at the point of manufacture. Indeed, the font size used for digital instructions can be changed to facilitate the most comfortable way of working for each individual worker. So the 'clunky' and bureaucratic traditional image of the early ISO 9001 standard may be a thing of the past.

In short, ISO 9001 and its direct link to the competitive priority of quality makes it a very powerful skeletal framework for managing a business and cash flow then moving to new models of manufacturing. It can be no surprise that many businesses have factories where parts will work with lean and other parts with IoT or lean and agile combined or, more likely, lean Six Sigma has been introduced to create a tightly controlled flowing process of goods and cash.

The irony of a high-level structure (such as Annex SL) is that it is the standardization of standards writing and this has been heralded as a new era too, one that is very much more sympathetic to businesses that operate more than one standard; the following chapters will focus on these other standards and the ability to use them with ISO 9001 (the world's most popular certified standard). ISO standards have requirements and there are a lot of good supporting guides to help business managers and owners to build the right approaches and to fit the needs of their business and its context. ISO standards are applicable to all businesses and provide an effective foundation upon which to achieve operational excellence. Conformity to ISO standards is also an expectation of many customers so using them to achieve internal operational excellence and to delight customers is a 'win-win' solution. Not just that – ISO standards demand that there is documented evidence of learning and improvement as well as audits that show where a business has weaknesses in its systems to support excellence in whichever standard they have implemented.

Seminars topics and examination questions

Here are a few questions that the reader may want to consider:

- How would you ensure that 'controlled documents' are updated as a result of team improvement activities?
- Compare and contrast the lean and Six Sigma approaches to operational excellence.
- Can a business be agile without perfect quality?
- Is there a point when it costs too much to be perfect and Six Sigma becomes too much?
- If you are only making bespoke items that are never going to be made again using a 3D printer – why bother with ISO 9001?
- Will a lean business using ISO 9001 ever create a defect?
- What is the best way to achieve operational excellence? Involve everyone as a lean business would or go for a very talented elite group of Six Sigma black belts?

Further reading

An internet search will yield many interesting professional articles and books on the subjects outlined in this chapter. The references at the end of the chapter are also a good foundation and signpost to useful texts.

Notes

1 Shroeder, R and Flynn, B (2001) *High Performance Manufacturing: Global perspectives*, John Wiley & Sons, Inc. See also Fast, L E (2015) *The 12 Principles of Manufacturing Excellence: A lean leader's guide to achieving and sustaining excellence*, 2nd ed, Taylor and Francis Inc

2 Hopkins, A (2007) The Problems of Defining Highly Reliable Organizations, *Working Paper 51*, Faculty of Arts and National Research Centre for OHS Regulation, Australia National University

3 Womack, J and Jones, D (2015) *Lean Solutions: How companies and customers can create value together*, Free Press, New York

4 Kumar, M et al (2008) Common myths of Six Sigma demystified, *International Journal of Quality & Reliability Management*, **25** (8), pp 878–95, https://doi.org/10.1108/02656710810898658 (archived at https://perma.cc/A9JV-2LAZ)

5 Kidd, P T (1994) *Agile Manufacturing: Forging new frontiers*, Addison Wesley, New York

6 Tracy, J A (2011) *Cashflow for Dummies*, For Dummies Publishing

7 Gillet, J, Simpson, P and Clarke, S (2015) *Implementing ISO 9001:2015: Thrill your customers and transform your cost base with the new gold standard for business management*, Infinite Ideas Limited

8 Mitchell, J (2015) *Operational Excellence: Journey to creating sustainable value*, Wiley-Blackwell, London

9 JMA (1986) *Kanban Just-in Time at Toyota: Management begins at the workplace*, Japanese Management Association, Tokyo

10 Ohno, T (1988) *Toyota Production System: Beyond large-scale production*, Productivity Press, Portland

11 Pyzdek, T and Keller, P (2014) *The Six Sigma Handbook*, 4th ed, McGraw-Hill Education

12 Suri, R (2010) *It's About Time: The competitive advantage of quick response manufacturing*, Productivity Press, Portland OR

13 Greengard, S (2015) *The Internet of Things*, MIT Press, Cambridge, MA

14 Womack, J, Jones, D and Roos, D (1990) *The Machine That Changed the World*, Rawson Associates

15 Ohno, T (1988) *Just in Time for Today and Tomorrow*, Productivity Press, Portland, Oregon

16 Glenday, I and Sather, R (2013) *Lean RFS (Repetitive Flexible Supply): Putting the pieces together*, Productivity Press, Portland, OR

17 Womack, J and Jones, D (1996) *Lean Thinking*, Simon and Schuster, New York

18 Monden, Y (2011) *Toyota Production System: An integrated approach to just in time*, 4th ed, Productivity Press, Portland, OR

19 Liker, G and Convis, G (2011) *The Toyota Way to Lean Leadership: Achieving and sustaining excellence through leadership development*, McGraw-Hill Education

20 Monden, *The Toyota Production System*

21 Olofson, O (2016) *Succeeding with Standardized Work: Through teamwork, on-the-job training, and coaching*, WCM Consulting AB

22 McCarthy, D and Rich, N (2014) *Lean TPM,* 2nd ed, Butterworth-Heinemann, London

23 Cragan, J, Wright, D and Kasch, C (2009) *Communication in Small Groups: Theory, process, and skills*, 7th ed, Cengage Learning Inc., Lyn Uhi Publishers

24 Brussee, W (2012) *Statistics for Six Sigma Made Easy!* 2nd ed, McGraw-Hill

25 Bicheno, J and Catherwood, P (2005) *Six Sigma and the Quality Toolbox*, Picsie Books, Buckingham

26 Pyzdek, T (2003) *The Six Sigma Project Planner: A step-by-step guide to leading a Six Sigma project through DMAIC*, McGraw-Hill

27 Blokdyk, G (2018) *Quick Response Manufacturing: A clear and concise reference'*, 5 Star Publishing

28 Wang, L and Wang, X V (2017) *Cloud-Based Cyber Physical Systems for Manufacturing*, Springer Publishing

29 Home, R and Housman, K K (2017) *3D Printing for Dummies*, For Dummies Publishing

30 Winman, C (2013) *3D Printing: The Next Technology Gold Rush – Future Factories and How To Capitalize on Distributed Manufacturing*, CreateSpace Independent Publishing Platform

31 Lazaro, O, Cavadini, F and Soldatos, J (eds) (2019) *The Digital Shopfloor: Automation in the Industry 4.0 Era*, River Publishers

32 Calosoft (2018) Internet of Things (IoT) 2018: Market statistics, use cases and trends [online] Available at: https://www.telecomcircle.com/wp-content/uploads/2018/04/eBook-Internet-of-Things-IoT-2018-Market-Statistics-Use-Cases-and-Trends.pdf (archived at https://perma.cc/D2RH-E2W6)

Environmental management systems standards (EMS) 06

The natural resources of the world are being depleted and poor attention to the sustainability of the natural environment has resulted in a need to protect it and redress, if possible, the damage done by industry thus far.[1] In the long term, the rate of depletion and harm to the environment is unsustainable without action taken now to protect future generations of the population. The sustainability of the natural environment is a strategic issue, and leaders of business now have a much sharper and greater interest in seeing a production business as part of a greater environmental ecosystem.[2] This new sensitivity to the natural world is important if businesses are to adapt and support the natural environment upon which they and their respective supply chains depend. The past two decades have also witnessed the ability of pressure groups to 'name and shame' businesses that deliberately ignore their environmental management responsibilities[3] and are detrimental to the natural world. With all this in mind, organizations have become more responsible, starting with company management, in making decisions and goals and finding ways to reduce the negative impacts of business on the environment.[4] They must do this whilst seeking ways to contribute positively to its sustainability locally and globally.

The environmental consciousness of business supply chains to protect the environment is perfectly captured in retailer Marks & Spencer's corporate programme 'Plan A'. Environmental improvement of every aspect of its business and its manufacturing suppliers is pervasive and parallels initiatives promoted by many businesses at the top of supply chains. Even businesses that are much earlier in such supply chains will be expected to play their part and adapt to protect the natural environment and exploit any opportunities presented by being better at environmental management. Knowing where to start and what to do is the remit of ISO 14001 – one of the world's most popular management standards.[5] It may help the reader to think of an environmental management system (EMS) as the application of the logic and structure of a quality standard – the application of environmental quality systems - in effect. Having understood the basics of ISO 9001 (and its guides), the use of ISO 14001 is easier to understand as it follows a similar structure whilst having some unique differences too.

LEARNING OBJECTIVES

At the end of this chapter, you should be able to:

- understand the importance of the natural environment for business and stakeholder engagement;
- describe and explain the major elements of an effective environmental management system (EMS);
- understand the influence of Annex SL on the structure of ISO 14001;
- understand the key elements of ISO 14001 and if it truly leads to an environmentally friendly product or service;
- describe the business benefits of a formalized approach to managing environmental processes of production and design.

Introduction

Business managers are aware and conscious of the natural environment and powerful consumers are taking more interest in organizations and their environmental policies. Large or small, it does not matter what sector you are in – due consideration must be given to the environment and a full systems approach needs to be adopted to support the business in these endeavours.

From business needs, EMS systems have evolved to help focus business leaders, their staff and their organizational resources on conformance with environmental management 'best practice'. Implementing environmental policies to set out the direction of improvement needed and to support a company's overarching objectives is a wise business decision but so too is the development of practices that support better environmental management actively and for all staff. An effective EMS can reduce the negative impact of an organization's operations and outputs and it can release enormous savings too – a common falsehood is that being environmentally responsible costs money and is a drain on business resources! Enlightened and modern businesses see the environment as a source of innovation, supporting better design and improving operational efficiencies to save money whilst making money through delighting customers.[6]

Using an EMS not only benefits the organization but also the employees, the consumers and the community by delivering sustainable solutions that comply with environmental regulations. Having a framework through which to achieve this is very important and that is why companies turn to tried and tested EMS frameworks that they can tailor to their own personal needs, be that their objectives, policies, targets or continual improvement of their environmental performance. One such framework is the standard ISO 14001, but there are others out there too that organizations turn to, such as BS 8555 or Eco Management and Audit Scheme (EMAS II). Regardless of which framework is used to develop and implement an organizational EMS, commitment and awareness is required, not just strategically but at all levels of the organization to ensure that an EMS is effective.

The benefits shown in Table 6.1 are just a few of many. This chapter will present the evolution of EMS systems and show how they guide 'best practice' management and employee behaviours.

What is an EMS?

An EMS is a system of structures, roles, processes, procedures and controls, audits and improvements that is designed, implemented and improved by all company staff for the protection of the environment by reducing risks and finding innovations that will support the environment so that an economically and environmentally sustainable business results. The British Standards Institution (BSI) originally defined an EMS as 'the organizational structure, responsibilities, procedures, processes and resources for implementing environmental management' (BS 7750). The BS 7750 standard was the first major EMS and was later adopted by the ISO to create ISO 14001 (and ISO 14000 series of guides). ISO 14001 added the word 'practices' into the definition[7] and proposed that ISO 14001 was 'the organizational structure, responsibilities, practices, procedures, processes and resources for implementing and

Table 6.1 The benefits of environmental consciousness and improvement for sustainable business

Stakeholder	Interest
The planet and future generations of citizens	Ecosystems are fragile and easily disturbed so embedding environmental thinking to shape business decisions will enhance the environment and prevent its depletion. There is little to no evidence that there is any trade-off of increased business costs because of engaging with environmental stewardship.
The customer	Environmental credibility is very important to the modern customer and this interest covers all customer segments. Customers will avoid dealing with businesses that cannot validate their environmental approach and actual improvements. Having an EMS gives credibility to the claim that the business regards the environment as important and has invested in management systems to protect it. The consumer also benefits from knowing every effort has been taken in the design and production process to protect the environment and engage with good practices including reducing harm, recycling, and reuse of materials and by-products.
The producer	The use of an established and recognized EMS is often considered by customers 'as expected' and a precursor to doing business. An EMS can dramatically improve business performance (operationally and financially) and lead to a sustainable business model where the environment is improved along with business performance.
The employee	An environmentally sensitive business and EMS systems require that employees engage and are empowered to find innovations that will protect the environment from adverse impacts, depletion and catastrophe. Working for such an enlightened employer brings pride and the knowledge that business leaders are investing in the future of the business in the long term (which brings employment stability and an enjoyable working life).
The local citizens	The devastating impact on the local environment caused by the historical industrial depletion of resources caused by mining and primary production is avoided. The natural environment looks better and medical conditions that result from 'dirty' producers are avoided.
The national government	Environmental resources and protection (including regulation) must be enforced and the widespread adoption of EMS systems supports the national agenda to protect the environment but also allows tax revenues from profits of such businesses to be received.

maintaining environmental management'. Therefore, an EMS is a system to manage anything concerning the environment using a portfolio of activities that are voluntarily undertaken by the management and employees of a business to conform to documented 'best practice' (remember a standard is just a document). An EMS is important for a number of reasons,[8] some being:

- Consistently complying with environmental laws and building compliance into business practices:
  - Ensuring that an organization is operating within the requirement of the country where they are working. This could include ensuring the organization is on top of regulations (and the obligations that come with these) such as obtaining:
    - waste management licences;
    - water abstraction licences;
    - consent to discharge waste into bodies of water;
    - authorization to produce greenhouse gas emissions;
    - authorization to transport hazardous waste.
- Improving overall environmental performance in a way that can be measured.
- Addressing environmental liability from current or past practices and ensuring that this educates an organization to bring about positive change internally.
- Facilitating a more environmentally proactive and efficient organization:
  - maximizing investment in environmental affairs;
  - integrating environmental objectives into an organization's overarching business objectives or targets.
- Ensuring that an organization provides an environmentally safe workplace for staff which can also positively impact on health and safety conditions at work.

It is important to note that an EMS cannot replace regulatory requirements and cannot guarantee regulatory compliance. An EMS ensures conformity to a set standard (such as the requirements for conformity to ISO 14001:2015) but compliance with regulations is a very different and legally bound matter. The quality of implementation of an EMS is therefore important and achieving conformance does imply that an organization is environmentally sensitive and responsible but progress and measured achievements in protecting the environment still have to be proven. To put it simply, a business can conform to a standard and offer a basic assurance that it has procedures in place to protect the environment but, because the senior management sets the goals and objectives it seeks, these may be less than would be optimal (they could be easy to achieve). Hence ISO 14001 is not in itself an assurance of environmental performance – the quality of the implementation and goal setting/actual performance is!

Learning point: Winning orders or qualifying for an order with a customer?[9]

A consumer or customer (B2C) will have a set of expectations when doing business with a potential supplier. They will have a set of order qualifiers, which are requirements that must be met by a potential supplier 'to get through the door to the negotiation table' with the customer. These could be that the company has ISO 9001 and has great quality processes. If a potential supplier passes the order qualification stage then it can differentiate itself by offering a customer/consumer an 'order winner', which is an additional benefit of working together that goes beyond a qualifier. So offering the ability to work on environmental protection programmes using the supplier's conformity to ISO 14001 could win business as it sets the supplier apart from its competition. Alternatively, perhaps ISO 9001 and ISO 14001 are just qualifiers? Therefore, it is the demonstrated performance of the supplier with these standards that differentiates them with new and existing customers.[10]

An EMS is a systematic approach to managing environmental issues that gives confidence that an organization's environmental policy objectives and targets are being managed. Hence an EMS can contribute to improved environmental and business performance initiatives and lessen the enforcement burden of regulators.

Key standards

Three dominant environmental management systems have been developed historically. The BSI standard, named BS 7750, was the first published standard to support the establishment of an organizational EMS. The European Commission developed an EMS known as the Eco-Management and Audit Scheme (EMAS) – a management instrument that can assist an organization to improve environmental performance. The ISO, absorbing BS 7750, developed the ISO 14001 standard and this is considered the international benchmark of all organizational standards (BS 7750 was withdrawn when ISO 14001 was published). ISO 14001 is perfectly aligned to support EMAS implementation. The third standard is the BSI standard BS 8555:2016 'Environmental management systems – Phased implementation-Guide' and is considered an important five-phase approach to create an EMS that will only assist an organization aiming to obtain ISO 14001 certification (essentially for small businesses).

The 1980s were a dynamic decade for environmental awareness and in 1987 the United Nations World Commission on Environment & Development (WCED) published *Our Common Future*[11] which stressed the global importance of 'sustainable development' and called for the development of effective environmental management systems by organizations regardless of sector. Four years later, in 1991, the ISO and IEC (International Electrotechnical Committee) worked together to form the Strategic Advisory Group on the Environment (SAGE).[12] The aim of SAGE was to make recommendations regarding the environment, and to take such recommendations to the 1992 United Nations Conference on Environment and Development (UNCED) in Rio de Janeiro. One of the SAGE recommendations was to establish EMS's in addressing environmental issues arising from organizational operations and by January 1993, ISO technical committee TC 207 had started the development of an international EMS[13] – which has always held the anecdotal record of being the fastest standard ever developed! It became ISO 14001 (Figure 6.1).

The BSI-published standard BS 7750 'Specification for environmental management systems' (1994)[14] provided much of the structure and logic for the ISO standard. By 1996, ISO had published a series of supporting documents known as ISO 14000 series, with ISO 14001 being the requirement

Figure 6.1 ISO 14001 development and revision timeline

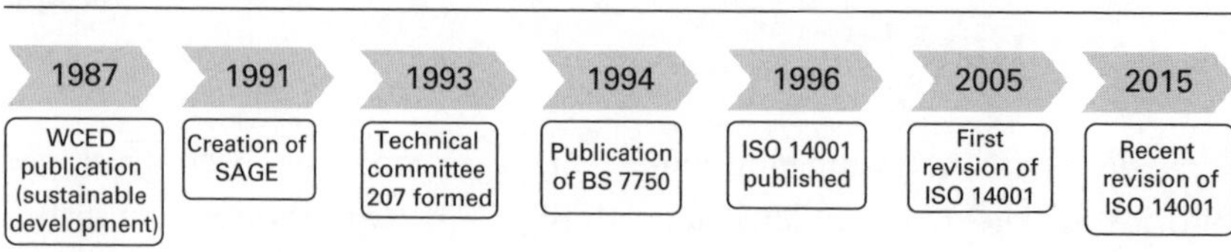

standard. BS 7750 was then withdrawn, which left BS 8555 as a supporting approach to assist organizations in developing an EMS and aligning with ISO 14001 over time.

BS 8555:2016

BS 8555:2016 has five phases, allowing organizations to progress 'a step at a time' and stop at any point to suit their circumstances, needs or capacity (resources). The standard is highly relevant to small and medium-sized enterprises (SMEs) of any sector and location. Larger organizations have often used BS 8555 as a manageable approach to implementing an EMS at multiple sites at the same time – to frame the change process and remain true to the ideals of ISO 14001. The lower pressure associated with a phased approach rather than a conformance requirement audit helps to motivate staff internally in feeling a real sense of satisfaction and achievement each time a phase is implemented rather than becoming overwhelmed with having to implement a fuller EMS (which takes time, investments, patience and due thought, consideration and planning). Some benefits of BS 8555:2016 for organizations are that the standard:

- assists in the management and reduction of environmental impacts;
- improves resource management by efficiently and mindfully using these resources, thus reducing costs (ie reducing waste and cutting energy costs);
- helps organizations meet regulatory requirements;
- increases leadership and employee engagement around the environment and becoming aware and responsible;
- encourages innovation that improves management system processes;
- enhances their reputation with investors, customers, the public;
- creates an economic growth focus that is linked in with keeping a handle on reducing environmental impact;
- is aligned to ISO 14001;
- whilst voluntary, is a logical, systematic approach to implementing an EMS at a pace that is dictated by the organization in question;
- gives information on the use of environmental performance indicators enabling organizations to assess their environmental impact using meaningful data/information.

The five phases of BS 8555 (each has three to seven steps) help an organization to build a robust system. Each phase has an 'overview' element, stage-specific 'achievement criteria', 'how to do' guidance, and 'example outputs'. The staged approach gives the user a list of tasks that they must achieve through its approach to a phase, with distinct stages and tasks to be conducted, which adds user friendliness and an easy methodology to follow (Figure 6.2). The phases are:

1 **Leadership, context and commitment:** a commitment is made by the organization to establish a baseline of an EMS.

2 **Ensure compliance:** here the organization not only identifies legal and other requirements but ensures that they are complied with.

3 **Plan and develop the EMS:** the organization develops objectives (targets/aims) through their policies and strategy and plans out processes that will assist in achieving them.

4 **Implement the EMS:** the operation of the processes and EMS planned in the earlier stage is implemented.

Figure 6.2 BS 8555 five-phased approach

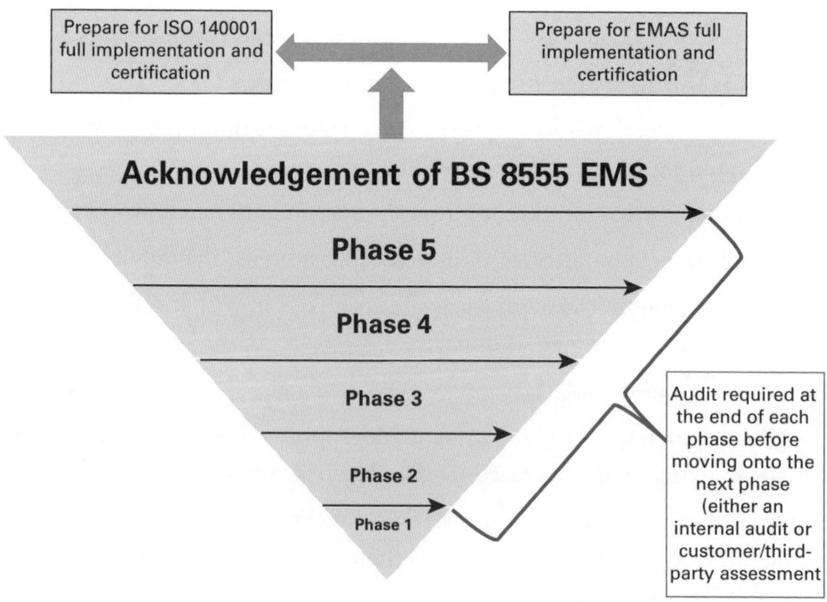

5 **Check and update the EMS**: the organization checks, audits and reviews the EMS and how it is functioning to ensure it is doing what it was supposed to and whether it can be improved.

Whilst the final phase specifies checks, there is an audit requirement at the end of each phase which is a 'go-no go' review to see if the company is fit to move to the next phase (assessment is either an internal audit or customer/third-party assessment). With all five phases in place, an organization can seek EMS acknowledgement (sometimes known as the sixth phase in this standard) which is a more formal recognition of BS 8555:2016 and from here go further to achieve BS 8555, EMAS or ISO 14001 certification.

EMAS[15] (eco management and audit scheme)

EMAS is a voluntary initiative aimed at improving an organization's environmental performance. The final version was issued in 2001 (known as EMAS II) and was revised to align it with ISO 14001 EMS requirements. This European-wide scheme seeks to 'recognize' and 'reward' organizations that go 'beyond the minimum legal compliance' with regard to their environmental performance and obligations. Initially it was restricted to only industrial companies but since 1995 it has become universal in application. To gain EMAS registration an organization must:

- carry out an environmental review and establish an EMS based on the five-phase approach;
- carry out an environmental audit of the organization (eg look at policy, performance and legal requirements);
- prepare an environmental statement based on the organization's environmental objectives;
- independently verify and audit the above and use audit evidence gathered after each of the five phases to demonstrate the effectiveness of the EMS.

ISO 14000 series[16]

The ISO offers a comprehensive environmental management system portfolio called ISO 14000 series, which has ISO 14001 as the conformance requirement standard. The portfolio includes:

1 guidelines/criteria for an organization to set up an EMS:
   - general organizational policies and procedures that govern the EMS.

2 auditing of EMS;
3 evaluating performance:
   - organizational evaluation;
   - product and process evaluation.
4 environmental labelling;
5 lifecycle assessment of products.

There are many additional ISO documents and standards relating to the environment, including around 570 standards covering air monitoring, water, soil, noise, radiation and transport of dangerous goods to name just a few. It is a much broader portfolio than series ISO 9000 and includes:

- ISO 14001: Environmental management systems (Requirements and guidance for use).
- ISO 14004: General guidelines on implementation and maintenance of an EMS.
- ISO 14005: Guidelines for phased implementation of an EMS including performance evaluation.
- ISO 14006: Guidance on incorporation of eco-design for those who've implemented an ISO 14001 EMS.
- ISO 14010/11/12: Guidelines for environmental auditing of EMS.
- ISO 14015: Environmental Assessment of Sites and Organizations (EASO).
- ISO 14020–14025: Environmental labels and declarations.
- ISO 14030: Green bonds.
- ISO 14031/32: Environmental performance evaluation guidelines.
- ISO 14040–14049: Environmental management (lifecycle assessment pre-production plans).
- ISO 14046: Environmental management (Water footprint requirements and guidelines).
- ISO 14050: Environmental management glossary.
- ISO 14062: Environmental management (integrated into product design and development).
- ISO 14063: Environmental management (environmental communication guidelines).

- ISO 14064: Greenhouse gases; measuring, quantifying and reducing greenhouse gas emissions.

ISO 14001 is the main focus of this chapter and it is often used in conjunction with ISO 9001 as two certificates of competence for business.[17]

ISO 14001 logic and structure

The ISO 14000 family of standards is designed according to the same PDCA cycle used to support all ISO system standards (see Figure 6.3). The same clauses (of ISO Guide 83 in 2011, which became Annex SL) are applied to ISO 14001 (see Chapter 4) with the first three clauses covering scope, normative references and terms etc, before getting to the main operational clauses 4 (context of organization) to 10 (improvement):

Plan:

- Clause 4: Context of organization
- Clause 5: Leadership
- Clause 6: Planning
- Clause 7: Support

Do:

- Clause 8: Operation

Check:

- Clause 9: Performance Evaluation

Act:

- Clause 10: Improvement

The other document guides of the ISO 14000[18] family support ISO 14001 and assist the PDCA cycle (examples of which are illustrated in Figure 6.3) so there is a lot of support for the development of the certifying business as an 'environmental learning organization'. For instance, an organization can refer to ISO 14001 and follow guidance for use and implementation of an EMS; however, 14004 and 14005 could also come in useful in the planning phase of the cycle. Moving on to the 'do' phase, ISO 14040 to 14049 can assist an organization implementing an EMS to assess its operation and use pre-production plans.

Figure 6.3 ISO 14000 family of standards and the PDCA cycle

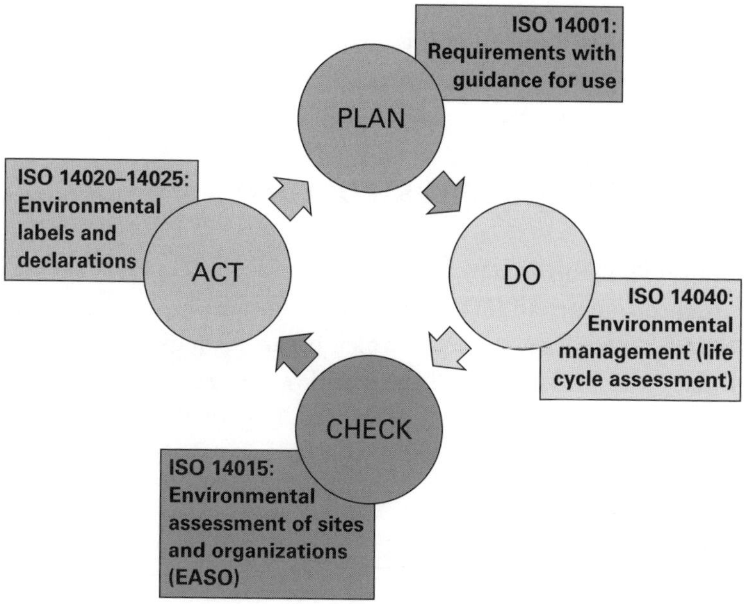

Just like any management system, checks and audits are essential to an EMS (see ISO 14015 and Environmental Assessment of Sites and Organizations (EASO)) and can help to assess the performance of the EMS. ISO 14064 – a standard covering measuring, quantifying and reducing greenhouse gas emissions – can also be of use when in the 'check' phase of EMS implementation and ongoing management, as well as the auditing standards.

The evidence of the 'check' phase allows organizational changes such as amending environmental labels and declarations (see ISO 14020 to ISO 14025) to create a robust EMS. Interpreting the data/information gathered from an organization means ISO 14031/32 (on environmental performance evaluation guidelines) will help managers to shape working practices that are effective and meaningful. Whilst ISO 14001 is the conformance requirement standard, these other documents are highly valuable and relevant for managers in thinking through what suits the business.

The PDCA cycle of ISO 14001 is illustrated in Figure 6.4. The PDCA cycle takes account of the context of the organization, which sets the scope of the environmental management system that the PDCA cycle will work in to achieve the intended outcomes of the EMS. Hence, internal and external

Figure 6.4 PDCA cycle of ISO 14001

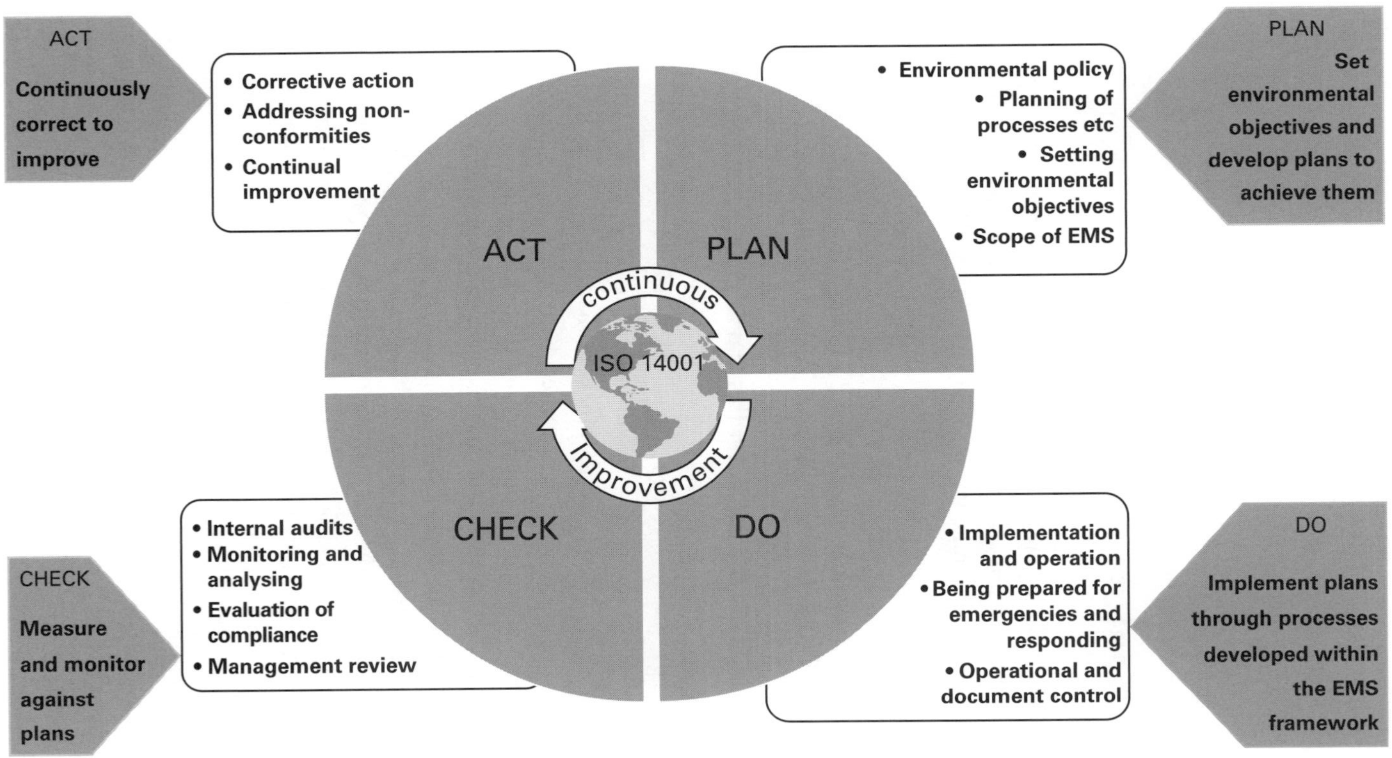

issues will be identified and taken into account along with the needs and expectations of interested parties; after all, an organization does not work in a sterile environment and must be aware of the impact that the society they are operating in can have on them, along with the political environment.

The PDCA model encompasses the high-level structure (HLS) of Annex SL as discussed earlier and in Chapter 4.

The features of ISO 14001

ISO 14001 is an international standard that certifies an organization has environmental policies, strategic improvement objectives and processes to manage all environmental interactions. ISO 14001 implementation means that an organization will establish and implement monitoring and control processes to make sure that they take action to improve performance (with an environmental focus) and will have the same audit functions as described for ISO 90001. This standard is extremely popular and is likely to become more so with the growing global concern around the environment and the sustainability of the planet for this and future generations; above all, it is a voluntary standard where businesses seek to achieve certification. The latest ISO 14001 standard to be released is ISO 14001:2015.

ISO 14001 can help an organization to demonstrate conformance with its own environmental policy and compliance with environmental laws and regulations, but it is not a guarantee. Having a policy is one thing; adhering to it and achieving its objectives is something else. However, ISO 14001 EMS does demonstrate a determination and commitment towards conformity and continual improvement.

The introduction of Annex SL has meant that ISO 9001 and ISO 14001 look similar and share a common structure but with different intent, text and vocabulary. ISO 9001 naturally requires information on the process approach of the organization and empowers an organization by setting out a systematic approach to meet customer needs by providing goods/services of consistent quality using QMS. ISO 14001 requires that an organization determines how they will scope and satisfy the EMS requirements of the business, how it will empower an organization with a systematic approach to measuring and improving on their environmental impact using EMS, and how the EMS will be seamlessly integrated with all business processes. The two management systems and international standards share the principles of CLIPS CFM explored in Chapter 2 and rely heavily on PDCA and auditing/review structures for continual improvement. Today, both standards have the same high-level structure of 10 clauses.

Even though the first three clauses have the same titles (scope, normative references and terms and condition), there are some differences, as these two standards are referring to different subject matter (quality verses environment). Scope naturally concerns the boundaries of the environmental management for ISO 14001 and clause 3 (terms and definitions) has only 22 common terms for both these standards.[19] The main operating clauses of ISO 14001 are the most interesting from a management perspective.

Clause 4 commences 'the thinking' that underpins the environmental system (context of the organization) and operates with four sub-clauses. The first sub-clause addresses an 'understanding of the organization and its context' and requires that the leadership of the organization must assess the internal and external environment (context) that could influence the outcomes sought of the EMS. The other sub-clauses include reviews of customers, suppliers, distributors and users and how the management system engages and uses an ongoing process of change (resulting from PDCA management cycles). For an effective EMS, the leadership of an organization will address the risk and opportunities of interactions with the environment and also the needs and expectations of interested parties (business stakeholders within and beyond the company).

Clause 5 concerns **Leadership** and has three sub-clauses on the context of environmental performance and the EMS. The clause focuses on enacted and well-crafted company policy and the importance attached to it by top management and all staff. The clauses also demand evidence of widespread engagement and promotion of the EMS goals and EMS itself with all 'interested parties'. Top management leaders must adhere to this clause by assigning roles and responsibilities that are relevant to those within the organization and investing heavily in communication on a perpetual basis. Hence, top management must demonstrate leadership of the EMS and reinforce this commitment with specific and aligned actions in which they are actively involved and accountable for. Such clauses help engage a committed leadership team with the protection of the environment.

Commitment is one indicator of an effective environmental business and clause 6 (**Planning**) continues to add detail to the EMS by demanding all risks and opportunities that arise from evaluating external/internal issues are addressed and aligned. Linking policy and objectives is a key activity so that corporate resources are most effectively used to deliver company goals. The clauses also demand ISO 14001 is integrated with the organization's processes, especially when other standards are in place (such as QMS).

Clause 7 takes Planning and adds greater detail to the **Support** that is required by an organization to provide for the management system by ensuring the right people are aware and competent in the processes, tasks and procedures of the EMS. This set of sub-clauses reinforces the importance of internal and external communication so that it is consistent, reliable, constantly reinforced, and consequentially trusted by all staff.

Clause 8 concerns the **Operation** and operational planning as well as control of the EMS and sets out requirements on how the organization will stay alert in identifying potential negative environmental hazards or threats. It also demands very detailed responses and processes for how an organization will respond if such a problem arises. The clauses demand high levels of detail in terms of how operational processes are managed and very detailed procedures (with tasks, sequences and named responsibilities for staff members) that are enacted should an environment catastrophe happen. This element of ISO 14001 ensures there is control around all environmental aspects that are influenced by administrative and technical processes upstream and downstream (including outsourced processes), all of which are defined within the scope of the EMS. Clause 8 has a distinct relationship with the risks and opportunities identified by clause 6 and thus creates an integrated system of controls and alignment in activities, controls and audits. Clause 8 is very important and focuses on the need to plan, implement and control the processes to mitigate risks identified and maximize on opportunities recognized.

Clause 9 concerns **Performance Evaluation** and covers the need to monitor, measure, evaluate, analyse and document evidence of conformance. The clause is a means of evaluating the entire EMS performance. For an effective EMS, it is necessary that the organization determines the criteria it will use to evaluate and analyse its performance through well-defined and regularly conducted reviews of key indicators. This clause concerns the assessment of the business performance and improvement to the environmental aspects/impacts of production and the associated Overall Significance Ranking (OSR) changes (this will be discussed later in this chapter because it is a key and distinguishing feature of ISO 14001). Essentially, the business and its leaders must assess and evaluate the impact of environmental performance and evidence how the business has improved and how its risks have reduced.

Finally, clause 10 focuses on the process of **Improvement** and the mechanisms that capture issues in the system, how these are reduced and how problems are solved effectively. These activities are very similar to those discussed in the ISO 9001 chapter, but the issues are obviously environmental as opposed to quality related.

To summarize, ISO 14001 has the same high-level structure as ISO 9001 but is less prescriptive than ISO 9001 due to its focus (a very wide definition of the environment and the processes of the organization). Being less prescriptive means that the emphasis falls on effectively engaged and educated leaders of the business to empower staff and design processes that work effectively and conform. The lack of an established performance benchmark for ISO 14001 and measures of 'good practice' means comparing one organization's performance against another's is difficult – so the challenge to management is to build the best organization they can. Nowhere in ISO 14001 does it declare what measures should be used and what makes a good target or not – the critics of ISO 14001 have always targeted this aspect of management but these are voluntary standards and improvements must be evidenced to maintain conformance, so all positive progress is good progress even if it is suboptimal.

ISO 14001 also focuses on the conformance of the environmental management system but it does not fully test the compliance of the business with regulations and the law – the latter are aspects of the context, leadership and other clauses and a competent leadership team will integrate the processes of conformance with good compliance too.

Distinguishing features of ISO 14001: environmental aspects and impacts

There are some distinguishing features of ISO 14001 that are worthy of highlighting, especially as the new high-level structure has made much of ISO 14001 look like ISO 9001 – except that it has an environmental rather than quality management focus. The terms 'environmental aspect' and 'environmental impact' have been used but what is the difference between an environmental aspect and environmental impact?

An **environmental aspect (cause)** refers to any element of an organization that interacts with the environment. This could be any such activities (within the operation processes), the end product, or services. An example could be the emission of toxic gases during the manufacturing processes, or the recycling of waste within a company.

An **environmental impact (effect)** refers to any impact an organization's activities, products or services have. This impact could either be environmentally adverse or beneficial in part or in whole, such as pollution of the air/water/soil (resulting from the emissions – cause) or more waste going into landfill (due to poor recycling within a company – cause). Hence, we can see a clear cause and effect (ie an aspect's impact on the environment). Some examples of impacts an organization's activities or operations can have in terms of cause and effect on the environment are given in Table 6.2.

Table 6.2 Aspects and impacts

Activity or operation	Environmental ASPECT	Environmental IMPACT
Operating vehicles	Air emissions	Poor air quality
	Use of natural resources	Depletion of natural resources
Car cleaning	Cleaning agents used	Soil and water pollution
	Use of water	Depletion impact on the natural resource
Rubbish disposal	Recycling of wastes	Less landfill
Heating a building	Boiler emissions to the air	Air pollution

When assessing the environmental aspects (causes), it is important that an organization rate them in terms of low, medium or high risk. An example of this is shown in Table 6.3, assessing aspects under four essential or significant criteria, namely legal liabilities, public concern, frequency and severity. When assessing environmental aspects (such as air emissions or waste pumped into water bodies), these significant criteria can be used to ask questions about the aspect and to rate the answers to these questions so a significance rating can be attained. This can assist an organization that has more than one aspect that they need to potentially address and this rating scheme can allow them to assess which (if any) of the aspects they need to direct their attention and resources to first.

Table 6.3 Rating schemes

Significance criteria	Result of a failure	Score
Legal liabilities *Is the aspect (cause) regulated?*	Criminal action will result	**High** eg worth 3 points
	Violation or possible fine	**Medium** eg worth 2 points
	Issue is unregulated	**Low** eg worth 1 point
Frequency *What is the overall frequency or probability of the aspect's impact?*	Occurs monthly or more frequently	**High** eg worth 3 points
	Occurs between monthly and annually	**Medium** eg worth 2 points
	Less than once per year	**Low** eg worth 1 point
Severity *What is the overall severity for the impact of the aspects Identified?*	Detrimental impact to humans, fauna, flora and the environment	**High** eg worth 3 points
	Impacts on water, air or soil quality	**Medium** eg worth 2 points
	Impact is aesthetic	**Low** eg worth 1 point
Public concern *Has the public ever expressed concern about the aspect?*	Often	**High** eg worth 3 points
	Sometimes	**Medium** eg worth 2 points
	Never	**Low** eg worth 1 point

NOTE Each organization will have to establish their own calibrations for each of the significance criteria and weightings in order to create an overall score.

This table is typically presented as a significance matrix that organizations can use to obtain an **overall significance ranking** (OSR). This matrix assists in helping to rank environmental aspects by assigning significance to each of them, aiding in the determination of whether or not each of these aspects could (or do) have a significant impact on the environment (this could be positive as well as negative impacts). Hence, one aspect such as air emission is assessed in terms of its risk of legal liabilities, whether or not it is of current public concern, the frequency of this aspect and the severity of it (or other concerns that an organization may wish to assess and address). Each of these is then used to obtain an OSR (Figure 6.5). Considering public concern is important, as this can directly affect revenue, depending on the

Figure 6.5 Ranking schemes used for environment overall significance ranking (OSR)

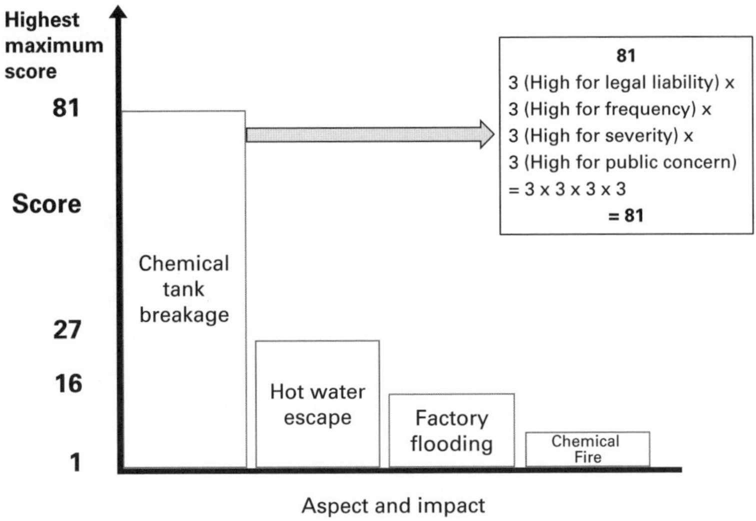

public image resulting from environmental impacts and how an organization manages it. The duration and scale of impact is also something that organizations should appraise.

The worst type of impact is one that has criminal action (scores 3), high public concern (scores 3), high frequency of occurrence (scores 3) and high severity (scores 3). An approach is simply to add these scores up to get an overall score (3+3+3+3 = 12) or multiply them (3x3x3x3 = 81). There is logic to the improvement of this rating system. If a business can reduce the severity of the impact then that will be a valuable activity. If a business can reduce the frequency of a problem, that would also be worth doing. If both severity and frequency are reduced then the issues of legal liability and public image may also reduce. The real leadership issue is in investing in processes and technologies that will reduce the OSR score. When all aspects and impacts have been assessed then it is possible to rank them from high criticality to low criticality. Such a ranking shows the management and leadership of a business what needs to be improved and which aspects will generate the best returns to the business. The risk matrix is a key distinguishing feature of ISO 14001.

Distinguishing features of ISO 14001: emergency preparedness

Anyone who has ever been on a plane, passenger train or commercial boat will have experienced 'emergency procedures' and a demonstration – such as the 'brace' position if a plane is forced to crash land. Well most planes, trains, and boats do not crash but the demonstration is a means of being prepared just in case an emergency happens. Applying the same logic to business and environmental management in particular means any business that has a risk should have a procedure that is available, well documented, up to date, and relevant should an environmental catastrophe take place. This is known as emergency preparedness. Emergency response procedures (Figure 6.6) are written to cope with such an event and represent a sequence of activities involving staff and stakeholders (internal and external) to restore an environmental catastrophe to stability and control. These are highly detailed documents with contact details and all the information necessary to enact a safe and speedy resolution to a catastrophic situation. A

Figure 6.6 Emergency preparedness and emergency response

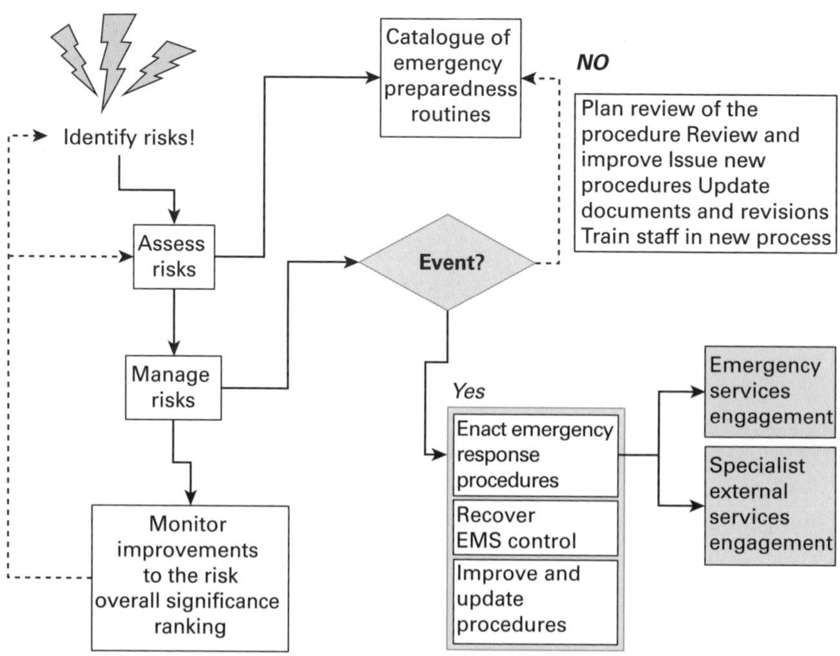

good example is seen in the world of commercial passenger flights; the procedures for fitting face masks, putting on a life vest, bracing, getting to the nearest exit and activating the life vest are all practised on every flight. This attention to detail and responsibility is the same as is used for businesses should there be a failure of a chemical tank on site, the failure of sewerage systems, the escape of gas, the flooding of a facility or any other negative environmental scenario that can be predicted. It can be seen that it is clearly important that an organization has some form of emergency preparedness and responsiveness when it comes to emergency potential environmental impact issues. Procedures need to be in place within the organization to identify the risk of operational activities on the environment (and humans) and to have appropriate courses of action that will be carried out in such circumstances (emergency response procedures). An example could be transporting hazardous waste and the risk associated with this activity, such as an unforeseen accident. An organization needs to plan what they will do in such emergencies and how they will respond; this should be tested and reviewed to ensure that the organization has the capacity, expertise and awareness around such risks and is always prepared. This would all be part of a robust EMS.

So, crudely, aspects and impacts with emergency preparedness are distinguishing features of ISO 14001. These features allow a business to be prepared for managing the business and its environmental relationships. These methods also focus the thoughts of staff and improve the response time to a catastrophic event.

The new high-level structure (Annex SL) has a new emphasis on risk thinking and generating processes that can identify, predict and be enacted to restore stability if a catastrophe were to happen. The processes associated with risk analysis and recovery are important and support an effective environmental management system. With the common high-level structure, it is easy to see how multiple ISO standards are easier to combine and manage.

EMS implementation

Committing to EMS implementation and certification is an important business decision, which has major implications for all staff and demands a continued commitment to learning, improvement and evidenced conformity. The standard is not easy to achieve, and all aspects of the system must align and self-reinforce, such that educating staff is reinforced with training records and such like and can be measured if it is a major goal/objective of the organization. Several steps are involved when establishing an EMS, including:

- **A strong and demonstrable commitment from top management to environmental management as a strategic imperative:**
  - gain commitment from top management in leading and communicating the strategic importance of good environmental management and a total business commitment to its systematic implementation, management and control;
  - gain awareness via research and 'white paper' reports;
  - define responsibilities and appoint management representative(s) to communicate and lead the awareness raising, training and implementation of the EMS;
  - identify business benefits of implementing an EMS;
  - establish an EMS steering committee to project manage the implementation process:
    - develop implementation plan and resourcing needed;
    - source external support if needed;
    - initial training on EMS.
- **Planning for implementation:**
  - identify all environmental aspects and assess their possible impact;
  - assess legal and other requirements from the business context;
  - formulate the environmental policy and vision – promote policy and gain staff 'buy in' to the business direction;
  - establish environmental objectives and targets for the business;
  - visit certified companies to see the standard 'in action' and talk with manager working with ISO 14001.
- **Implementation and operation:**
  - develop documentation and processes (ie develop processes for monitoring and measurement along with any corrective and preventive action).
- **Develop and deliver:**
  - increase awareness within an organization and introduce in-house training and presentations to assist with wider appreciation of the skills and demands for certification and effective management processes/ daily management processes.

- **Establish internal audit programme:**
  - carry out internal audits to evaluate conformity to requirements (such as that of ISO 14001) and identify and close any identified gaps in the system;
  - follow up internal audit with improvements to system using reports and support for staff to make systems 'easy to do right and difficult to do wrong'; maintain the right amount and type of evidence to support the needs of the auditors.
- **Review:**
  - conduct reviews of the initial EMS by management as a formal and significant business review of departmental and process performance. Review goals, objectives and measures for the business and amend where necessary.
- **Improve:**
  - using the review-stage information along with the audit data to focus and implement improvements into the standard, processes and system.

The implementation of the standard will initially attract non-conformances because very few organizations have all the necessary policies, processes and procedures in place and good internal auditors will help prepare the business for certification so that the official third-party process will be as painless as possible.

ISO 14001 certification

Gaining certification for the current ISO 14001 standard generally requires around 12 to 18 months of concerted effort from many business leaders, managers and teams, although the time is typically dependent on the complexity of the organization. If an organization already has an existing EMS in place, then this can make it easier for them to adjust and improve their EMS within their continual improvement cycle. If an organization wishes to gain certification in ISO 14001, then they need to select a competent **certification body (CB)** and apply (complete a questionnaire for the CB to understand the organization and help give them context) for an accredited conformity assessment body that is allowed to certify ISO 14001. A services contract is often written between the CB and the organization, following a quote for the services being acceptable to the applicant business. As each organization is different, and with some being more complex than others, the assessment process may require more skill, expertise and time and so the quote will reflect this. Organizations that are more complex will require more help and time, whereas small businesses may be able to make very rapid progress. Having established a contract, the CB will carry out a review of the organization's processes and documentation to establish whether the organization's EMS is aligned and capable of conforming to the ISO 14001 standard requirements. A preliminary audit and report is conducted by the CB (carried out on site to evaluate the EMS in action) and a **first-stage assessment (FSA)** is completed and presented back to the team at the applicant company. The report will identify weaknesses and improvement opportunities for the existing system in operation.

The next phase of the assessment process involves a **certification audit.** Typically, this will happen at least one month after the FSA and the evaluation is much more thorough and detailed (effectiveness of implementation against the ISO 14001 standard and the organization's own internal requirements). Upon completion of this phase, the findings are written up by the CB and discussed with the organization. If there are no issues then the CB will recommend the company for ISO 14001 certification or, if nonconformities are found, the organization will be requested to address these by implementing corrective and preventive actions. A 'follow up' site visit to the applicant company will be carried out by the CB to ensure that the necessary actions have been implemented and if so recommendation of ISO 14001 will be made. Upon this positive recommendation, an independent review is carried out on the report generated by the CB and a satisfactory review will result in certification of the business to the latest version of ISO 14001. From here, certification is granted for only three years and is subject to surveillance visits every six to twelve months. The last of these surveillance visits in the three-year certification period is termed a **renewal visit,** from which the CB can either recommend certification for renewal or to make changes and improve the EMS. When going down this renewal of certification (if or when ready), then the renewal is independently reviewed and if successful the organization is certified for another three-year period. After a while, the ISO 14001 standard will be revised and businesses will have around **three to five years to transition from the old standard to which they are certified to the new revision.** The process described above is the same as that of ISO 9001 conformance.

Once a business has been certified to the current ISO 14001 standard, the management standard should be self-sustaining and allow teams to improve each day, for issues to be problem-solved, for management reviews to identify system weaknesses, and for the organization to get better and better when working with its stakeholders to support its environmental performance. It is at this point that the benefits of ISO 14001 can be realized.

Benefits of being ISO 14001 certified

ISO 14001 certification and ongoing improvement helps businesses:

- satisfy the requirements of their customer base;
- meet industry requirements (or third-party requirements such as those in the supply chain or a funding requirement);
- support a differentiated market strategy;
- enhance the perceived value and motivate staff to engage with the environment, harness the talents of the workforce to achieve environmental objectives and enact policies;
- create an environmental management system that gives satisfaction for all staff and stakeholders;
- generate pride and enjoy the learning experience of a new method of demonstrating the EMS compliance of the business;
- create pride in the public declaration of their EMS and the esteem it brings;
- enjoy the challenge of solving environmental issues and supporting the business to innovate.

Whatever the reason for implementing ISO 14001, organizations declare many benefits. A 2011 BSI study reported a number of benefits in several areas for those organizations who have implemented ISO 14001.[20] Six of the areas that have enjoyed positive results included:

- Management benefits:
  - 37 per cent performed better in terms of average profitability;
  - 65 per cent found that their company image improved.

- Operations and facilities:
  - 98 per cent made savings that they attributed to waste that did not end up in the landfill;
  - 98 per cent felt that their emergency preparedness was enhanced.
- Product development:
  - 96 per cent enhanced their products' environmental performance.
- Sales and Marketing:
  - 55 per cent had additional public sector opportunities as a result;
  - 75 per cent attracted new customers.
- Finance:
  - 65 per cent made savings of up to $25,000 in their first year of being certified ISO 14001;
  - 27 per cent saved up to $100,000;
  - 66 per cent found that implementing this standard reduced their operating costs.
- Legal:
  - 84 per cent had fewer permit violations;
  - 55 per cent improved on their legal compliance.

The general findings show ISO 14001-certified companies improve performance, enhance their reputations, increase sales, open market access, avoid litigation issues, differentiate their products and create a positive impact on the bottom line of the business. Therefore, whilst it is not a standard that focuses on finance, by improving environmental quality performance positive financial returns are yielded. So again, we can see that an ISO standard offers a payback to fund its own introduction! That is without assessing the new levels of innovation and creativity generated by the implementation process and new product designs.

In summary

In today's competitive world, perhaps ISO 9001 quality standard is not enough for modern stakeholders and ISO 14001 is needed to add a new level of management competence. The operational benefits of an effective quality system and the knowledge gained from implementing such a system are easily applied to ISO 14001 and environmental management practices to support a business now and create a sustainable long-term future. On the 'flip side', the penalties for ignoring environmental requirements are harsh and the internet (eg social media) is a very effective way of disgracing businesses that transgress or attempt to hide poor performance. Customers and local stakeholders are powerful allies when their interests and views are integrated with a business's ISO 14001 system (and deserve to have a role in supporting a local business) because they can help a business's top management make sense of the organizational context and provide resources to support an organization that it would not normally think about accessing. The financial community, the lenders of business capital and finance, are also acutely aware that environmentally well-managed businesses are good for business and that 'dirty' businesses are bad investments. So, overall, ISO 14001 certification is good for business and the environment too. It harnesses staff and supplier innovations and challenges the organization to 'step up' and perform at a higher level of environmental competence.

ISO 14001 offers many benefits to product designers too and also provides a structure to channel the challenges of designing products that are 'environmentally friendly' and can positively contribute to environmental sustainability. Design initiatives such as Design for the Environment (DFE) and operating models such as using materials from 'cradle to cradle' or 'cradle to grave' create an exciting working environment for designers. They create 'stretch challenges' that release the innovative potential of the design team and also enlist their skills when looking at how best to improve processes and eliminate materials that may deplete resources and threaten the long-term future of the business and its natural environment. The direct connection between the design of a product, the implied production process needed to make it, and reduced impacts on the environment is very clear. A simple change to a design may allow a lot of weight of materials to be removed without compromising the functionality of the product, or a substitution of materials could make financial savings whilst using a more sustainable material. The challenge of better environmental management presents many opportunities to stretch the talents and capabilities of engineers and designers in a way that brings out innovation and offers much greater satisfaction and sales revenues. The skills of all workers will be needed to ensure that ISO 14001 – the requirements standard – is used to build a learning organization that embodies good practice. ISO 14001 cannot, by itself, guarantee a product is the most environmentally friendly but it is a starting point and will, as the organization learns and receives greater feedback from workers and stakeholders, start to transform the organization, its products, its technology and its sustainable future.

Seminar topics and examination questions

- Do you really need a standard to prove your environmental credentials?
- With ISO 14001, do you really have an environmentally friendly product? Or just a management system that documents that what you do is sympathetic to the environment?
- Should regulators demand ISO 14001 for every company within an industry sector?
- Compare and contrast the latest versions of ISO 9001 and ISO 14001 – how are they similar and how do they differ?
- Does ISO 14001 have a much better approach to embedding risk thinking than ISO 9001?
- Should commercial buyers only trade with ISO 14001-certified supply partners?

Further reading

There are many great resources on the internet provided by the ISO and national bodies. These are invaluable for both ISO 9001 and ISO 14001. YouTube also has some very good information that is provided by certifying bodies and their client case studies.

Notes

1 Hedstrom, G (2018) *Sustainability: What it is and how to measure it*, De JG Press
2 Belcham, A (2014) *Handbook of Environmental Management*, Routledge Press
3 Stuart, T (2009) *Waste: Uncovering the global food scandal*, Penguin Books
4 Klein, N (2015) *This Changes Everything: Capitalism vs the climate*, Penguin Books
5 Grover, R and Grover, S (2017) *Winning the Environmental Challenge with ISO 14001:2015: Implementation of environmental management system*, Notion Press Inc
6 Gulnik, L and Gulnik, J (2017) *Serving Clients and Community through International Standards: Quality and environment ISO-9001, ISO-14001*, 90daysoulmate.com

7 Jaju, S B (2011) Implementation of ISO 14000 in luggage manufacturing industry: a case study, DOI: 10.5772/17278

8 Price, T (2016) *Environmental Management Systems: An easy to use guide to boosting your organization's environmental performance*, 2nd ed, CreateSpace Independent Publishing Platform

9 Hill, T (2000) *Manufacturing Strategy: Text and cases*, 3rd ed, Irwin McGraw-Hill, Boston

10 Horte, S and Hakan, Y (1997) The firm and its customers' views on order-winning criteria, *International Journal of Operations and Production Management*, **17** (10), pp 1006–19. Read more: https://www.referenceforbusiness.com/management/Ob-Or/Order-Winning-and-Order-Qualifying-Criteria.html#ixzz5gZaZ7dX8 (archived at https://perma.cc/69RL-BX7L)

11 WCED (1987) *Our Common Future*, Oxford University Press

12 Jackson, S (1997) *The ISO 14001 Implementation Guide: Creating an integrated management system*, Wiley & Sons Inc. Publishers

13 ISO (2018) ISO/TC 207 Environmental Management [online] Available at: https://www.iso.org/committee/54808.html (archived at https://perma.cc/DB9A-87WC)

14 Rothery, B (1993) *BS7750: Implementing the environment management standard*, Gower Publishing Limited

15 Daddi, T, Iraldo, F and Testa, F (2015) *Environmental Certification for Organizations and Products: Management approaches and operational tools*, Routledge Research in Sustainability and Business

16 www.iso.com (archived at https://perma.cc/N4G8-E3EQ)

17 It should be noted that whilst ISO 14010/11/12 gives guidelines for environmental auditing of EMS, ISO 19011 is also relevant to this series as it has guidelines for auditing management systems for 14000 series standards

18 Ambrose, P (2016) *ISO 14001:2015 Audit Guide and Checklist*, SystemsThinking.Works.

19 Kleinova, R, and Szaryszova, P (2014) Comparison of new drafts of ISO 9001:2015 and ISO 14001:2015 Standards in term of integration [online] Available at https://www.sjf.tuke.sk/transferinovacii/pages/archiv/transfer/29-2014/pdf/171-180.pdf (archived at https://perma.cc/UWD2-QW4J)

20 BSI: https://www.bsigroup.com/LocalFiles/en-AE/Sustainability/ISO per cent2014001/ISO14001_per cent20Benefits per cent20spidergram.jpg (archived at https://perma.cc/RP2N-BDTN)

Occupational health and safety management systems

07

Technology and equipment may determine what a business can potentially produce each day but the staff who operate the technology determine what is produced. Most items of equipment used in a factory cost many times the average wage of the people who operate them so why wouldn't business leaders invest in the processes needed to support workers whilst 'at work'. Responsible organizations take responsibility for the health and safety of their workforce and any other persons performing work for them. There is much talk, in management books and at conferences, about employees and workers being the No.1 asset of any organization (especially world-class businesses) so a standard that supports workers whilst at work is a critical addition to any business. The implementation and management of a systematic approach to occupational health and safety (OH&S) is important and the ISO offers ISO 45001 standard as a modern support to businesses seeking to enhance their health and safety performance at work and to better manage OH&S risks.[1]

LEARNING OBJECTIVES

At the end of this chapter, you will be able to:

- describe the reasons why a business would want to improve its occupational health and safety management systems and performance;
- understand why standards are required to protect the interests of the employer and employees;
- describe the main features of ISO 45001 and its historical development (OHSAS 18001);

- understand the importance of complying with current legal requirements and regulations in a manner that embodies the key principles of involving everyone, taking a risk-based thinking approach to the business, auditing and improving business processes.

Introduction

Occupational health and safety (OH&S) is a core competence of all manufacturing businesses. Many (but not all) countries have laws that need to be complied with and an international standard allows businesses to conform to accepted good practices that help businesses to achieve their compliance requirements (although a standard does not replace the need for a business to comply). Such standards are good for all workers too so it is no wonder that many businesses choose to connect their systems together and use ISO9001 with ISO 14001 to manage processes that involve people whilst at the same time using ISO 45001 as the standard for workplace and staff welfare management. The World Health Organization (WHO) define occupational health as dealing with '...all aspects of health and safety in the workplace and has a strong focus on primary prevention of hazards'.

OH&S is a complicated area of management that involves knowledge from many different disciplines including psychology, industrial engineering, human resources and more. The purpose of an effective OH&S system is to:

- Design and cultivate a **healthy working environment** resulting in a reputation as an employer that is safety conscious.
- **Reduce stressors and risks** in the workplace for a worker and their co-workers as well as their families.
- Reduce the number of accidents and the causes of 'near misses'.
- **Comply with national and international regulations** concerning workplace management and protection of workers. An OH&S management system can help an organization to be aware of and manage compliance to applicable legal requirements, although conforming to an OH&S system international standard cannot be used as a proof of compliance to such legal requirements.
- **Protect employees** from harm and employers from litigation.
- Increase productivity with **better staff attendance** at work.
- **Reduce insurance premiums** by receiving fewer claims.

The purpose of an OH&S system is primarily to protect workers whilst at work. The term worker, for ISO 45001, concerns any managerial or non-managerial person and any person performing work under the organization's control – so it covers volunteers, contractors, interns and such like.

ISO view of occupational health and safety[2]

According to the ISO:

- The purpose of an OH&S management system is to provide a framework for managing the prevention of work-related injury and ill-health.
- The implementation of an OH&S management system is a strategic organizational decision to eliminate or reduce workplace risks of injury or ill-health by taking appropriate preventive measures.

When an OH&S management system (supported by the use of appropriate methods and tools, at all levels in the organization) is introduced proactively it will help prevent injury and ill-health, improve and enhance the safety and health of its workers and the other persons under its control, and improve staff morale and performance in general. Occupational health and safety goes by a number of names, which often doesn't help and underpins the need for international standardization. For example, OSH (Occupational Safety and Health) and WHS (Workplace Health and Safety) are both used in addition to OH&S but all have the same or very similar meanings.

ISO 45001 'Occupational health and safety management systems – Requirements with guidance for use' is the world's first international standard for OH&S.[3] It provides a framework to increase safety, reduce workplace risks and enhance health and well-being at work, enabling an organization to proactively improve its OH&S performance. It is unnecessary to review the plan, do, check and act (PDCA) cycle that underpins this standard as it has been covered in previous chapters (the PDCA cycle is built into all ISO management standards). The enablers for PDCA and the development of a company-wide systems approach to OH&S are shown in Figure 7.1. The level of detail, the complexity, the extent of documented information, and the resources needed for an organization's OH&S management system will depend on a number of factors. These factors include the organization's context (eg the number of workers, company size, its geography, its culture, its social conditions, its applicable legal and other requirements), the scope of its OH&S management system, the nature of its activities, its products, its services, and its OH&S risks.

Figure 7.1 The enablers for a successful and effective OH&S ISO 45001 system

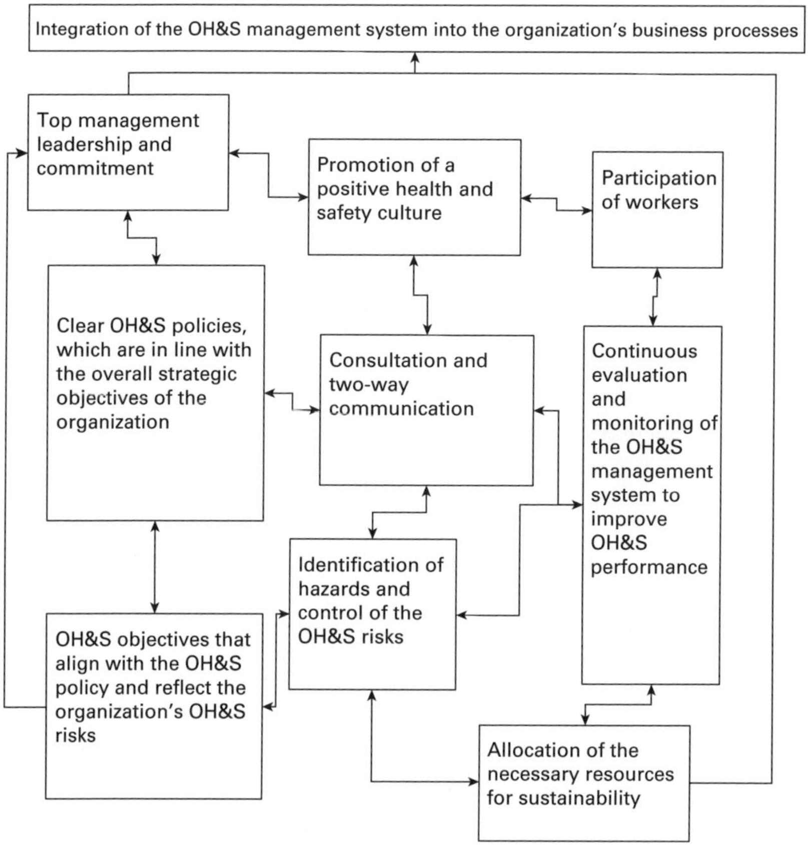

History of occupational health and safety standards

Various industrial occupational health and safety standards were being operated in the United Kingdom and other countries by the 1990s. The standards were managed and governed by different groups. Each standard had common features and slightly different aspects too. Taking the approach of combining 'the best' of each standard into a single standard, BSI published the OHSAS 18000 series and OHSAS 18001 requirements standard. The BS OHSAS 18001 occupational health and safety management system framework[4] was designed to provide practical assistance to business owners and managers with structures, policies, procedures and controls needed to manage an organization. The purpose of the standard was to create a system that yielded the best workplace conditions and health and safety for employees of large and small businesses alike. The standard never became ISO 18000 (series) because this is an existing standard that related to radio frequency identification (and BS 5750 for quality became ISO 9001 and BS 7750 became ISO 14001 standards so there is no precedence for just adding ISO to an existing country standard). Whilst it never became an ISO standard it was developed by experts from a wide range of countries and was used around the world. OHSAS 18001 was withdrawn (as is the protocol when an ISO standard is published and a country adopts it) and ISO 45000 series was introduced. Companies operating OHSAS 18001 systems need to have migrated to ISO 45001 by 2021.

The ISO 45001 development programme began in 2013, and ISO/PC 283 committee was established to oversee the process. Over 70 countries engaged with the drafting process (this process of new proposals has already been covered in Chapter 3). The first committee draft was revised as it failed to gain sufficient approval from ISO members to progress to DIS but eventually, after revisions, it gained approval in 2018. The main differences between OHSAS 18001 and ISO 45001 include the latter having greater emphasis on the accountability of top management and multiple requirements concerning worker participation and consultation. It covers the context of the organization (clause 4.1) and the issues that are relevant to the business and its control of an OH&S management system, and places greater emphasis on committed leadership, internal and external stakeholder engagement, and processes to manage organizational risks. These additions are the direct result of the adoption of Annex SL, the initial high-level structure. These additions include the positive and negative aspects of using the OH&S system, and understanding the expectations of workers and other interested parties (stakeholders in the business). Interested parties include any person or organization that can affect, perceive being affected, or be affected by a decision or activity related to the OH&S system, with an emphasis on leading and changing the business culture by top management setting the example (clauses 4, 5 and 6).

ISO 45001: an integrated management system

To create a management standard that results in an effective process of improving workplace and occupational health and safety, a systems approach is undertaken which begins with the strategic direction of the OH&S system, its leadership, assessments, processes and improvement/reviews. The key elements of an effective system are shown in Figure 7.2.

Figure 7.2 The key features of ISO 45001

OH&S system ISO 45001 Elements	
	Developed and implemented OH&S policy and OH&S objectives
	Established systematic processes aligned to the 'context' of the organization
	Understanding of the risks, opportunities, legal requirements and the other requirements impacting on the business
	Determining the hazards and OH&S risks associated with the activity of the business, including eliminating or controlling the risks to minimize their potential effects
	Establishing layers of operational controls to manage OH&S risks and to comply with legal and other requirements placed on the business
	Increased business and staff awareness of OH&S risks
	Evaluating OH&S performance and improving performance continuously
	Establishing the necessary competencies to effectively operate and manage the OH&S system
	Developing a positive health and safety culture throughout the organization so that OH&S is engrained in all working practices and decisions
	Ensuring consultation and participation of the workforce is practised so that everyone is informed and aligned with OH&S requirements

The international standard has adopted the Annex SL high-level structure of clauses and interoperability with other ISO international standards such as quality, environment, security, etc. The features in Figure 7.2 directly reflect the new influence of the Annex SL structure. Although we have reviewed Annex SL many times in previous chapters, it has three clauses that set up the standard, its relationship to other documents, and then its scope and terms that follow the main mechanisms used to manage a system. These include the setting of the standard and generalities of its relationship with other standards etc in clauses 1–3:

1. scope;
2. normative references;
3. terms and definitions.

Clauses 4–10 contain the requirements used to assess conformity as with other standards that use this high-level structure and provide the staff of conforming businesses with the key processes needed for an effective system to be embedded.

Clause 4: The context of the organization

The main clause and sub-clauses demand that all external and internal issues affecting the purpose and objectives of the organization and the enablers to achieve the intended outcome(s) of the OH&S management system shall be reviewed and understood by all staff, especially the leadership team. Such an understanding must extend to the needs and expectations of workers, other interested parties and must be applicable to legal requirements. The organization shall determine the boundaries and applicability of the OH&S management system, and this shall be formally documented.

Clause 5: Leadership

Clause 5 concerns the direction of efforts, worker participation and consultation processes surrounding the OH&S system. The leadership of an organization play a crucial role and have overall responsibility and accountability for the protection of worker health and safety. Ultimately, the senior leadership team must take responsibility for the effectiveness of the OH&S management system and managing all hazard sources/situations that have the potential to cause human injury or ill-health. This section/clause and sub-clauses require that the organization's context as well as OH&S risks/opportunities are considered when establishing the OH&S management system. Furthermore, the leadership of the organization must ensure that OH&S management system nonconformities and opportunities to improve are identified and prompt action taken in response to enhance OH&S performance.

The standard also demands that leaders ensure work-related hazards are systematically identified, the risks evaluated and prioritized, and countermeasures introduced to reduce risks (such a risk management process has many similarities with the risk assessments that characterize ISO 14001). The standard also demands that leaders resource the system effectively, set performance improvement objectives, and remove obstacles or barriers to staff participation.

The embedded theme of 'constant communication' is also a responsibility given to the organization's leadership in terms of its importance, conformance to the standard and communication of the progress towards the intended outcomes of the system. In this manner, the leaders must promote continual improvement and lead with words and behaviours that set and reinforce a positive culture. The key features of effective OH&S leadership include:

- **policies derived from the strategic direction** of the business by top management and specifically for the OH&S policy;
- ensuring the **fitness for purpose** and appropriateness of the system;
- ensuring a **commitment to the control of OH&S risks** through a hierarchy of control and its continual improvement;
- ensuring **worker commitment via active participation and consultation** concerning the documented OH&S policy and its periodic review for appropriateness;
- **top management shall ensure that the responsibilities, accountabilities and authorities for relevant roles within the OH&S management system are assigned, communicated and documented at all levels within the organization;**
- workers at each level of the organization shall assume responsibility for those aspects of the OH&S management system over which they have control;
- top management shall assign the responsibility and authority for ensuring that **the OH&S management system conforms to the requirements of this international standard** and must report on the performance of the OH&S management system;
- leaders must also create **processes that allow worker participation,** consultation and representation at all levels and functions of the organization.

Clause 6: Planning clause

The planning features of an OH&S standard include actions to address OH&S risks and opportunities and the provision of assurance that the management system can achieve its intended outcome(s) to prevent, or reduce, undesired effects. Once again, staff participation is a key theme of the clause as well as technical reviews of OH&S risks (related hazards and applicable legal and other requirements). The organization 'shall' maintain documented information to provide confidence that OH&S decisions and procedures have been conducted as planned. An effective OH&S planning process also demands the proactive identification of hazards arising in the workplace and to workers for both routine and non-routine work activities. The areas covered by the standard are shown in Figure 7.3.

Figure 7.3 Planning and ISO 45001

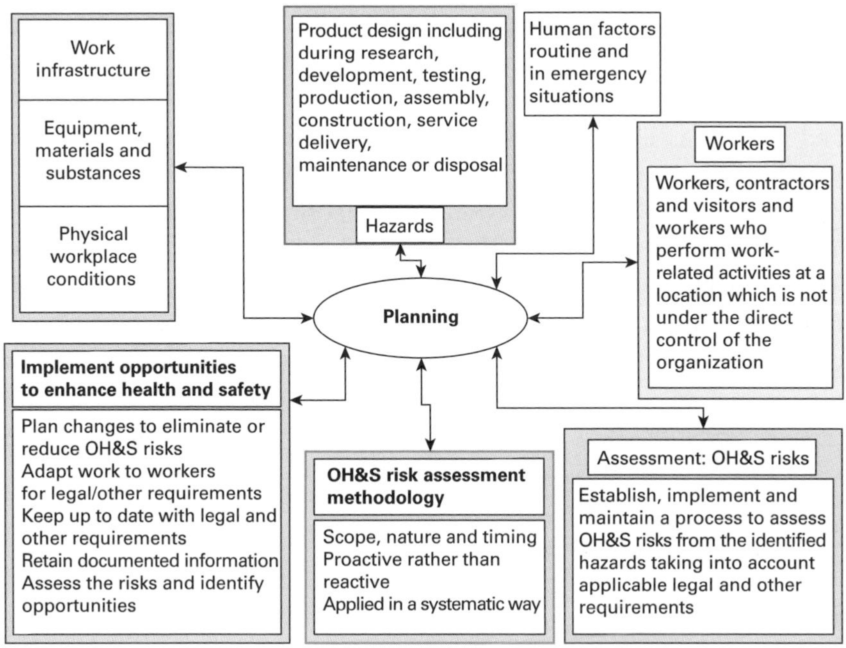

The standard places great emphasis on planning an organization's operational activities. This includes the design of work areas, processes, installations, machinery/equipment, operating procedures and work organization as well as the planned adaptation of these processes. The clause also covers the social aspect of work and the development of the human capabilities to work safely, recognize and manage hazards. The standard is also very specific about the planning of action within a business to address risks and opportunities as well as actions to prepare for and respond to emergency situations (preparedness and emergency response).

Learning and the time to reflect (and challenge the effectiveness of the OH&S management system) is also emphasized in the standard. The purpose of such evaluations is to test the system effectiveness, as well as the effectiveness of improvement interventions undertaken. It is also important that a management team shows how improvements are meaningful and beneficial to the business and its staff. To undertake such evaluations, system performance must be measurable and any improvements documented if practical so that they can be compared with the measurable OH&S objectives. The results of these evaluations must be shared across the business and its stakeholders. The standard also demands engagement and active involvement of staff from all relevant functions, levels of the organization and any worker representatives to maintain and improve the OH&S management system.

Further, the ISO standard also stipulates when setting the OH&S objectives of an organization that the leadership shall consider best practices, technological options, financial, operational and business requirements and harness as much good knowledge and intelligence as possible. The participation of all workers when conducting such planning routines is important in this respect. For conformance, organizational plans must be auditable in terms of what will be done, what resources are needed, who will be involved, when it will be complete and how (if practicable) the before and after can be measured and monitored. Audits of the planning process must also include the review of how the results are evaluated and how the actions to achieve OH&S objectives will be integrated into the organization´s business processes (standardized and engrained in daily working practice). The documentation concerning OH&S objectives and plans must be retained.

Clause 7: Support

The provision of the right resources of the right quality to support OH&S is key to a successful business and the achievement of high performance. ISO 45001 demands that an organization shall determine and provide the resources needed for the establishment, implementation, maintenance and continual improvement of the OH&S management system in order to enhance OH&S performance. Such support includes the knowledge necessary for the operation of its OH&S management system, which should be maintained to remain up to date and current. The fit of good knowledge and skills of staff and high-performance OH&S systems is logical and ISO 45001 demands that organizations shall determine the necessary competence of person(s) doing work under its control. Organizations must therefore demonstrate that staff are appropriately educated, trained, qualified and/or experienced. Where applicable an organization must take actions to acquire the necessary competence and evaluate the effectiveness of the actions taken. To manage the knowledge base of the organization it is necessary that appropriate documented information is retained as evidence of competence and for auditability. Actions taken to ensure competence of staff must therefore take into account the hazards identified and associated OH&S risks (assessed by the organization), preventive and control measures resulting from the OH&S risk assessment process, assigned roles and responsibilities, and individual capabilities, including experience, language skills and literacy. The maintenance of company knowledge is important, and competencies should be updated where made necessary by context or work changes. Necessary competencies also include those prescribed by applicable legal and other requirements; applicable actions can include the provision of training, mentoring, or the re-assignment of currently employed persons, as well as the hiring or contracting of competent persons to the business. The standard also promotes the engagement of workers in identifying needs and assisting in building necessary competencies; it also promotes 'on the job' training at no cost and during working hours. Other issues related to workers include improved awareness of persons doing work or work-related activities (regularly or temporarily) under the organization's direct and indirect control. This includes awareness of:

- the OH&S policy;
- the worker contribution to the effectiveness of the OH&S management system;
- the benefits of improved OH&S performance;
- the implications of not conforming with the OH&S management system requirements of their work activities, including the consequences, actual or potential;
- incidents and the lessons learned from them.

Support to organizational staff also includes the provision of internal and external information and communications relevant to the OH&S management system including decisions about what relevant information to disseminate and how to do it, when to do it and with whom – with contractors and other visitors, and with other external or interested parties. The standard also requires that organizations shall take into account diversity aspects (eg language, culture, literacy, disability) where they exist, when considering its information and communication processes. Again, documented information is important and must effectively support the OH&S management system. The main criticism of earlier standards was that they were bureaucratic but ISO 45001 (and all modern standards) are more sympathetic and understand that the extent of documented information for an OH&S management system will differ from one organization to another, due to size, technology, products and services and complexity. Modern technologies and other forms of evidence are now acceptable instead of traditional manual records, but each company must convince its certifier/auditor that these forms of evidence are robust and reliable. The 'importance' of supporting documentation is shown in Figure 7.4.

The ISO 45001 conformance standard (like all others) relies heavily on documented information as necessary; this does not mean it has to be exclusively a printed or paper-based document but could include a poster, a spreadsheet or a tablet. The purpose of such information is to provide evidence to prove that an organization does what it says it does. Hence, documented information is relevant to auditing internally and by second- and third-party auditors. Documented information provides structure to the OH&S system and is a living system that adapts and adjusts with the business to support it. Documentation does not need to be onerous but the 'downside' of getting OH&S wrong is significantly negative and inhibiting to a business and its workers, so a business must develop systems and evidence that are coherent, robust and in place to protect workers. Documents also support the effective management of the people and processes of an organization – its value adding and operations – and are the basis of continuous improvement efforts.

Figure 7.4 Documentation and ISO 45001

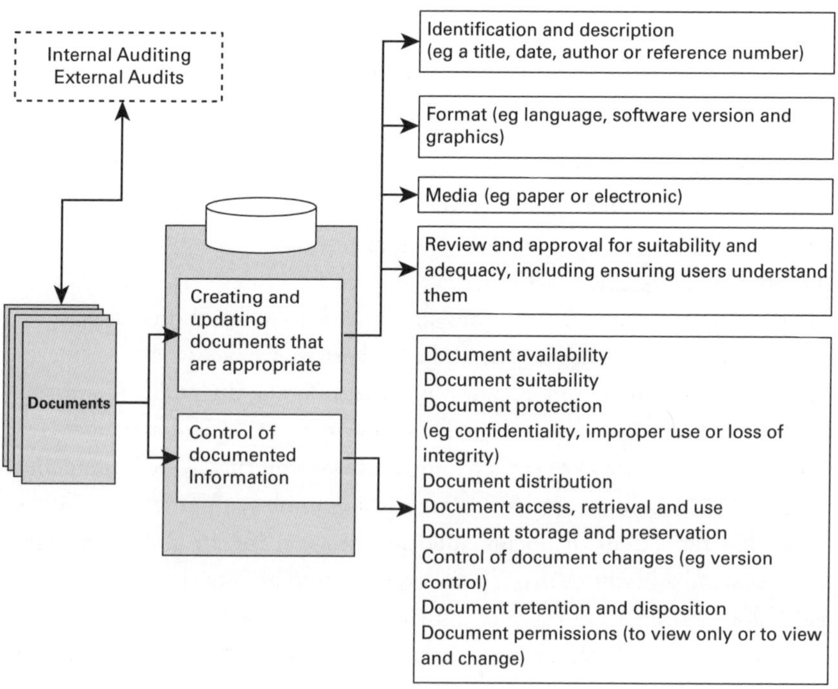

Clause 8: Operation

Operational planning and control are the main activities of a business and are the way of enacting objectives and document control. Within this clause an organization must determine and identify the hazards associated with its manufacturing and operations and determine where the implementation of controls is necessary to prevent or reduce OH&S risks. All processes must be systematically reviewed to understand how they are to be controlled and for the verification of the effectiveness of the controls applied. Businesses must also keep documented information about what controls have been used and the extent of confidence that the processes have been carried out as planned. Managing the core process of routine (and non-routine) work means a hierarchy of control needs to be implemented and deviations in the process must be understood from an OH&S perspective.

The standard advocates the use of a hierarchy of control – which is what gives ranges in the effective solution of the OH&S risk (Figure 7.5). The least effective solution is to provide personal protective equipment to the worker and the most effective is to eliminate the root cause of the hazard itself. An effective OH&S system will focus on the elimination of risks and may combine multiple controls to ensure the protection of workers and those in the workplace.

Every international standard demands that processes and procedures will change and improve over time so an organization shall plan and manage temporary or permanent changes to the OH&S management system to ensure they do not have a negative impact on OH&S performance. Such changes may include the resolution of incidents and nonconformities, the introduction of new products, processes or services at the design or redesign stage, changes in knowledge or information about hazards and changes to work processes, procedures, equipment, organizational structure, staffing, products, services, contractors or suppliers. New developments in knowledge and technology (and changes to the applicable legal or other requirements) constitute changes and require intervention by the organization. Such change must be implemented in a planned and controlled manner with the identification of any OH&S risks. To ensure change is successful it is also expected that an organization will review the consequences of unintended changes and take action to mitigate any adverse effects.

An ISO 45001-certified organization shall also ensure that outsourced processes which impact on its OH&S management system are controlled and the organization shall establish controls for procurement (eg of products, hazardous materials or substances, raw materials, equipment, or services

Figure 7.5 The hierarchy of controls

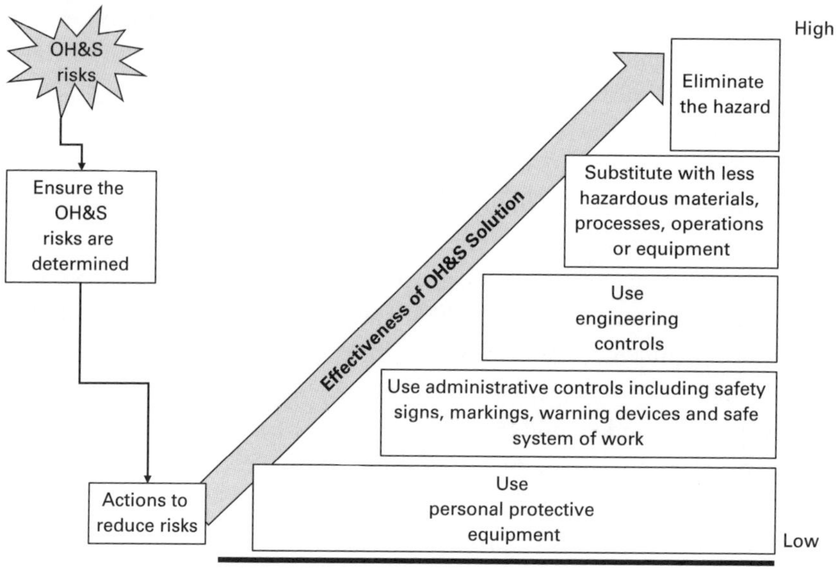

and selection of contractors) so that these items conform to its OH&S management system requirements. The standard also covers the management of contractors and processes to identify and communicate, evaluate and control the OH&S risks arising from the contractor's activities and operations to the organization's workers, from the organization's activities and operations to the contractor's workers, and from the contractor's activities and operations to other interested parties in the workplace. For organizations with multi-site operations then co-ordination mechanisms will be needed across the group.

In a similar manner to ISO 14001, the OH&S system must operate with a process of emergency preparedness and response. The organization must identify emergency situations and establish, implement and maintain a process to anticipate, prevent or minimize OH&S risks from potential emergencies. Such routines include the identification of and planning for potential emergency situations and the preparation of a detailed planned response. The procedures shall be periodically tested, rehearsed and revised as necessary. Information availability plays a large part in these routines, as do training of staff and information/training of contractors, visitors, relevant emergency response services, government authorities, and the local community. The organization shall keep up-to-date documented information for the process and on the plans for potential emergency situations.

Clause 9: Performance evaluation

Every 'world class' organization has a passion for measuring and using such data to carry out better planning, make more effective business decisions, and for improvement purposes. In general an organization shall determine what needs to be monitored and measured to conform, the measures concerning the applicable legal (and other) requirements of its operations with identified hazards, and OH&S risks and opportunities, operational controls, and measured progress towards the organization's OH&S objectives.

The organization must be clear on the methods for monitoring, measurement, analysis and evaluation (as applicable) to ensure valid results. The organization also needs to outline when monitoring and measuring shall be performed, and how results are analysed, evaluated and communicated to the workforce and interested parties. Again, the participation of workers in these activities is promoted. The organization shall evaluate the OH&S performance and determine the effectiveness of the OH&S management system. The organization shall retain appropriate documented information as evidence of the monitoring, measurement, analysis and evaluation of results.

An essential element of any organization is to ensure the measurement equipment in the factory is calibrated (and/or verified), monitored and maintained as appropriate. In this manner, routines are needed to manage the process of verification of this form of control equipment (such as calibrating weighing scales). Further evidence is also required to capture the fact that such testing has happened, and the organization shall retain such appropriate documented information as evidence of the results of these routines.

Measurement in the form of compliance evaluation along with evaluating compliance in line with legal requirements and other requirements to which the organization subscribes is important. Once again, these routines must be formalized with documentation. The organization must also provide documented evidence that the frequency of data capture, the methods of capture, and the actions following measured deviations in performance are undertaken in a systematic manner as well as evidence that shows compliance with legal and other requirements.

The internal audit process can also be considered as a series of control measures and an organization must establish, implement and maintain an audit programme(s), again with details concerning the frequency of conduct, methods, responsibilities, planning requirements and reporting. These audits shall take into consideration the importance of the process, OH&S risks and opportunities, and the results of previous audits. Such audits need to be defined and conducted by competent, trained, objective and impartial auditors. The audit results shall be reported to relevant management, workers and interested parties (see ISO 19011 for details on the practice of auditing).

Any audit will provide good feedback to senior management and therefore such intelligence should be used to determine the success and continued suitability, adequacy and effectiveness of the OH&S system and whether improvement actions have been undertaken or sustained. Such a 'management review' shall include consideration of improvement actions, changes in external and internal issues as well as any changes to legal and other requirements. The management review should also review the OH&S risks, OH&S opportunities and how well the OH&S policy and objectives have been met (including trends). Any incidents and nonconformities should be reviewed, and workers encouraged to participate in consultations. The outcome of the management review shall include conclusions about the OH&S system effectiveness, decisions related to continual improvement opportunities, actions needed, and details/information when objectives have not been met. Again, the report should be widely communicated for all staff and interested parties and all documents that support the management review process should be retained.

In summary, measuring and taking action as a result of learning is critical to the PDCA cycle of improvement and this section of the standard offers many valuable insights for top management. The quality of information generated by the effective implementation of ISO 45001 is critical because it triggers a process that allocates scarce business resources to improve the welfare of its workforce.

Clause 10: Improvement

Improvement is the result of good management and an effective ISO 45001 system implementation will indicate where the performance of the business is insufficient and offer an opportunity to perform at a higher level.

Reactive improvements result from incidents and ISO 45001 requires (using the standards terminology: an organization 'shall') the instigation of defined processes to correct the situation (as illustrated in Figure 7.6).

Corrective actions shall be appropriate to the effects (or potential effects) of the incidents and unsurprisingly all documents concerning the improvement process must be retained as evidence of the nature of the incidents and any countermeasure actions (along with the results of corrective actions and their effectiveness). Understandably, the results of the process must then be

Figure 7.6 Reactive improvement

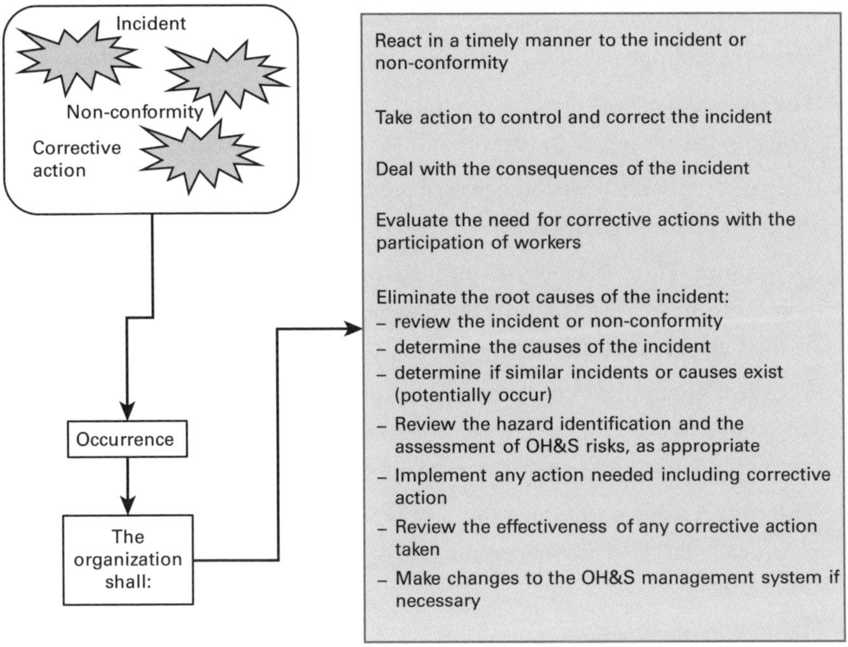

communicated to all workers and interested parties. More generally, the standard requires that an organization shall establish, implement and maintain a continual improvement process(es) in consultation with its workers and shall retain documented information as evidence of the results of continual improvement. Naturally, as with all ISO standards, the auditing of a standard for conformance is governed and dictated by ISO/IEC TS 17021, which sets out the technical specifications and competence requirements for auditing and certification of ISO 45001. The results of audits and nonconformances will be catalysts for the improvement process.

The trilogy

This chapter has presented an overview of the ISO 45001 standard and has outlined the systems, processes and procedures for the protection of the workforce whilst at work. Many organizations combine ISO 9001 (quality) and ISO 14001 (environmental management) with ISO 45001 (occupational health and safety) and there are many benefits in doing so:

- Problem-solving and improvement activities conducted by workers will be based on a true understanding of quality improvement methods and a good knowledge of occupational health and safety. The result is a better standard of improvement, solutions and work that is easier to do right.
- The risk assessments used by the standards means that staff have a greater focus on the design of processes and the physical working environment.
- The risks associated with the presence of chemicals and other products in the workplace fit well with the intention to protect the environment.
- The combination of analyses needed to understand the context of the organization will lead to more robust decision making and a holistic view of the business and the value it generates.
- The strong emphasis on leadership and communication means that the workforce will have a greater say and engagement with the future competitiveness and prosperity of their employer.
- The engagement of suppliers and other interested parties makes a huge resource available to an employer without having to pay for such involvement.
- An improving business is good for everyone!

In summary

Designing and managing safety in the workplace is a key responsibility of the modern manufacturing and business leader and no one can claim ignorance of its importance. If the workplace is dark, dirty, and dangerous then progress with ISO 9001 quality systems and ISO 14001 environmental systems is unlikely to be sustainable. ISO 45001 is an important addition to the competitive arsenal of any business, and it protects the most important of all assets that are available to an organization – its workers! In the campaign for safety in the workplace, the role of the designer and draftsperson is key. To enhance and maintain an audit trail of improvements, technical drawings are needed for the fabrication of work stations. New ways of presenting materials to workers in a safe and controlled manner are necessary and allow workers to visualize what the new workplace will look like and how best to manage it. Designers are critical to solving identified risks in the workplace and converting ideas into visual representations of what the work environment could be.

The involvement of engineers and designers with the process of managing occupational health and safety is critical. The design of the workplace is fundamental to ensuring workers are safe. Furthermore, team leaders and operational staff rely upon engineers and designers to enact changes to the workplace that result from learning how to best implement ISO 45001 and conform to its requirements. Operational staff have great ideas but will get frustrated when they do not have access to designers who can draw and print out the modifications that are needed to ensure a safe and healthy workplace. A light, bright and ordered workplace is safer and also has many benefits in terms of pride and good mental health, so this standard is one of the most important that industrialists rely on. Designers play a big part in this and can help minimize workplace stress by creating an attractive workspace for all workers and visitors. One of the most powerful sales propositions to a new customer is to show them a workplace that is in conformity with ISO 45001. Most customers will visit to inspect (and often audit) their suppliers so for them to take back hard evidence and the mental images of a fantastic workplace is important, and shows them how much attention is spent on occupational health and safety.

Ensuring workers are cared for and integrated with the ISO standard is also good for morale and many other key business measures including quality and productivity. Workers make great salespeople too, and a disciplined approach to occupational health and safety is a very clear reflection of the company's culture and how well workers are engaged with the process of managing with ISO 45001. It can be little surprise that the standard is such an important addition to any other standard to which the organization is certified.

ISO 45001 is well designed and provides significant advice to all staff about how to optimize and exploit an effective occupational health and safety system. The standards document and the clauses within it represent latest 'best practice' and are a great way of making a complicated issue – OH&S – easier to understand and manage effectively. The international standard is applicable to all organizations that intend to implement and maintain an OH&S management system. This standard also assists in ISO 45001 nonconformities through continual improvement and ensuring the engagement of all staff and stakeholders. OH&S is so important it is likely that this standard will continue to have high relevance for business leaders as a standard where conformance has a strong personal meaning for each member of staff.

Seminar topics and examination questions

- When there is a breach of company safety, should the leaders of the organization blame the individual involved or the system that the leaders have helped to design?
- What occupational health and safety factors would you look for if you audited a fast food restaurant?
- As a leader of a small machining company making steam valves, what activities would you undertake or request to be undertaken to communicate the OH&S plan and performance of the business to its staff?
- Does the use of ISO 45001 apply to temporary workers?
- Many businesses outsource aspects of the production process to other businesses, so is the external organization within the scope of the management system? Is the outsourced function or process within the scope? And what does this mean for managers of the relationship with the external supplier?

Further reading

The subject of occupational health and safety dominates a lot of the internet and national government ministries as well as business trade bodies. The British Health and Safety Executive is a good source of information.

Notes

1 The Chartered Quality Institute (2018) *ISO 45001:2018 Understanding the International Standard*, Kindle Edition, The Chartered Quality Institute, London

2 Occupational Health and Safety: ISO 45001, PDF file available at www.iso.org (archived at https://perma.cc/SS92-MT2P)

3 Dentch, M (2018) The ISO 45001:2018 *Implementation Handbook: Guidance on building an occupational health and safety management system*, Kindle Edition, ASQ Quality Press

4 Lakhe, R and Dharkar, K (2018) *ISO 45001:2018 Occupational Health & Safety Management System*, Kindle Edition

Information security management 08

Historically, criminals on horseback who aimed to take money from 'passers-by' practised highway robbery. Often armed, they held up travellers and business professionals and demanded 'monies with menaces'. The legends of Dick Turpin and Robin Hood live on, but today, theft of valuables usually happens in the form of data and the robbers are almost impossible to find. In the digital age, theft of data and information is a much more significant and lucrative issue for the robber. There have been many high-profile and headline-grabbing cases where business corporations have been hacked and information stolen, or information held on USB memory sticks has been lost by employees whilst travelling. One simple USB stick can hold the details of millions of customer accounts; if this was to fall into the wrong hands it could result in serious fraud and brand damage for the company involved.[1] In the digital world, where information is key and an asset, it is understandable that businesses will seek to protect it and themselves. In history it was scandalous to think that a 'highway robber' would steal from passers-by at gunpoint, and yet today the scandal of losing data or being deliberately 'hacked' by cyber criminals can damage businesses that are unwittingly targeted by such thieves. Organizations must be vigilant and act defensively, as the smallest of leaks of information can cause major embarrassment or loss of customer confidence. Information security is now a major issue; it has joined the main standards of quality, environmentalism and occupational health and safety as a major standard to demonstrate to stakeholders that an organization is serious about the treatment of customer, employee, commercial and supplier information. ISO 27001 (officially titled ISO/IEC 27001) is the international standard that supports business to develop information security management processes and conform to 'best practice'.

LEARNING OBJECTIVES

At the end of this chapter, you should be able to:

- define the importance of information security;
- understand why businesses need to consider protecting data in an increasingly digital society;
- understand ISO 20000 series and its relevance in information technology service management systems (ITSMs);
- understand the major features of ISO 27001 and why it is important for effective information security management;
- explain how other organizations are important in the field of information security management, such as ISACA, AXELOS and the CMMI Institute.

Data is valuable for businesses seeking to deliver high levels of customer service. Data drives everything – it triggers the production process and it is essential for managing cash flow. Today a lot more is known about consumers and employees than ever before but with data expansion come risks and issues, the biggest of which today is protecting information. Cyber-attacks, corporate hacking and data breaches pose a real threat to the operations of a business. An effective management system will protect against external threats posed by malicious attempts to get data and internal failures or human error.[2] Furthermore, there are now severe sanctions and penalties for companies that experience breaches, in addition to any loss of brand image. What is needed is a systematic specification and standard to protect such information.

The effective use of an information security management system (ISMS) provides a structured and holistic approach to data protection for policy-driven goals and improvement targets, as well as a series of procedures that are used to control risk-sensitive aspects of the business and reduce the likelihood and severity of any preconceived or human error source of data breaches. The ISO 27001 requirements standard and series of supporting guides are world leading and will become even more important as the world continues to become more reliant on digital and mobile technologies.

Information security

Information security management (also referred to by many in the field as infosec) refers to the implementation of action, policies and procedures to ensure that information is secure and protected so that it cannot be accessed

Figure 8.1 An effective information security management system (ISMS)

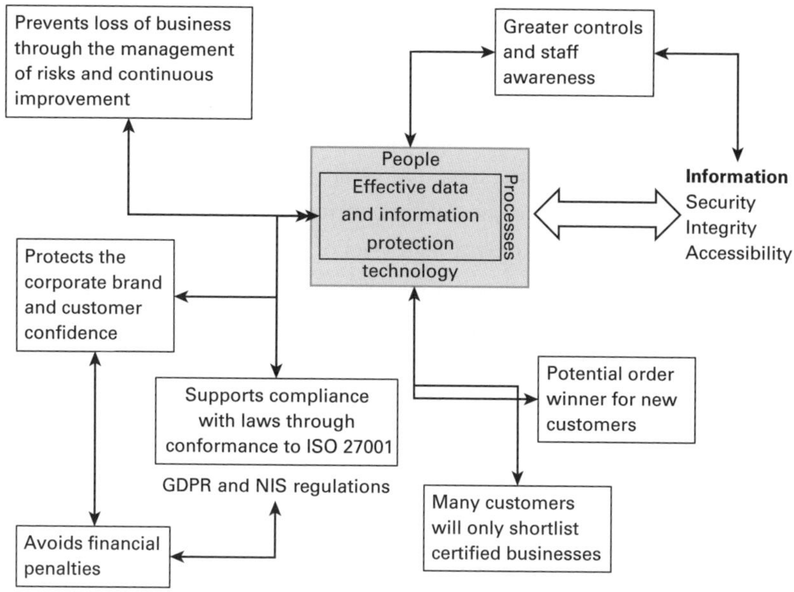

by those for whom it is not intended. Securing corporate information prevents unauthorized access so that it does not fall into the wrong hands or become manipulated, modified or destroyed, either maliciously or accidentally. Information can be stored physically (in a file, for example) or electronically (on a hard drive, USB stick or cloud, for example) and both formats need to be appropriately and proportionately protected to ensure the integrity of the data is not compromised along with confidentiality (where applicable). With digitization of information also comes opportunities for organizations. Digital records are now, where necessary and sufficient (as well as sufficiently protected), capable of being used as sources of conformity evidence for auditors. The acronym CIA stands for the Confidentiality, Integrity and Availability of data as the key areas of protection needed in place for a business to operate an effective system (Figure 8.2). CIA provides the basic logic for organizations when designing, improving and auditing their information security policies and procedures. Each organization will need to design its own system, policies and procedures based on conformity to the ISO 27001 standard, to fit the unique contingencies of the exact business.

The confidentiality aspect of the CIA triad tends to receive the first consideration when implementing a standard in terms of how the information/data is being stored by the organization. Most businesses will have trained their staff in managing data in accordance with changes in the law and recent 'scandals' where businesses have 'lost' customer and other data. Access to the information that an organization stores must also be controlled, appropriately regulated and restricted. It is important to understand that even a simple organization will have many different types of information and so a 'blanket policy' for all information would be inappropriate. To make an informed judgement about what practices are best suited to the data and information under consideration, it is first necessary to understand the risks associated with the information. In this manner, there is no need to have a high level of confidentiality (and thus 'tight' security measures in place) for data that could be graded as low risk if it fell into the wrong hands. However, other information may be rated as high risk of causing a lot of harm if the wrong person got hold of it and used it maliciously. Therefore, grading 'information confidentiality' in this manner is usually the first practical step before an organization decides how best to safeguard the relevant information appropriately and proportionately.

Information integrity guarantees the reliability, incorruptibility and hence the trustworthiness of the information stored and the integrity of information for the lifetime of the information, after which procedures are necessary to ensure the effective disposal of the information in an appropriately sensitive manner. The availability of information provides an assurance that information can only be accessed by those who are authorized to do so and that the system(s), policies and procedures in place to achieve this are robust and proportionate.

Figure 8.2 The CIA triad

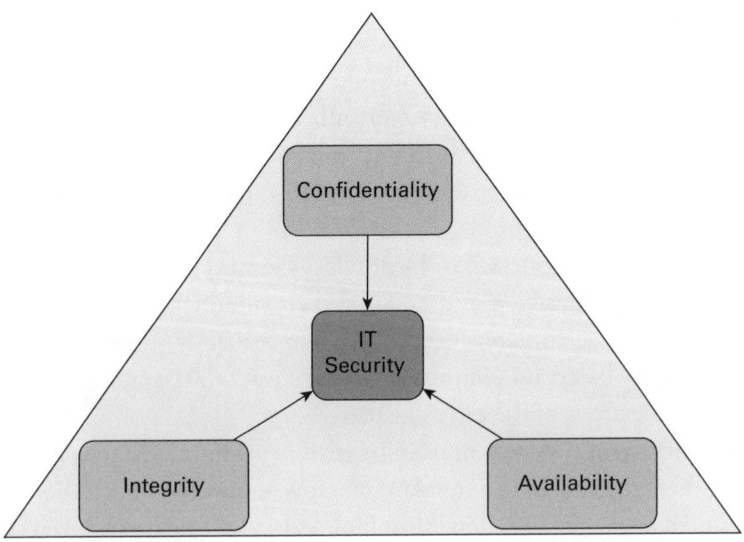

Organizations must draw on a number of different defences to ensure information confidentiality, integrity, availability and thus security. Such practices could include (but not exhaustively) password protection, biometric verification/login, key fobs, two-factor authentication, log in limitations if the wrong password/user name is input, and data encryption. Backed-up and stored data has to be managed and include organizational processes that detail the recovery steps necessary if there were to be a disaster of some kind (eg a fire or break-in to an office) or breach in the system (eg cyber threat or virus).

Information security management systems (ISMS)

The management of organizational information, be it physical (files, reports, paper forms etc) or electronic (accounting systems, HR data, payroll data etc) includes ensuring that the information is secure and protected from unauthorized access which could cause harm to individuals and the organization. Annex SL provides the structure to the ISO 27001 standard and outlines what the organization 'shall' do to ensure that information cannot be tampered with, modified or prematurely destroyed. ISO 27001 requirements standard is known as an information security management system (ISMS) which uses a structured approach to policy setting and information/data management all the way through to management reviews and improvement activities. The many considerations that must be reviewed by organizational leaders are shown in Figure 8.3 and ISO 27001 demands an alignment between the goals of the firm, its processes for information security, risk assessments and the improvement activities undertaken. These reviews will influence what is presented in the security manual (promoted and embraced by top-level management) and form a document that outlines the organization's strategic goals from which security rules and procedures can be written.

The 'context' of an organization is important and increasingly regulated (with fines for those organizations that do not comply) and business leaders must consider the current legislation and regulation impacting on the operations of the business. Compliance to such regulations is mandatory and having a dedicated information security team with knowledge and skills to ensure that the organization's data/information is secure is vital. The business context poses many threats/risks and opportunities that result from advances in technology and other means of sharing and remotely accessing information.

Figure 8.3 Typical considerations for an ISMS

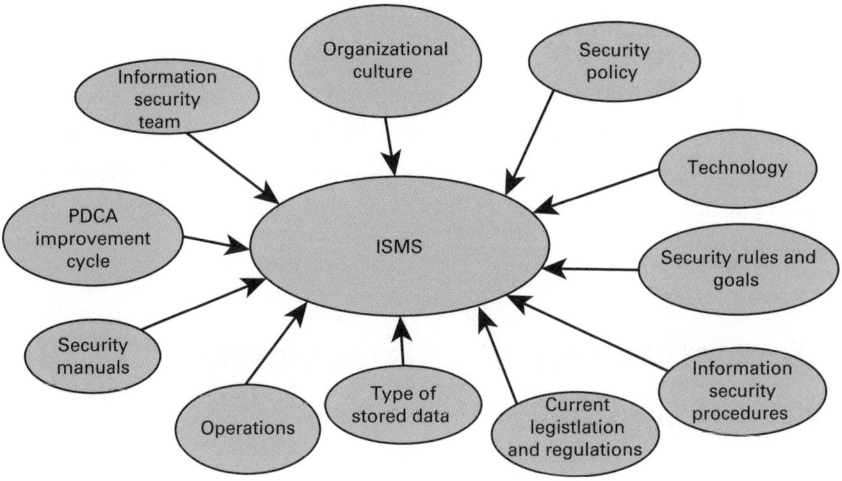

'Going paperless' may offer many new business opportunities but also poses many challenges in terms of the storage of digital data and its protection. Increases in digital literacy and customer demands have led to an explosion of information that is stored digitally (on hardware and/or software). Cloud storage, formed of hardware storage and fast servers based in a number of different physical locations, has added a new contextual feature that businesses must review. However or wherever data is stored, the internet is increasingly being used to maliciously access this data and tap into the hardware or software storage systems. This kind of cyber threat can come from anywhere in the world, hence organizations must establish robust defences that are 'up to date' and proportional.

Cyber security typically consists of a trio of controls, namely people, processes and technology (Figure 8.4). Improving each element of the model helps reduce such attacks or the risks posed by human errors, which can be as great as highly organized external attacks. The rapidly changing business context means cyber threats are increasingly difficult to detect and organizations must be agile and adapt their processes accordingly. The use of formalized management reviews and focused continuous improvement of ISO 27001 processes ensures an organization remains up to date and all staff remain supported with process documentation to mitigate any such cyber threats. Managing people skills and also the documented evidence and working documents for an ISO 27001-conforming business are key challenges and developing, maintaining and upgrading the cyber control systems of a business requires competent staff who are perpetually trained to stay up to date.

Figure 8.4 Cyber security controls

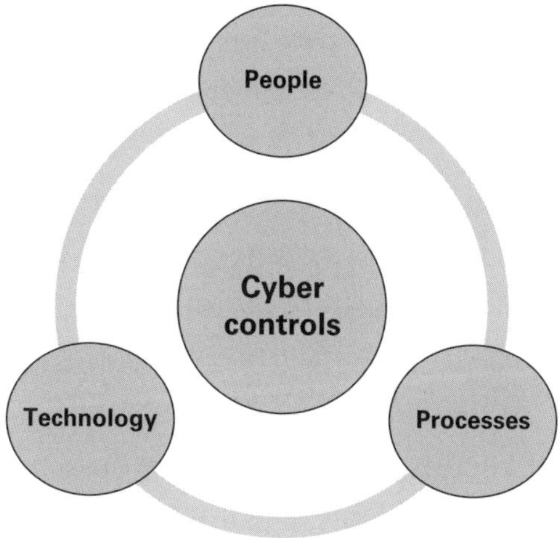

One of the major contextual changes for businesses has been the severe penalties for non-compliance with the General Data Protection Regulation (GDPR). The whole purpose of this regulation was to unify data protection and privacy for those who reside in the European Union and the European Economic Area, and it has been written into European law. GDPR does not specify how to comply necessarily but some security regulations can only be adhered to through, for example, data encryption such as SSL (Secure Socket Layer). Furthermore, INTERPOL (the world's largest international police organization) has a global mission to prevent cybercrime and this also impacts on businesses.[3] All these changes and organizations that require businesses to use more robust practices demand a systematic approach to creating defences against cyber security breaches. ISO 27001 provides logic, systems and an ability to improve practices so that they are increasingly robust and resilient. The main features of the ISO 27001 standard include:

- Management commitment to cyber security:
  - senior management commitment within the organization to cyber security;
  - emphasis of a robust cyber security system to management teams.
- Network security:
  - implementing good detection, prevention and protection of cyber threats;

- implementation of security measures with a robust network infrastructure;
- back-up measures for databases;
- passwords and secure network and architecture.

- Business continuity planning:
  - response and recovery planning in the event of a cyber-attack;
  - rigorous testing of recovery systems (being fully prepared);
  - risk management planning.
- Operational security:
  - governance, architecture and organizational culture;
  - ongoing audits of current systems to identify weaknesses;
  - cyber security response team within the organization to handle and deal with cyber threats;
  - security policies and procedures implemented within the organization.

Cyber security certification and standardization

Increasing organizational threats and risks of data storage have resulted in significant investments in staff training so that they can achieve **Certified Information Systems Security Professionals** (CISSP) status. Gaining the CISSP status ensures a staff member has the expertise and know-how to not only design and implement a first-class cyber security system but to manage one as well. Typically, those who are in charge of data security within an organization are ideally placed to benefit from such a certification, along with auditors, managers, executives and security analysts. CISSP is not the only certification, though; others include:

- **Certified Authorization Professional** (CAP) which covers security assessment and authorization.
- **HealthCare Information Security and Privacy Practitioner** (HCISPP) which is relevant for those involved with healthcare security and privacy.
- **Certified Secure Software Lifecycle Professional** (CSSLP) which covers secure software development.

- **Certified Cloud Security Professional** (CCSP) which is relevant for those who are involved in cloud security systems.
- **Systems Security Certified Practitioner** (SSCP) for IT/ICT security administration.
- **Certified Cyber Forensics Professional** (CCFP) which covers forensic standards of practice that are given value in courts of law.

ISC2, a cyber and IT security not-for-profit professional body, has developed these globally available certifications with the aim of unifying accreditation to standardize the industry of cyber security. ISC2 was founded in 1989[4] after the formation of a consortium of professional organizations in the field of information security. This group used its global expertise to develop standards in the cyber security curriculum in an array of fields, as mentioned above.

Security standards

As part of an organization's management system (MS), managers typically need to consider having an ISMS which includes policies and procedures for managing the information collected, stored and used by the organization. Such a system should reduce the risk of security breaches around the information whilst maintaining business continuity.

For some experts, **ISO 17799 Information Technology – Security Techniques – Code of practice for information security management** was the starting point when developing security standards (this ISO standard grew from **BS 7799 Information security management systems – Guidelines for information security risk management**). ISO 17799 covers a number of key management responsibilities and general guidelines that assist an organization to establish, implement and maintain an ISMS and is an evolution of Shell's corporate security standard. This ISO standard was eventually revised in 2005 to become **ISO 27002 Information Technology – Security Techniques – Code of practice for information security controls** and was written to align with the ISO 27000 series.

The ISO (International Organization for Standardization) and IEC (International Electrotechnical Commission) jointly developed the 27000 series of information security standards. Most of the 27000 series of ISO/IEC standards are listed here:

1. ISO/IEC 27000 Information technology – Security techniques – Information security management systems – Overview and vocabulary.
2. ISO/IEC 27001 Information technology – Security techniques – Information security management systems – Requirements (**the conformance standard**).
3. ISO/IEC 27002 Information technology – Security techniques – Code of practice for information security controls.
4. ISO/IEC 27003 Information technology – Security techniques – Information security management – Guidance.
5. ISO/IEC 27004 Information technology – Security techniques – Information security management – Monitoring, measurement, analysis and evaluation.
6. ISO/IEC 27005 Information technology – Security techniques – Information security risk management.
7. ISO/IEC 27006 Information technology – Security techniques – Requirements for bodies providing audit and certification of information security management systems.
8. ISO/IEC 27007 Information technology – Security techniques – Guidelines for information security management systems auditing.
9. ISO/IEC TR 27008 Information technology – Security techniques – Guidelines for auditors on information security controls.
10. ISO/IEC 27009 Information technology – Security techniques – Sector-specific application of ISO/IEC 27001 – Requirements.
11. ISO/IEC 27010 Information technology – Security techniques – Information security management for inter-sector and inter-organizational communications.
12. ISO/IEC 27011 Information technology – Security techniques – Code of practice for information security controls based on ISO/IEC 27002 for telecommunications organizations.
13. ISO/IEC 27013 Information technology – Security techniques – Guidance on the integrated implementation of ISO/IEC 27001 and ISO/IEC 20000-1.
14. ISO/IEC 27014 Information technology – Security techniques – Governance of information security.
15. ISO/IEC TR 27016 Information technology – Security techniques – Information security management – Organizational economics.

16 ISO/IEC 27017 Information technology – Security techniques – Code of practice for information security controls based on ISO/IEC 27002 for cloud services.

17 ISO/IEC 27018 Information technology – Security techniques – Code of practice for protection of personally identifiable information (PII) in public clouds acting as PII processors.

18 ISO/IEC 27019 Information technology – Security techniques – Information security controls for the energy utility industry.

19 ISO/IEC 27021 Information technology – Security techniques – Competence requirements for information security management systems professionals.

20 ISO/IEC 27031 Information technology – Security techniques – Guidelines for information and communication technology readiness for business continuity.

21 ISO 27032 – general guidance on cyber security best practice.

22 ISO/IEC 27033 (all parts) Information technology – Security techniques – Network security.

23 ISO/IEC 27034 (all parts) Information technology – Security techniques – Application security.

24 ISO/IEC 27035 Information technology – Security techniques – Information security incident management.

25 ISO 27799 Health informatics – Information security management in health using ISO/IEC 27002.

The standard and guides named above provide a comprehensive portfolio of assistance to organizations from financial information, employee and customer details to intellectual property management. The first standard of the sequence is **ISO/IEC 27000 Information technology – Security techniques – Information security management systems – Overview and vocabulary**, which helps organizations understand not just the vocabulary used by this family of standards but also how the standards in the series fit together.

ISO/IEC 27001

ISO/IEC 27001 Information technology – Security techniques – Information Security Management Systems (ISMS) – Requirements is the conformance standard that specifies the requirements of an organization's ISMS so it can be certified and audited, and its evolution is given in Figure 8.5.

Figure 8.5 ISO/IEC 27001 timeline

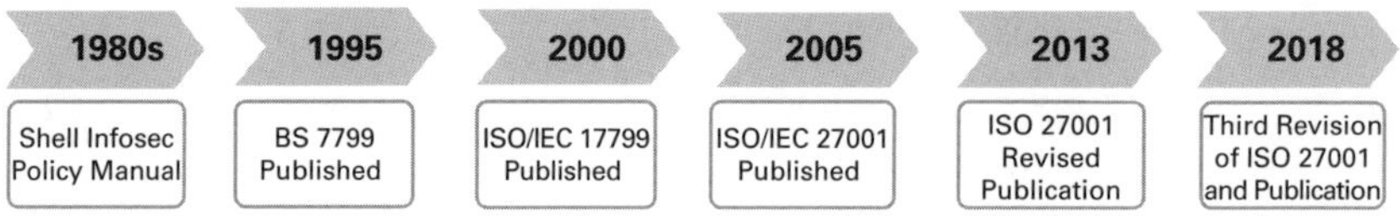

This standard specifically addresses the implementation of a robust and resilient management system that focuses on information security in any sector/business of any size. ISO 27001 is the most well-known standard in the ISO 27000 series. ISO 27001 helps and guides organizations to implement an ISMS framework that keeps data secure along with establishing a system that incorporates legislative and regulatory requirements, and allows them to demonstrate that their system complies with this legislation. This management standard is not obligatory, but it is not difficult to see how certification is essential when it comes to reassuring customers and stakeholders that best practice is being followed.[5] It is critical that information security within organizations continuously seeks to improve and stay on top of the latest technological developments to reduce the very real risks of the threats that can breach such a system. Hence, in the same way that the other ISO management standards have been developed to follow the PDCA (plan–do–check–act) cycle of continuous improvement, ISO 27001 is no different and flows with the same high-level structure that has been mentioned in earlier chapters. ISO 27001 is thus compatible with the other management system standards that the ISO have developed, having adopted the Annex SL of the MS standards. The clauses and sub-clauses of ISO 27001 are given below:

Introduction

1 Scope

2 Normative references

3 Terms and definitions

4 Context of the organization

- **4.1.** Understanding the organization and its context
- **4.2.** Understanding the needs and expectations of interested parties
- **4.3.** Determining the scope of the information security management system
- **4.4.** Information security management system

5 Leadership

- **5.1.** Leadership and commitment
- **5.2.** Policy
- **5.3.** Organizational roles, responsibilities and authorities

6 Planning

- **6.1.** Actions to address risks and opportunities
- **6.2.** Information security objectives and planning to achieve them

7 Support

- **7.1.** Resources
- **7.2.** Competence
- **7.3.** Awareness
- **7.4.** Communication
- **7.5.** Documented information

8 Operation

- **8.1.** Operational planning and control
- **8.2.** Information security risk assessment
- **8.3.** Information security risk treatment

9 Performance evaluation

- **9.1.** Monitoring, measurement, analysis and evaluation
- **9.2.** Internal audit
- **9.3.** Management review

10 Improvement

- **10.1.** Non-conformity and corrective action

Implementing all the requirements of ISO 27001 assists organizations including government agencies, companies of all sizes and not-for-profit charities to establish, implement, maintain and constantly improve their ISMS. The top management of an organization shall evaluate the performance of the ISMS and instigate corrective and/or preventative actions to ensure that it is updated and improved. The standard adheres to the classic PDCA cycle and hence the 'plan' element is covered by clause 4 (Context of the organization), clause 5 (Leadership), clause 6 (Planning) and clause 7 (Support). The 'do' element is covered by clause 8 (Operations), the 'check' element is covered in clause 9 (Performance evaluation) and finally action is taken through the evidenced improvements to conform to clause 10.

Other security standards and regulations

There are other security standards and regulations, including the following:

ISACA (Information Systems Audit and Control Association)

In 1967, a group of expert individuals in the field of auditing and computer systems controls sought to provide a centralized source of guidance and information for the use of information technology.[6] The group became known as the EDP Auditors Association (in 1969) and **ISACA (Information Systems Audit and Control Association)** in 1976. ISACA is a global, independent not-for-profit association that works to serve professionals in the field of IT governance through globally accepted, acknowledged and adopted practices of information systems; it supports individuals/organizations that are responsible for auditing and/or setting standards, and the ISACA certified areas are:

1 **Certified Information Systems Auditor (CISA) certification**
   - This is aimed at those working in the areas of information systems audit, control, monitoring and assessment of information technology systems.

2 **Certified Information Security Manager (CISM) certification**
   - This is aimed at those who manage information security.
   - It is relevant for individuals developing and managing an information security program.

3 **Certified in the Governance of Enterprise IT (CGE IT)**
   - This is aimed at those IT professionals who need or want to have formal recognition of their IT governance and knowledge.

4 **Certified in Risk and Information Systems Control (CRISC)**
   - This is aimed at those who manage risk 'through the development, implementation and maintenance of information systems controls'.
   - The certification links IT risk management to enterprise risk management.

5 **Cybersecurity Nexus (CSX and CSXP)**
   - This assists individuals in demonstrating that they are up to date with the most current cybersecurity standards and that they have the necessary skills in this field.

The ISACA certifications for IT professionals also assist with guidance on auditing, controls, management, cybersecurity etc, and are a means of giving confidence to employers that an individual they employ is competent. The organization has a global membership and has created a holistic **Business Model for Information Security** (**BMIS**). ISACA realized, though, that professionals around the world, in different sectors and different-sized organizations, have an array of at times very different requirements such as auditing. Hence ISACA have developed the following:

1. **IT Assurance Framework (ITAF)**
   - This framework is aimed at individuals who audit information systems along with those who are required to give assurances around information systems.
2. **Control Objectives for Information and Related Technology (COBIT)**
   - This is a framework that shares good practice around IT governance and management.
   - It provides IT controls that can be implemented.
   - There have been different versions created to keep up with current standards, issues and thinking within the field (each new version has built and expanded on the previous version).
   - Current version is COBIT 5, which has incorporated other standards and frameworks such as Val IT, Risk IT, ITIL (Information Technology Infrastructure Library) and ISO-related standards.
3. **Val IT™**
   - This framework is based around value creation in IT.
   - It is integrated with and complements COBIT.
   - It provides a governance framework for IT investments.
   - It focuses on decision making and on benefits.
4. **Risk IT**
   - This is a framework to manage IT risks and complements COBIT (in fact it is fully covered in COBIT as part of the control objectives).
   - This assists IT professionals to fulfil their responsibilities in the area of IT governance and minimize the very real business risks associated with the use of IT.

AXELOS

ITIL (Information Technology Infrastructure Library) is owned by **AXELOS** (ie a joint venture between the UK Government and Capita plc). AXELOS develops and promotes best practice frameworks and methodologies in a number of fields, of which IT service management (ITSM) is one. The aim of ITIL is to help an organization in aligning its ITSM with the organizational needs and strategy (with a minimum competence from which it can build). ITIL certification can only be obtained by individuals and there are five certification levels:

1. foundation level;
2. practitioner level;
3. intermediate level;
4. expert level;
5. master level.

Another AXELOS best practice framework is **RESILIA**, which focuses on cyber security and resilience best practices and helps organizations to understand decision making and its positive/negative impacts. RESILIA certification assists professionals in building cyber resilience into current systems and processes and seeks to compress response speeds if a breach occurs. There is a RESILIA foundation level of certification and a practitioner level.

ITIL and ISO 20000 series

ITIL is an essential support to the effective exploitation of the **ISO/IEC 20000 Information technology Service management** series (a standard that came out of the BSI's standard BS 15000) to ensure an ITSM aligns organizational needs with best practice. ISO 20000 sets standards and ITIL provides a best practice framework (Figure 8.6) and creates a pyramid of controls to support core business functions (which themselves could include other standards and management systems). The second pyramid tier exploits best practice IT service management (ITSM), drawing from ITIL to integrate such practices within the core business of an organization. The top two tiers of the pyramid are covered in part 1 and part 2 of the ISO 20000 series, and set out the requirements in part 1 (the specifications or the whats of a system) and the code of practice in achieving this in part 2 (the hows) when implementing an ITSM. An organization can implement ITSM processes using ITIL's best practices and later build on this by adopting ISO 20000-1. Hence ITIL and ISO 20000 are symbiotic.

Figure 8.6 ITIL and ISO 20000

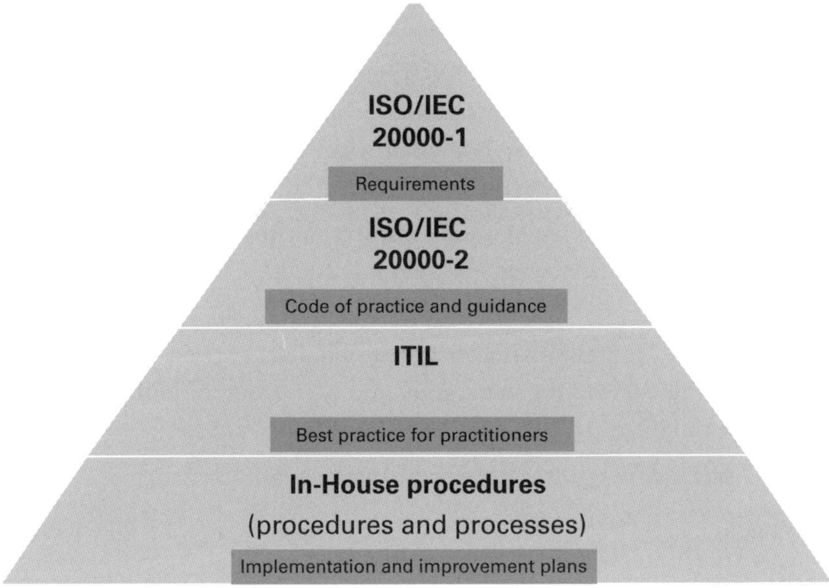

There are several parts to ISO 20000, some of which are:

1 **ISO/IEC 20000-1:2018 Information technology – Service management system requirements**
   - This part 1 sets out the requirements for an IT service management system (ITSMS).
   - This standard is useful for those in an organization who develop and implement an ITSMS along with maintaining it.
   - It specifies the requirements needed to implement an SMS.

2 **ISO/IEC 20000-2:2012 Guidance on the application of service management systems**
   - Part 2 works within the scope of ISO 20000-1:2011 (ie part 1 of ISO 20000) and sets out the standards for the processes of an SMS.

3 **ISO/IEC 20000-3:2012 Guidance on scope definition and applicability of ISO/IEC 20000-1**
   - Part 3 here sets out guidance on writing a scope for an SMS that is set out in ISO 2000-1.
   - This standard helps organizations with implementing an ISO 20000-1 SMS.

4. **ISO/IEC 20000-5:2013 Information technology – Service Management – Part 5: Exemplar implementation plan for ISO/IEC 20000-1**
   - This standard sets out an exemplar implementation plan for an SMS that fulfils the requirements of ISO 20000-1.
5. **I.SO/IEC 20000-6:2017 Information technology – Service Management – Part 6: Requirements for bodies providing audit and certification of service management systems**
   - Part 6 of this series of standards sets out the requirements around auditing and certifying of an ISO 20000-1 service management system.
6. **ISO/IEC PDTR 20000-7 Information technology – Service management – Part 7: Guidance on the integration and correlation of ISO/IEC 20000-1:2018 to ISO 9001:2015 and ISO/IEC 27001:2013**
   - This standard is currently under development.
7. **ISO/IEC 20000-10: Information technology – Service management – Part 10: Concepts and vocabulary**
   - This standard sets out the key concepts of the ISO 20000 series (ie all parts).
8. **ISO/IEC 20000-11:2015 Information technology – Service management – Part 11: Guidance on the relationship between ISO/IEC 20000-1:2011 and service management frameworks: ITIL®**
   - This part in the series is a Technical Report.
   - The standard gives guidance on the relationship between ISO/IEC 20000-1 and ITIL (a service management framework that is commonly used).
9. **ISO/IEC TR 20000-12:2016 Information technology – Service management – Part 12: Guidance on the relationship between ISO/IEC 20000-1:2011 and service management frameworks: CMMI-SVC**
   - Part 12 of the series focuses on the CMMI Institute's model for services (CMMI-SVC).
10. **ISO/IEC NP TR 20000-13: Information technology – Service management – Part 13: Guidance on the relationship between ISO/IEC 20000-1:2018 and service management frameworks: COBIT**
    - Currently under development.
    - This standard will tie into ISACA's Control Objectives for Information and related Technology (COBIT) mentioned earlier in the chapter.

It should be noted here that ISO 20000-4, part 4 in the series, has been withdrawn along with ISO 20000-9, part 9. Like other standards, this series is often revised and updated to reflect changes in market trends along with new knowledge and technology.

CMMI Institute

Capability Maturity Model Integration (CMMI) is a process-focused improvement training programme linked to ISACA. The CMMI Institute is an organization whose aim is to benchmark and elevate performance in a variety of fields, some of which include cyber security and data management. The CMMI draws upon expertise from government, industry and the software engineering institute to develop these models to assist organizations in improving their processes.

The ISO have acknowledged the importance of standards to cover models and frameworks that have been developed by organizations in the field of information security such as ISACA, AXELOS and the CMMI Institute. Therefore, we see part 12 in the ISO 20000 series (ISO/IEC TR 20000-12) as providing guidance on the relationship between the standard ISO 20000-1 and CMMI's service management model (CMMI-SVC). CMMI-SVC looks at the establishment and management of service provider organizations. As such the information security fraternity and associations of practising managers are very closely linked to this standard and both active networks have championed the development of ISO standards/guidelines (see also ISO 15408 – Evaluation for IT security and standards for payment card industry data security standards (PCI DSS)).

In summary

Information security is a major issue that senior managers of business must control, and effective senior management teams will spend a lot of time promoting security standards to staff and building layers of defence against wilful or accidental breaches. The widespread influence of digital technologies and the fourth industrial revolution (including the IoT) brings with it enormous opportunities but also enormous threats. A single event where security is compromised is enough to damage a manufacturer's brand and send entire supply chains into chaos. ISO standards provide new capabilities for organizations and allow a top management team to build resilient business systems by focusing on the key organizational practices that experts have determined to be good practice. With new technologies and the widespread use of consumer-enabling/mobile technologies increasing, the ISO cyber security standards will become more useful and will proliferate, with new guides and support for 'best practice' management over time. These standards help to protect the value that is represented by data, and businesses with good defences against innocent breaches and cyber-attacks will be considered prudent and reputable.

With specific reference to the operations and needs of product designers, the international guides and requirements standards for information security are critical to good practice. The design process is a strategic corporate capability and data must be protected and governed effectively (as well as archived). With large data use and with greater levels of 'home working', and therefore more exposure to events where data can be lost or stolen, there are new responsibilities for designers, and being cognizant of good data security practices is vital. Such standards support collaboration between designers and other staff regardless of country of residency and time zone, and provide a systems approach to ensuring data is managed and secured to protect the business from harm.

The dimension of a business context used to be comparatively simple until the advent of the internet and the digitally enabled business environment. In the 1980s, Hollywood made films about hackers who had accessed NASA or the FBI, and have continued to dramatize the impact of getting through information security in films such as *Skyfall*, and yet today cyber threats pose a major problem to business leaders. The value of conformity to ISO standards helps to build a robust and resilient business that can withstand sabotage attempts and honest lapses in information security.

Seminar topics and examination questions

1. Who owns the Cloud and is it secure? Discuss.
2. What damage could a hacker do to a business like a high street clothing retailer or a high street bank?
3. What exposure does a university face?
4. What types of accidental failures could result from the carelessness of employees?
5. Who should 'own' this standard in a business?
6. Should information security be considered a quality issue and integrated with ISO 9001?

Further reading

There are a whole range of books that deal with professional training and all variants of security issues (many books also focus on sector-specific issues) so an internet search will generate a lot of good books in this area, as will a quick search of YouTube.

Notes

1 Taylor, A et al (2013) *Information Security Management Principles*, 2nd ed, BCS Publishing
2 Sutton, D (2014) *Information Risk Management*, BCS Publishing
3 Steinberg, J (2019) *Cyber Security for Dummies*, John Wiley and Sons, London
4 https://www.isc2.org/about (archived at https://perma.cc/T7XQ-J89E)
5 Sutton, D (2017) *Cyber Security: A practitioners guide*, BCS Publishing
6 https://www.isaca.org/About-ISACA/History/Pages/default.aspx (archived at https://perma.cc/9NF8-W7VS)

Business continuity and uninterrupted product flow

09

Modern supply chains are so effective that it comes as a shock when things fail. Consumers just expect things to work without a hitch and will, within seconds, post information on the internet if the service they received is, in their opinion, anything less than perfect. There is bewilderment when we do not have the products we want on the supermarket shelf, or we run out of petrol at the filling station. In fact, it is such a shock that it often features on the national news broadcasts. Other 'headline grabbing' news includes product recalls and catastrophes that affect manufacturing facilities (such as flooding or fires). These are 'freak events' but they do happen, and they can be planned for. As modern supply chains operate with less stock, they become more vulnerable to these catastrophes and modern purchasing professionals have been quick to demand business continuity plans from each supplier as an assurance that risks of interrupted trading have been assessed and the supplier has the procedures necessary to protect itself and recover. In addition, large projects and 'high profile' national events are managed in this manner and lead organizations have also demanded such 'continuity' capabilities from construction, ticketing, security, food and beverage, cleaning, and other suppliers of goods and services. Of all the 22,000 ISO standards, there is one that covers business continuity: ISO 22301. Yet again, the learning from experts that is contained in this standard is invaluable and provides an effective structure to mitigate any issues that threaten the continuity and cash flow of an organization.

LEARNING OBJECTIVES

At the end of this chapter, you should be able to:

- describe the factors that could lead to a catastrophic failure in business continuity and the need for a resilient manufacturing capability;
- understand the major features of the ISO 22301 standard and its terminology;
- describe the benefits of managing to the ISO 22301 standard and its key features;
- explain the fit between the standard and those covered in previous chapters.

Responsive and resilient manufacturing

An organization that presents certifications of its management systems to ISO 9001 (quality management), ISO 45001 (Occupational Health and Safety), ISO 14001 (Environmental Management), ISO 27001 (Information Security) and then declares it is certified to ISO 22301 has the necessary management competence and business resilience to assure processes are in place just in case a catastrophe was to strike! It is quite an overwhelming offer to a commercial customer/buyer. It is a demonstration that the business has covered all its bases. It is also good for other interested parties such as investors and staff too. It is a strong signal that the company will make a great and long-term business partner. To give the standard its correct title, as per the ISO Technical Committee 223 now 292, it is 'Societal security and business continuity management systems – Requirements'.

Business continuity systems are designed and implemented to allow an organization to predict, risk assess and develop contingency plans to protect the continuity of its product flow into, within, and from the business. Freak events, acts of nature, sabotage and other sources of disruption can stop the flow of work in a factory in an instant and bring chaos to a supply chain. It is critical for business leaders today to understand the risks that could impact on a business and then develop countermeasures and emergency preparedness routines. Every business will face a unique set of risks but some of the most common are listed in Figure 9.1.

For the most part, businesses will function without issue or with the occasional minor interruption but there are potentials for failures of materials coming in, the processes and operations of the factory itself, and the outputs of the business and its relations with stockholders and customers. Latent

Figure 9.1 Sources of business catastrophe

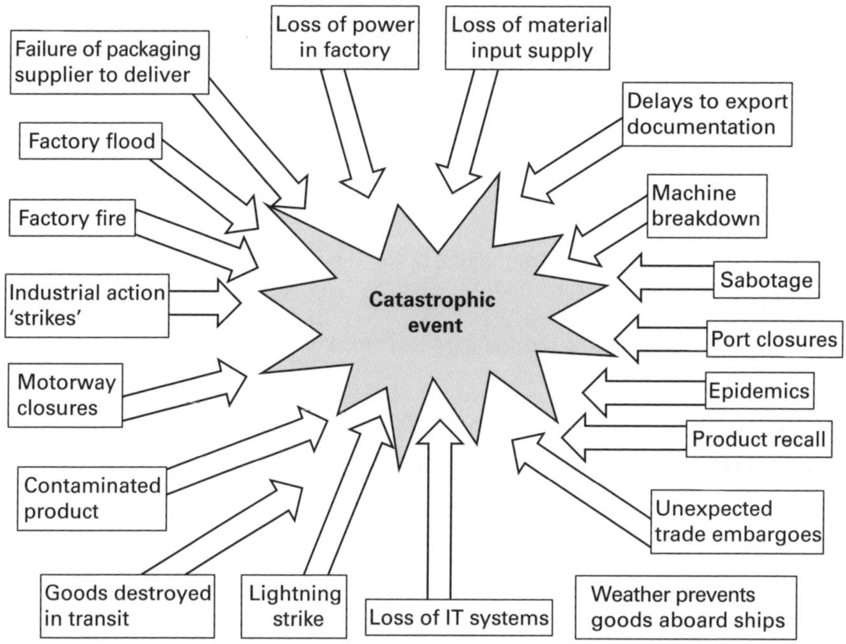

risks do exist and whilst they may never actually happen there is always the possibility that they will and when they do, they have a dramatic impact on the business and its partners. The result is that customers do not get their orders for a period before the supply chain can be recovered and normal service resumed. The adoption of business continuity standards for an entire supply chain creates a resilient system of product supply.[1]

Historically, when the importance of understanding business risks was less sensitive, supply chains tended to work with large amounts of stock so interruptions could be absorbed by selling the stock from the warehouse. Recent destocking of supply chains and just-in-time manufacturing systems mean that such stock no longer exists and therefore there is no buffer to protect businesses from the impact of failures. In Japan, a supplier to Toyota would have only a few hours of finished good stock and would deliver eight shipments of products each day, so a major stoppage of just a single supplier to the vehicle assembler could cause chaos for all suppliers and halt vehicle assembly. Even if a business does not operate to such high levels of logistics reliability, a competent business leadership team will therefore plan for contingencies that could interrupt the flow of goods and cash flow, and practise the countermeasures to any such interruption should one happen. Further still, many customers have penalty clauses should a supplier fail to deliver products, which, if enacted, would result in even more financial penalties for the supplier. But not just that – industry gossip will inevitably lead to brand damage for the business that fails to plan, and this is at the heart of this standard, which takes risk management to a whole new level.

So, business continuity is a major issue that cannot be ignored, and ISO 22301 specifies the requirements for establishing, managing, sustaining and improving an effective business continuity management system. The standard emphasizes the importance of understanding organizational needs and risks and embodying them within a formalized business continuity policy and objectives. As with all ISO standards it is important to design and formally document procedures, operating controls and measures for managing the organization's overall capability to deal with a disruptive event or incident. Monitoring and reviewing of the management system and its performance, coupled with continuous improvements (based on non-conformance gaps and gaps between the business's objectives and its actual performance) creates a resilient learning organization.

The Business Continuity Management (BCM) standard has adopted the high-level structure approach (originally called Annex SL) of most other standards, which includes the needs (or 'shalls' in ISO speak) of leadership and policies: personnel with defined responsibilities, effective and formalized processes that support effective policy making, planning, implementation, operations, performance assessment, reviews and improvements of the entire management system. The standard demands evidence, and proof of conformance and documentation (in all its acceptable forms) must be provided to evidence that the BCM process is being operated correctly and is reviewed frequently. Just like all others, the implementation of this standard is dynamic and will adapt using the plan–do–check–act improvement cycle and changes in the context of the business (and its interested party stakeholders – customers, laws, etc). The ISO claims that the standard is suitable for all businesses of all sizes but that each business must use the standard to develop systems and processes that suit its unique context and needs. The 'appropriate' application and demonstrated proof of BCM system effectiveness will also include the inclusion of legal, regulatory, organizational and industry sector requirements to allow working practices and organizational goals/objectives to 'fit' together seamlessly. Again, the standard is certified on a voluntary basis and independent certification bodies ensure that an organization meets all the clauses necessary to gain certification to the most recent revision of the standard of 'best practices'. A company may buy the standard but may decide to implement the clauses without gaining formal certification.

The standard and its features

The common features of business system scope, normative references and terms (definitions) are included as the first three introductory clauses before the true operating mechanisms (major clauses) of the standard are declared. One of the key parts of the initial clauses is the setting of the scope (the activities covered by the BCM system) and organizations will have to justify any exclusions from the scope of the system. The scope must be available as formalized documented information. Before exploring the key clauses, it is worth contextualizing some of the terms used (Table 9.1).

Table 9.1 Key terms

Term	Definition
Business continuity	The capability of normalization (returning to normal operating conditions) to continue to deliver products and services at acceptable performance levels following a disruptive incident.
Business continuity management (BCM)	A holistic and systematic management process of leadership, staff, policies, processes, procedures that are established to operate, monitor, review, maintain and continuously improve the business continuity processes and resilience of an organization.
Business continuity plan (BCP)	A set of formalized procedures designed to respond and return business operations to a normal level following an incident or adverse event. The plan is triggered by a process of invocation and details who and what will be undertaken to resume and restore normal operations.
Corrective actions	Actions taken by an organization to restore a process to conformity with the standard.
Disruptive incident	An event that interrupts or causes a catastrophic failure in the operations of a business.

(*continued*)

Table 9.1 *(Continued)*

Term	Definition
Exercise	A learning event designed to simulate a catastrophe so that those involved and the organization can develop and practise the countermeasures needed to restore business continuity.
Impact analysis	The systematic analysis if a risk to a business is realized, which shows the severity of the adverse condition created.
Invocation	The act of declaring that an organization's business continuity arrangements need to be put into effect in order to continue delivery of key products or services.
Maximum acceptable outage (MAO)	The time it takes for adverse impacts (which might arise as a result of not providing a product or service or performing an activity) to become unacceptable. Maximum tolerable period (MTP) is the maximum period of disruption of time that it would take for the adverse impact to become unacceptable (from the company perspective).
Minimum business continuity objective	The minimum level of services and products acceptable to the organization to achieve its business objectives during disruption.
Mutual aid agreement	An agreement between two organizations or more to work together and support each other.
Recovery time objective	The period of time following an incident within which a product or activity must be resumed or resources recovered. The recovery time objective must be less than the time it would take for the adverse impacts that would arise as a result of not providing a product/service or performing an activity to become unacceptable.
Risk and risk appetite	The effect of uncertainty on the objectives of the business and its risk appetite being the amount and type of risk that an organization is willing to pursue or retain.
Risk assessment	The overall process of risk identification, risk analysis and risk evaluation.

At first sight, the terms used can be quite baffling and almost like learning a new language, but they soon become apparent in terms of setting internal company goals for minimizing disruption (setting levels of acceptability) and those for recovery. The main implications of the standard require that an organization shall determine the external and internal issues that are relevant to the purpose of the business and issues that affect the ability of the business to achieve its intended BCM outcomes. The context of the organization contains trading partners, supply chains, communities and legal and regulatory requirements which must all be reviewed to ensure the leadership of an organization takes a holistic approach to BCM. The conformance standard is structured in full compliance with Annex SL:

- Scope.
- Normative references.
- Terms and definitions.
- Clause 4 – The context of the organization and determining the strategic issues, interested parties and scope of the BCMS.
- Clause 5 – Leadership, commitment, policies, responsibilities and authorities.
- Clause 6 – Planning to address risks and business continuity objectives and associated plans to achieve them.
- Clause 7 – The resources, competence, awareness, communication methods and documented information for the BCMS.
- Clause 8 – The operational planning and control, risk assessment and impact analyses. The clauses contain the continuity strategy, the establishment and implementation of business continuity procedures as well as procedures for exercising and testing the invocation of key procedures.
- Clause 9 – The measurement of the system, audits and management review learning processes.
- Clause 10 – The management of non-conformities and corrective actions as well as processes for continuous improvement.

The standard in more detail

The standard is an important one and the clause structure is quite demanding in terms of the emphasis on identifying risks and managing them so that disruption of the business and its value-adding processes does not occur.

Leadership

Leadership must demonstrate commitment to setting a strategic direction for the organization and integrating the BCM system requirements so that they are built into business processes. Leaders must ensure adequate resources are available to make the continuity system work and must widely promote and communicate the strategic importance of business continuity.

Business leaders must ensure the system supports its intended objectives by directing and supporting people to contribute to the effectiveness of the system and promoting continuous improvement of the system and of its actual achieved performance. So once again, this standard demands that top management must champion BCM and display the leadership behaviours that reinforce its importance (including responding to audits and reviews with countermeasures and improvements). This standard also promotes the role of leadership in supporting the engagement of staff with the practice of invoked emergency procedures through the conduct of simulated failures, mock exercises and periodic testing of the BCM system.

Top management must also develop business continuity procedures that are appropriate to the organization and include the necessary resources, objectives and continuous improvement activities to engrain BCM into daily activities. The system must be documented, widely communicated and available to all interested parties (as appropriate). Furthermore, top management leadership and others must periodically review the system to ensure it remains relevant. To achieve these outcomes, the organization's leadership must demonstrate how responsibilities and authorities for operating the system have been assigned and ensure the conformance of the business to the standard.

The objective for any system is to prevent failure or identify the early signs that failure may be happening; this is a major role for the top management in helping employees to engage with this agenda. It is also expected that should failure happen then the business must be capable of correcting the situation quickly and recovering as soon as possible to avoid the negative consequences for cash flow, profitability and branding.

Planning

Planning converts the leadership intent and a contextual assessment into actions to ensure the actual management system can achieve its intended outcomes to prevent or reduce the undesired effects of adverse incidents.

Planning must also ensure continuous improvement results from the plans to address business risks and support the improvement of the business. These improvements must be integrated with other processes and the effectiveness of any actions taken must be reviewed. As such, plans must be consistent with the policy set by the top management team. To achieve its business continuity objectives, an organization should determine who is responsible, what will be done, what resources will be required, when it will be completed, and how the results will be communicated and evaluated.

Support

Support demands that the BCM system shall have the resources to help establish the business operations and the education and training of staff. The main push for the organization is to provide resources for the BCM system in terms of people, time and all the necessary inputs to build a robust system. The big challenge is to communicate and maintain the awareness of all staff. Keeping staff aware of what situations could lead to disruption is important because when normal production pressures happen it is easy to forget to look for signs of deterioration in processes or potentials for failure outside of the business. The key message to the staff is that no sales means no income and that is not good for the business. So a robust manufacturing system is key. Everyone should be aware of the policy and able to meet their own roles during disruptive events and incidents should the worst happen. Communication must be formalized (internally and externally), especially during disruptive events (external communication demands that the testing of communications capability for use during such disruptions is very detailed and has been tested/simulated). Again, the standard also demands that creating, revising and archiving of documents should be controlled and standardized in terms of format, frequency of use etc.[2]

Operations

The **Operations** section of the standard outlines the requirements for effective operational planning and outlines the controls needed for processes and documented information that evidence practice, ensure and prove practices are the most up-to-date versions, and evidence confidence that the processes conducted by the organization are being carried out as planned. The main activities to ensure business continuity include business impact analysis and risk assessment procedures, which are at the very heart of this standard.

These routines establish and maintain a formal documented process for analysing the impact and systematically assessed risks to the control of the business. The process is like that of ISO 14001 and managers must set out the criteria for the evaluation of the potential impact of a destructive event or incident. Such an evaluation should also take into account legal and other requirements to which the organization subscribes. Such systematic analyses must prioritize risks, impacts and costs to the business and procedures must be in place so that the assessment is kept up to date. A multi-professional perspective is required to analyse the root causes of failures and to 'engineer' the best form of solution or recovery plan.[3]

Business impact analysis is conducted to analyse the negative impact on the provision of products and services, initially and over time so that priorities and timeframes can be established for the correction of the problem and the restoration of the organization to normal operating conditions. To be effective, the organization must understand timeframes and specify the minimum acceptable level for which a business can operate at 'sub-normal' levels (tolerate such underperformance) and then how quickly it can recover. This section of the standard demands that the organization must identify all dependencies and supporting resources of these activities including suppliers, outsource partners and other relevant interested parties. The latter activity will also include which (if any) emergency services are needed for each contingent event. In this manner, the BCM system has a very effective focus on risk assessment; the organization shall identify the risk of disruption to business and prioritize activities that are core to doing that business. In effect, the business must protect its value-added processes and material flow. This is the correct approach for supply chains that operate 'just in time' models of production rather than managing huge warehouses full of dormant or slow-moving stock.

In conducting the risk analyses, an organization shall also look at the dependencies that exist between the production system (information, people, assets, outsourced operations, business partners and other resources) and must have a holistic approach to identifying all factors and organizations that can help keep the manufacturing system in balance and in control. The quicker the initial signs of failure can be identified, the quicker and timelier an intervention can be implemented to protect the production system. In this manner, a very thorough and detailed evaluate of failure sources (disruption and related risks) is needed, as well as the alternative courses of action should something untoward materialize. The identification of counter measures that are commensurate with the business objectives (for recovery to normal operations in a given time and to a minimal standard of business performance) is key to directing the right level of resources for the recovery of the business and to mitigate and respond to potential negative business impacts.

The organization must also prove that it has established the optimal level of resources (people, information, buildings, facilities, information technology, transportation, finance and partners and suppliers) to support continuity plans and goals, and must allocate, for any identified risks requiring treatment, proactive measures to reduce the likelihood of disruption, to shorten the period of destruction and limit the impact of disruption. Such activities could include operating with alternative suppliers, maintaining weekend capacity, using more sophisticated maintenance and predictive maintenance routines and such like.[4]

Plans are rather useless unless the organization has established, reviewed and implemented business continuity procedures. These procedures shall establish an appropriate internal and external communications protocol, be specific regarding immediate steps to be taken during disruption, be flexible to respond to anticipated threats and changing internal and external conditions, and must focus on the impact of events that could potentially disrupt operations. The sophistication of these activities will pay dividends if a latent source of failure was to become real. The procedures must be developed based on stated assumptions (about recovery and mitigating impact) as well as on an analysis of the independencies involved so that minimizing the consequences of a potential through implementation of appropriate mitigation strategies is established and all key staff know why it is in place.[5] As such, there is a requirement for the standard to establish and operationalize an **incident response structure** that:

- enables individuals to know their roles and the process;
- documents and implements procedures;
- is trained and capable to respond to disruptive incidents using personnel with the necessary responsibility, authority, competence and ability to manage an incident;
- includes the identification of 'impact thresholds' to justify the initiation of a formal response by the organization to a disruptive event (invocation).

The incident response structure is therefore a coordinating mechanism used to assess the nature of the event and trigger the activation of an appropriate business continuity response to protect the business. Such individuals represent a command centre and once the activation of a response is deemed necessary they coordinate with 'one voice and one process' all other employees in the structure to invocate the necessary processes and procedures for the activation, operation, coordination of effort and communication of the response throughout the business and potentially beyond it to other interested parties. In summary, the Incident Response Team that operate the planned response must have the necessary resources to support them to manage the disruptive event in order to minimize its impact as well as ensure good communication with interested parties, support organizations for which a mutual agreement exists, as well as the media if appropriate. In summary, the Incident Response Team should ensure the following activities are conducted:

- **Warning communications** (WC) are also important so that clear communication, in a time of crisis, is used to control the response in the most effective way. As such, the organization is expected to implement and maintain procedures to record vital information about the incident and any actions taken as a result. Post the incident, this information is critical for new rounds of problem solving and the generation of new learning/improvement to the system. Alerting interested parties potentially impacted by an actual impending disruptive incident must also be included and integrated with all future contingency plans.
- **Business continuity plans** (BCP)[6] must also be documented as procedures for responding to disruptive incidents and all recovery plans to restore the business to normal operating conditions within a predetermined timeframe. The plan itself should, in great detail, assign the roles and responsibilities for activating the response, and give details for managing the consequences of a disruptive incident with keen regard to the welfare of individuals, strategic, tactical operational options, and prevention of further loss. The plan should also detail how and under what circumstances the organization will communicate with employees as well as other interested parties and emergency services.
- **Operate plans** that prioritize activities within predetermined timescales and details of the organizations as well as plans for 'standing down' once the incident is over.

The key features of this standard include the business continuity objectives, activation criteria, procedures, assigned staff roles, authorities of staff members, communication, resource requirements and the flow of information. The recovery of the organization can only happen if procedures are anticipated and documented.[7] The testing of the system must be ongoing and periodically a **full exercise and simulation of a potential disruptive incident** must be undertaken and fully reviewed. Testing continuity procedures and ensuring the business can deliver the business back to normality within the business continuity objectives is key. The latter is a difficult task that requires significant expert input and, even in the simplest business, will have a range of scenarios that must be reviewed and validated. Formalized 'post exercise' reports including recommendations for improvement will also be expected of the organization in order to be certified. Whilst this section may seem onerous, these are the processes that support the business and the real value of the standard. If the same levels of contingency planning were applied to organizations as with the safety of aircraft, then business resilience would improve and supply disruptions would reduce to a minimum.

Performance evaluation

Performance evaluation contains a set of organizational routines that determine what aspects of the business continuity management system needs to be monitored and measured (including determining the methods for measuring and monitoring to ensure valid results as well as when measuring should take place). The organization must also ensure that action is taken to redress any non-conformity and retain relevant information as evidence. The company should have a procedure for monitoring performance and setting appropriate performance metrics for the organization, which are regularly reviewed and measured. Periodic evaluations must be undertaken to establish trends and detect deviations so that the organization may evaluate compliance with other applicable legal and regulatory requirements and industry best practices. In effect, a comprehensive and focused measurement system will help assess the health of the system as well as the ability of the organization to increase the mean time between any forms of failure.

To support such evaluations, internal audits are necessary, with the reports of this form of testing being invaluable to the top management and incident response structure team. In this manner, the organization shall plan audits including the frequency of, methods for and definition of audit criteria, selection of competent auditors, and reporting of findings to the relevant management processes. Documentation for this process must be available for inspection and auditing by a third party.

The final cycle of learning for this standard is the operation of a periodic and effective management review process where top management shall measure the status of actions from previous management reviews, changes in the business continuity system, information on business continuity performance (including trends) and details of any detected non-conformities. Such information supports the top management team to audit results and look for opportunities for improvement especially when setting priorities, setting goals, and maintaining the risk analysis register of the business. The outputs of the review should look at variations to the scope of the business and its improvement in terms of changes to any aspect of the system and any new 'best practice' that has been embedded in the working practices of the organization.

Improvement

The final clause concerns **Improvement** and taking actions to make the management system perform to a higher level of resilience and robustness; this activity relies upon undertaking corrective actions as a result of identified non-conformities. When a non-conformity occurs, the organization shall – to be certified – identify the non-conformance and react to it by taking adequate controls to deal with it and its consequences. The corrective actions should eliminate the causes of non-conformity in a formalized manner and once a countermeasure has been completed it is the responsibility of the organization to review the effectiveness of the action/solution and any new documentation released as a result. As such, continuous improvement processes ensure the business continuity management remains adequate and effective. After all, the BCM system is an assurance to the business that it operates with the highest levels of control and an assurance to external interested parties that the management of the business is competent and committed to maintaining an uninterrupted supply of products to the market. Improvement and learning is important, especially for business continuity purposes. Most businesses rarely predict what could go wrong and interrupt the cash flow cycle, and fewer still will have formal documented plans that can be enacted if things do go wrong. In this respect the pre-emptive processes of business continuity are invaluable to supporting business and ensuring customers get the products for which they have paid.

The standard in summary

The use of business continuity standards and supporting information is growing by the month and organizations implementing the ISO 22301 standard will be able to demonstrate to legislators, regulators, customers, potential customers, the local community, the financial community and other interested parties that they are adhering to the latest best practice in business continuity with the ISO management system. For operational staff and designers of products (who hold the blueprints for products) it is important that, should a catastrophe happen, key data sources and emergency plans are in place to recover. The design team may very well use back-up data systems and 'recovery points' to allow designs and key product documents to be recovered with minimal disruption. The standard naturally creates a level of conformance that many businesses struggle to achieve and – when they do gain certification – the achievement is received with pride and the certification is a 'badge of honour'. The gap between a normal business and a certified one is huge and ISO 22301 provides a significant gap analysis between ideal conformance with the standard and what companies actually have in place when they start. This gap is quite alarming given the amount of workers who depend on an organization as employees, or employees of suppler businesses. Again, it is a voluntary standard, but the amount of effort expended to fulfil the clauses of the standard means it is highly likely that certification will be pursued.

The best way of finishing this review of business continuity management is to review what most world-class organizations would want of their suppliers:

- they are safe;
- they have high quality;
- they support the environment;
- they are so reliable that the flow of goods is never interrupted (information and business continuity).

As such, this standard offers a final level of competence for an operating model that is designed to protect the business from threat and disruptive influences. These capabilities are the highest levels of the sand cone model introduced in Chapter 1. The most demanding of customers will also expect that a business has the necessary processes and procedures in place so they can be assured that all major eventualities are formally controlled and have plans attached to them should anything untoward happen. Certification to the business continuity standard is therefore a direct and unmistakable attempt by a supplier business to show it is competent but also capable of responding to a catastrophe in its own operations and those of its suppliers. Such a certification and conformity is an investment made by an organization to protect the trading relationship with its customers; the combination of quality management standards, occupational health and safety standards, environmental management standards, security standards and business continuity standards is a very powerful assurance to existing customers and a potential order winner with new customers. Most customer businesses these days have plenty of alternative suppliers available, but aligning a supply chain of the right type of suppliers, who will invest in the business relationship and continuously improve performance, is an order winner for most customers.

Seminar topics and examination questions

Here are a few questions to think about:

- What internal failures could beset a business?
- If you were a member of the Incident Response Team, what information and process could you enact to recover from a major failure of your key supplier to provide materials to you?
- What steps would you take if a fire was detected in the factory?
- What practices and other countermeasures would you introduce if your business operated in a geographical area that was prone to flooding?

Further reading

The certification of an organization to ISO 22301 is a major achievement and there are a growing number of case studies on how things go wrong and certification auditors who can help to direct you to good advice and 'benchmark companies' that are worth visiting. Remember not to copy what you see though, because this standard (like all others) relies on your context and aligning the most appropriate processes for your operating conditions.

Notes

1 Barnes, J (2001) *A Guide to Business Continuity Planning*, John Wiley and Sons, London

2 Fulmer, K (2007) *Business Continuity Planning: A step-by-step guide with planning forms*, 3rd ed, Rothstein Associates

3 Estall, H (2012) *Business Continuity Management Systems: Implementation and Certification to ISO22301*, BCS Publishing

4 Wong, W and Shi, J (2014) *Business Continuity Management System: A complete guide to implementing ISO 22301*, Kogan Page, London

5 Blythe, M (2009) *Business Continuity Management: Building an effective incident management plan*, John Wiley and Sons, London

6 Tucker, E (2015) *Business Continuity: From preparedness to recovery*, Butterworth-Heineman, London

7 Watters, J and Watters, J (2014) *Disaster Recovery, Crisis Response, and Business Continuity: A management desk reference*, A Press

Supply chain management, design and international standards

10

Introduction

There is an old belief that one business will compete against another in a marketplace. Whilst this is true at one level, it is actually more correct to state that supply chains actually compete.[1] The supply chain is the entire chain of businesses involved with the flow of materials (from raw materials to the hands of the customer) and these businesses are equally engaged in the competition. In addition, no company can keep poorly performing suppliers because these members of the supply chain will cause problems, 'noise' in terms of causing all other suppliers to have poorly flowing materials, and will limit any supply chain's responsiveness. They may also even affect the brand of the product because consistent failures to deliver materials result in consumer complaints. In this respect, picking the 'right type' of supplier is critically important. This chapter will explore the role of standards within the supply chain and how they can be used to improve performance.

LEARNING OBJECTIVES

This chapter will help the reader understand what is in supply chain management and why it is important by examining:

- the concept of the supply chain and how it supports competitive advantage for a business;

- the different approaches to relationship management within the supply chain and the application of standards to the supply chain;
- the features of supplier coordination and supplier development;
- the role of the Supplier Association (SA) as a learning and improvement mechanism;
- how supply chain innovation can lead to quicker product introductions and more effective customer product design solutions.

What is a supply chain and why is it important?

A supply chain is the total number of companies that come together to satisfy final consumers of a product and do so profitably. These businesses either have a direct relationship with the customer and are known as Business to Consumer (B2C), or will supply products and services to business customers, who may then supply the final consumer directly or through another business. Those companies that supply another business are known as Business to Business (B2B) suppliers.

Even the simplest of consumer products can have a very complex supply chain that may cover many continents and time zones.[2] A commonplace product – such as tubes of toothpaste – could have tubes made in the same country, with printing of the tubes conducted locally, the main ingredients for the paste from suppliers abroad, and specialist additions or colours processed by a few other businesses before they arrive at the factory where the paste can be blended and the toothpaste tube filled and packaged into cardboard shipping boxes (the boxes will be made by a supplier too!). Then there will be the delivery vehicle and process, which may be a service that is operated by a supplier too. All these businesses must perform well (and synchronize) for materials to be ready for conversion when they are needed. If any single item is missing then the efforts of the entire group of suppliers in the supply chain can be delayed and time/effort wasted.

Supply chain management is an area that covers many different types of organizational staff and specialist knowledge. It is useful to frame some of the terminology used in supply chain management:

- **Consumer** – the consumer is the final person in a supply chain. They use the product and often pay for it. In effect, these individuals or companies are the focus of effective product designs and efficient processing by all members of the supply chain.

- **Customer** – either a business or an individual that orders a product to be made and to whom the product is sold or leased. The customer may be the consumer of the product but not always – sometimes products are bought by one organization but used by others.
- **Retailer** – the organization that buys products and displays them in stores or uses the web to promote their products to customers and consumers.
- **Direct supplier** – the organization that makes and sells the product to a customer, retailer or consumer. This business may include production and assembly processes and is often a brand owner.
- **Tier One suppliers** – these businesses represent the suppliers to the direct supplier. They will sell parts, materials or subassemblies to the direct supplier (which the direct supplier will use to configure its product offering). If the direct supplier is a laptop manufacturer then Tier One suppliers may make keyboards, displays, memory chips and drives.
- **Tier Two suppliers** – the suppliers to the Tier One suppliers and will sell materials and parts, such as the basic circuit boards or wires etc that are made into products by the Tier One suppliers.
- **Warehouse** – a physical building in which products are stored securely and protected from perishing. The purpose of a warehouse is to hold stocks that are about to be shipped or are held because they have been made in advance of need. Warehouses may contain materials coming into a business as well as goods waiting to be sold to the next customer.
- **A supply contract** – a legal document that sets out the commercial arrangements between a buyer and a supplier. Often contracts are used between Tier One and Tier Two suppliers to outline the levels of service expected and any penalty clauses that may be invoked if a supplier fails to maintain their part of the agreement. Likewise, contracts may be used between Tier Two and Tier Three suppliers (and all the way back along the supply chain).
- **Relationship** – the inter-organizational approach and informal contract to supply that is used to work collaboratively or with a more adversarial approach to suppliers.
- **Cash flow** – the conversion of orders into sales revenues and profits. Cash flow involves buying goods at a price and selling them for a profit so that the monies received can be used to begin the buying of replenishment or new materials to build into a product and sell again (for money).

Figure 10.1 shows the typical ordering of the supply chain tiers to the focal producer and then on to the customer. Between each company and each tier there may be product warehousing and logistics companies that use air, sea, and road transport to deliver goods. Between each of the companies there will typically be a legal contract of supply and recycling activities. At each tier, from Tier Three to Tier One, the supplied materials and parts will be converted and value added to them. The intent of the entire supply chain is to be profitable and to give customers what they want, to the highest quality, when they want it. Deciding which companies to buy from, whether to treat them like business partners or not to trust the supplier are all decisions that a business must undertake. Suppliers are interested parties and stakeholders of a business so it is important to engage with them in an appropriate manner. All suppliers are important and some are strategically important to the success of a customer business. There are many advantages to a well-designed supply chain because higher customer performance is likely to lead to higher sales and that is good for all businesses in the chain.

Figure 10.1 Typical ordering of supply chain tiers

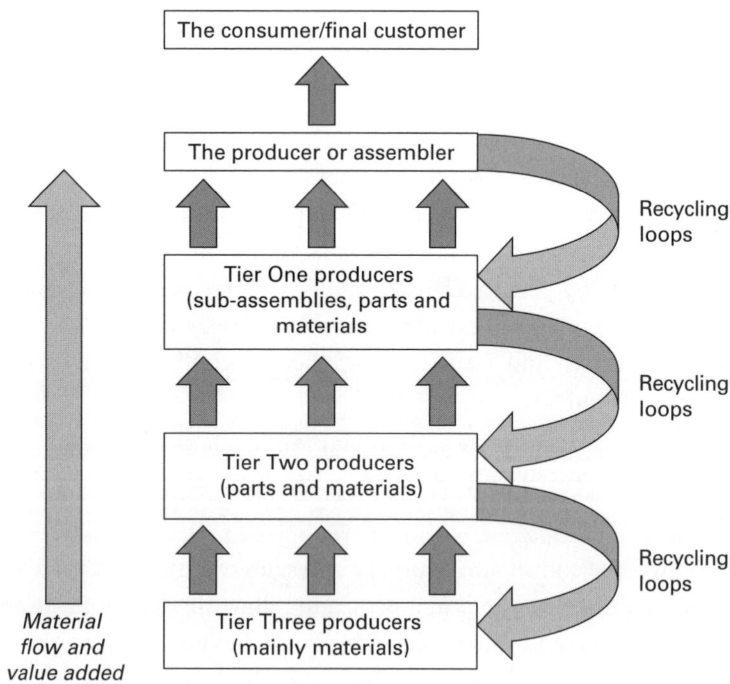

If a supply chain competes against another then the design of the chain and which companies are part of it becomes a strategic decision. Such decisions also mean a much deeper working relationship with the right type of supplier so that a good operational performance can be used to build a deeper relationship and collaboration (for higher levels of innovation and a form of co-management of the material and cash flow processes). Selecting suppliers and developing them or learning from them is very important and such forms of improvement are necessary to maintain a conformity with many international management standards. Incorrectly designing the supply chain can have devastating effects on the flow of production and the brand image of each business.

Another interesting fact for many supply chains is that most producers at the head of the supply chain (and the direct interface with the customer) do not make a lot of the final products they sell. In fact they will often spend a lot of time assembling the products that have been supplied by other businesses in the supply chain. A typical car assembler will actually 'buy in' around 80 per cent of all the parts and subassemblies that make the finished vehicle they sell to the public or fleet operators. Therefore, 80 per cent of the costs of making a product (in this case a car) are attributable to suppliers; more enlightened companies will identify key suppliers and work with them for mutual benefit. They will also work to improve the performance of the entire chain so products can arrive with the best quality assurance, in the shortest time possible, with product designs that are environmentally friendly and where the data across the whole supply chain is protected and secure. Perhaps even more illuminating for businesses is the fact that most supply chains operate with very little stock to act as a buffer in case a supplier fails or there are sudden uplifts in demand. Without high levels of buffer stock, suppliers must be able to deliver what is needed just in time for it to be used.

Despite the obvious importance of the supply chain concept for managers, it really only became a strategic issue in the West in the late 1990s (and the 1960s/1970s in Japan, where the just-in-time system originated). Prior to this point, supply chain management was limited to that of a clerical activity of getting suppliers to bid for contracts, buying products, placing orders for products and paying outstanding invoices. Today, the Internet of Things (IoT) and very complicated computerized planning systems can track deliveries throughout the work and can report on exactly where they are located.

Even though the supply chain was not popularized as a strategic concept until the 1990s through the work of Michael Porter (at a time when the benefits of closely working with suppliers was demonstrated by companies like Toyota and others), the original ideas of engaging with suppliers can be traced to the quality principles of the TQM guru W Edwards Deming. Deming would preach to Japanese businesses that they should cease doing business on price alone and really work with suppliers to improve their quality and improve the capability of suppliers to innovate too. His views were distinctly that you get the supplier you deserve – so if a business is for ever squeezing the prices and margins of a supplier it can be no wonder that the supplier will try to buy from cheaper and less reliable sources. Inevitably that form of supplier management will end in catastrophic failure as the supplier cannot make a profit and will walk away or worse (the supplier may create a defect that goes all the way to the customer or may go bankrupt so no parts will be received). The design of the supply chain (the numbers, types and strategic importance of each supplier) has implications for the focal producer and how international standards can be used to create a robust and reliable supply chain that is perpetually improving and innovating.

From purchasing to supply chain

Around the early 1900s, there was no supply chain department; instead it was a clerical activity. At this time, the dominant logic was to be vertically integrated and to make everything that was needed for a product in the factory itself. The time period had comparatively less technically sophisticated materials and this was a feasible option, although no single producer could actually be an expert in everything it bought. Vertical integration meant that only a few items were purchased from other businesses and therefore clerks could be used (under the direction of the factory engineers and designers) to order anything the company could not (or decided not to) make.

The purchasing department was subservient to the engineering and design departments that dominated every decision inside the factory at that time. Engineers and designers would issue specifications and provide drawings for suppliers and then it was the role of the purchasing clerk to go and get quotes from suppliers in response to these specifications. The belief was that each supplier would quote the lowest price for the product and therefore the clerk could select the lowest of all the bids and then place the order. This approach assumed that the suppliers were reliable and could provide the specification at the quality needed. This was not always the case. Mass production businesses therefore did not like suppliers and would change them often and place orders with the suppliers' competitors. Loyalty was seen as a weakness and a process that would allow the supplier to become more comfortable and less competitive to offer the best value for money. Suppliers were therefore seen as adversaries. It was believed they would, if allowed, try to put up their prices to profit from the customer and as a consequence were prohibited from developing long-term and collaborative business relationships.

The constant switching of suppliers, with perpetual tendering to see if another business would offer a lower price, meant that a lot of staff time was dedicated to tendering rather than developing more effective material flows. In addition, suppliers would not be allowed to design products or take specifications and offer a better way to make them (at a lower cost to the supplier and therefore a cost reduction to the customer). As such, the supplier had no way of sharing its specialist knowledge for improvement, and as a consequence no such innovations took place. The relationship was adversarial and a tactical exchange of materials in return for payment.

Suppliers that designed their own products would also challenge the power of the engineers in mass production systems even though the supplier could offer access to their specific sophisticated expertise and implicit knowledge about how best to deliver great product functionality at a lower total cost of supply. As such, engineering designs at this time were suboptimal and within the factories quality control processes were poor or bureaucratic (defects would be quarantined and scrapped or reworked). The belief was that suppliers would innovate to find ways of submitting the lowest prices per product item and that was as much innovation as was comfortable for the dominant engineers of the time.

Engineering changes did occur and it was common with complicated products such as vehicle assembly for engineers to place an order for a part and then request that 'the drawing' was modified. Suppliers of the part, who had offered a low and competitive price initially, would take such a request by the buying company (within the contracted supply time period) as a means of raising their prices; they would try to make a bit more profit even if the part was easier for them to make and would cost less. Such a reaction was used to justify the adversarial approach taken to all suppliers. To maintain the threat of moving work from a supplier, the mass producer would keep a very large number of alternative suppliers and would threaten to switch to another as a means of keeping the current suppliers subservient.

However, this approach was costly because it was seen as a clerical activity with purchasers having no way of contributing to the strategic success of a business.

It was not until Japanese producers started to build factories in the UK, Europe and the United States that supply chain management practices were seen to work in the West. These practices, operated at Japanese subsidiary companies from the 1980s, proved that collaborative relationships could work and could deliver superior business results for both the buying organization and the seller. Although many businesses in history have operated harmonious and collaborative relationships with their suppliers, few organizations have proactively developed their supply base in the same manner Japanese industries did, such as the approach taken by the Toyota Motor Corporation in particular. The development of suppliers was a quite understandable reaction to the post-Second World War condition where there was little to no material, technological or human resources. The Japanese nation, in a period of severe austerity, needed to make the most of everything and although the US occupation of the country outlawed close working relationships with suppliers (to prevent collusion), supplier practices did emerge that were collaborative and long-term in nature. Such relationships exist to the current day and collaboration, originally from the practices of the Japanese business model, now dominates Western management thinking.

The Japanese model was more holistic and purchasing professionals were treated with respect. Indeed, suppliers were seen as extensions of the producer's factory and collaboration was a natural way of improving both businesses. The Japanese and Toyota supply chain model was based upon:

- Lower total number of suppliers (by retaining only the best suppliers).
- Trusting that suppliers will behave in the best interests of the buyer because of the dependencies between the two businesses on the buying organization selling more products.
- Measuring suppliers on their quality, delivery, cost performance as well as the investments made by suppliers in the partnership with the customer and investments made by the supplier in the ability to design products.
- Ensuring the resources of the buyer were available to the supplier to help improve the supplier's performance. An explicit demand that all suppliers would implement total quality management in all their business affairs.
- Suppliers would be expected to provide the greatest levels of product quality and would assure/guarantee perfect quality to the customer.

- It was expected that all suppliers and the buying organization would share strategies and invest in co-destiny activities as well as risk reduction.
- All suppliers would offer improvement ideas and engage in a continuous effort to find ways of reducing product costs without compromising the quality of the product.
- Product specifications would be very broad and suppliers would be given a target price for their product which allowed the supplier to design the best functional product to satisfy the buying company.
- Suppliers would be given the right to supply a part exclusively for a specific car (if they were high performers) but one or two other suppliers would have the same exclusivity for a similar part used in a different car. The approach lowers the risks of a single factory failure and maintains the ability to switch production if a catastrophic event was to happen that halted material flow.
- Contracts would be issued for the lifecycle of the product unless under-performance occurred.
- Suppliers would be encouraged to buy and dedicate equipment and teams to the exclusive production of the buyer products.
- Demand for products would be tightly managed; to avoid peaks in demand followed by no orders, a steady state flow would be used (and variation kept to an absolute minimum).
- Suppliers would be encouraged to locate their factories as close to the buying company as possible to allow a 'no inventory' and just-in-time logistics system to operate.

Winning business with prestigious Japanese buyers was a major achievement and equally losing business could be fatal to the future of a company that failed to meet the demanding performance levels to which Japanese businesses aspired. It should be noted that when Toyota invested in its UK facility it required suppliers to operate with a defect level that was measured in defect parts per million shipments, whereas the UK – at that time – operated to a performance level of several percentage defects. For the appreciation of the reader, 1 per cent of defects is equivalent to 10,000 parts per million defects.

To ensure that the entire supply chain was a dynamic learning environment, the Toyota supply chain model involved high levels of supplier coordination and supplier development:[3]

- Supplier coordination is the executive-level sharing of strategic information and data concerning market trends and other valuable data sources (coordinating the strategic direction of all suppliers).
- Supplier coordination using common communication systems and plans (including production planning and coordinating material flows as well as design information). Smoothing information flows is important because companies can deal easily with a level and regular volume of orders. When demand is volatile and uneven it is difficult to plan and respond to sudden increases in demand. Many of these increases are created by poor and outdated computer rules rather than any real product sales uplifts. As such, the Japanese way of levelling demand to make the flow of products predictable is a major benefit – and it keeps cash flow moving too.
- Supplier development through the use of one-to-one specific improvement requirements as a result of monitoring and finding gaps in the supplier's production system.
- Supplier development using groups of suppliers formed because they shared a key material interest (such as steel, glass, plastic etc) or were suppliers that all supported a key element of the final product (such as braking systems, cooling systems and such like). These development activities were a direct means of transferring knowledge from the buyer to groups of suppliers and between suppliers for mutual improvement and mutual gain. Such group supplier development activities were conducted using a 'Supplier Association' where suppliers would meet often (typically monthly) to share information, visit each other's sites and work on major projects together. They are very powerful learning mechanisms that offer superior impact than attempting to develop suppliers one at a time.

The adversarial and the collaborative Japanese models have been presented to show the extremes of supplier management. A business that believes in teamwork and uses international management standards will see a repeated emphasis on teamwork, both within and beyond the factory. The best approach to supplier management will be specific to each buying business and what they buy, but looking at these two 'extremes' allows an appreciation of how supply chains are designed. It is also worth remembering that suppliers may be accountable for up to 80 per cent of the parts used in a product so there is much to gain from engaging with the supply chain.

Supplier management and the design process

Providing a product to meet a production schedule is directly related to the timely management of material and cash flow. The quality, delivery and cost performance of suppliers can be monitored and targets for improvement established for each business but this is only part of the process of supplier management. Beyond the materials transaction is a series of competences that are needed from a supplier to support its own future and to work more closely with buying customers. These are known as capabilities and competences. The two major business competences are those of partnering with a customer and achieving a preferred supplier status, and the key capability of being able to design new products. In Chapters 1 and 14 of this book, the modified 'sand cone' model will be discussed, which shows how a quality-first approach leads to few trade-offs and a greater performance for any business. A higher level of business competence is that of designing products in collaboration with and on behalf of a customer.[4] In contemporary times, the ability to design products compresses time in getting products from the drawing board to the hands of the customer, which is good for both sales and cash flow.

It is very difficult for any operations management department to lower costs without eventually looking at the costs of production that are determined by the design of the product itself. The selection of materials, the implied volume of the product, the amount of labour needed and the level of automation are all decisions derived from the product design. As such, it is necessary to gain access to designers to change and modify designs and maintain the functionality of the product but to reduce unnecessary costs. Working with suppliers with ISO 9001 or ISO 14001 provides a good structure to enact such changes. By working with suppliers using international standards as a means of focusing such improvement (such as ISO 14001 for better environmental product designs), major cost reductions for the product can happen as well as designing out unnecessary features, excessive waste and material usage.[5] The ability to work with suppliers on design issues opens up many potential collaborations in the form of:

- **Design for Manufacturing** (DFM) is a process where a product is designed or redesigned to make it easier for the supplier company to actually make. This approach will also include changes to the product design that allow a supplier to be more effective at assembling a product too. The latter is known as **Design for Assembly** (DFA).

- **Design for the Environment** (DFE) can be used to challenge the use of resources that deplete the environment or can represent an opportunity to change to a more sustainable material. In parallel, designers may also **Design for Disassembly** (DFD) to allow products made by the buying company to be dismantled and recycled more easily.
- **Design for Mass Customization** (DFMC) allows a generic product design to be customized easily (as such a product is partly built and finished to the exact order of the customer). Mass customization is often used by companies making laptops; a general laptop is built that has the keyboard and most common items but the design of the product allows customer-specific requirements like memory size, processing chips and sound systems to be added easily. Mass customization cuts down the need to hold finished products of any given product.
- **Reverse engineering** (and stripping down other people's products) is a core design competence that means a buying company and suppliers can learn from competitors' products by purchasing the item and dismantling it to see how it is made and how much it costs to make it. Such activities are useful and can result in major innovations in the design of the product.
- Greater engagement with the actual customer and consumer can also be conducted via 'voice of the customer' exercises and actually getting final consumers to feed back to the entire supply chain about their experiences and what they would like to see improved.
- Designers can also work to establish 'carry over' parts, which are parts that a supplier will continue to supply into the next generation of products offered to the customer and consumer. This improves the efficiency and cost effectiveness of future product designs (and any investments in automation by the supplier).
- Engaging suppliers with the design process can also be used to collapse the 'time to market' through better design process management from concept to final product. The approach allows for synchronous and concurrent engineering across the entire supply chain and therefore time compression.
- Target costing and a 'cost down' approach to product designs may also be introduced with suppliers. The approach starts with setting a target price for the finished product in the market and then working backwards from that price to find the best design. This is in direct contrast to a 'cost plus' approach, which takes the manufacturing costs of each stage and then adds a margin which may make the product far too expensive for the customer or consumer.

- The co-design of products also allows the potential for a perpetual use of materials[6] called a **cradle-to-cradle** (C2C) product or part. Such a part is recycled and reused indefinitely by a producer. Such products do not deplete the environment and are recycled into new products (when combined with the use of the product as a carry-over item), improving the environmental performance of the producer.

All too often, discussions concerning supply chain management will focus on supply and delivering products but this misses many potential activities for profitable collaboration. These opportunities are valuable and international management standards prompt for such engagement and improvement. Modern markets and products that offer greater personalization (bespoke or customized standard products) command higher margins. Managing the supply chain and improving material flows is therefore an area of management that offers high rewards and many commercial advantages. The product design functions (of suppliers and buying organizations) have a direct bearing on product costs, product quality, ability to assemble the product, the technology needed to make the product, and many other key responsibilities that the operations department and quality specialists will need to manage. A close working relationship between the engineering, operations, quality and supply chain teams and the design team is a very potent and powerful force for improvement.

The supply chain and international management standards

One of the most important aspects of managing a complex supply chain is being able to make decisions about products and services with the certainty that those decisions will be satisfied and the outcome the buyer expects will actually happen. Working with a high degree of certainty is so much easier when all businesses operate to international standards such as those of the ISO. Every certified or self-certified supplier that operates to an international management standard – such as ISO 9001 – offers a confidence that the necessary good practices are in place and are being managed. Operating ISO standards across an entire supply base is a major advantage and it is important because it also means the company shares a common language with its suppliers. Much attention by the ISO technical committee (TC) will have been expended to ensure the language of each requirement standards is clear and satisfactory to the experts and industry. The content of the standards also means that the latest requirement standard revision will contain the latest practices that support an effective and efficient business.

Any purchaser that has dealt with suppliers from other countries will know just how difficult it is to understand a foreign language and even commonplace words can often be misunderstood. The words used in international standards have been deliberately selected, reviewed by experts for clarity, and then published in supporting guides for use by all businesses. If a supply chain requires an improvement to its environmental performance then the supply chain-wide introduction of the standard is a major asset to a buying organization and transformation levels of change can be achieved with the combined efforts of all suppliers. The ISO approach also requires keen attention to risk management and to the needs of interested parties such as the supply base.

Developing suppliers also becomes easier because it is easier to perform customer-led second-party audits with supplier business to help and collaborate to make improvements that will benefit both businesses. Identifying gaps with a collaborative relationship with a buyer is a much less traumatic experience for a supplier or a group of suppliers. Opportunities for improvement therefore result from the adoption of international management standards.

As a buying business, ISO standards encourage audits of suppliers to be undertaken by competent staff and for the purpose of developing suppliers. These second-party audits are an important feedback activity and a means of targeting joint improvement projects. The audit serves as a means of testing for any potential risks in the supplier's operating model and sharing knowledge to assist the supplier to improve or the customer to modify their processes to make trading easier for the supplier. Audits and improvements lower the total overall costs of doing business together and will reduce further with every sustained improvement. Although supplier development may benefit other customers (who could be competitors) it is unlikely that any supplier will go to a competitor and offer to reduce their product prices and as such will probably apply the improvements throughout their business to improve performance and reduce operating costs.

ISO standards offer many benefits to product designers both at the buying company and in the supply chain. These benefits include:

- Formalization of design processes and key milestones in the project management and control of designs from concept to final product deletion for both parties.

- Controlled documents and standard operating procedures for both businesses.
- Improvement activities that allow designers to get involved with quality improvement through their own efforts within the department and also by receiving timely feedback from other areas of the organization and supply chain (including the sales and marketing teams and feedback concerning product performance from users, and product opportunities and innovations from material technologists).
- Greater integration of the design process with the strategic level of the business to promote the powerful capabilities of the design department for competitive advantage and time compression to get products to market quicker.
- Greater understanding of the design capacity of the business (including skills, competence and training) in areas where it would be considered non-traditional and unusual for designers to receive such investments.
- Designers have a strong contribution to lean and Six Sigma approaches.
- Better drawing and document control including numbering and controlled revisions of key documents.
- Enhanced data security to protect drawings and other commercially sensitive product information as well as greater exposure to digitized materials.
- A greater sense of pride and achievement.

The management of the supply chain and the extended design function to include supplier involvement in product designs is embedded in international standards and the high-level structure provides for the following:

- The role and performance of suppliers and product designs will be analysed during the review, focusing on the context of the organization. The supply chain, risks to supplied materials, the importance of product designs and future predictions of consumer tastes and trends are vitally important to review. These reviews inform the leaders by allowing them to form a future operating model of the company and its approach to supplier management.
- The supply chain department and design department are both internal stakeholders and suppliers represent external stakeholders and interested parties. As such these expert workers and organizations will have a view of the social, legal, political, technological, environmental and ethical trends

that will impact on the ability of the business to make money and command a profit. The design and supply chain teams will be expected to have established and monitored these business trends and be in a position to inform the business leadership team about what should be done to protect the business from risks and exploit any opportunities that may arise.

- The planning and support clauses represent areas of leadership and management that directly impact on the supply chain and design departments. As such these departments will need to bid for resources and develop worker skills, competences and talents to support the business.
- The business operation will outline the processes and procedures of each department, the control of documents, and measures used to assess performance. The performance evaluation clauses allow performance trending and can be used to identify performance gaps between what is needed to meet the goals of the company and the actual performance of the design process or supply chain team.
- The improvement clauses of any standard mean that supply chain specialists and designers will become increasingly involved in innovation and problem solving. It is likely that the supply base will be a focus for improvement once internal business processes of the certified or self-certified buying company are being effectively managed. Improvements made by the engineering and operations teams are also likely to require a new layout, operator workstation, product and other forms of drawing.

So the move from reactive and clerical purchasing with static designs and suppliers that are treated adversarially, to the proactive management of suppliers and product designs is a major transformation and a major addition to the competitive capabilities of the entire supply chain. The review of the supply chain will lead to many interesting and potentially revolutionary models that could see products that were sent to be made abroad (due to labour cost advantages) return to local production because everything is made to order. Reviews may also highlight the risks of buying goods from suppliers in faraway countries and suppliers that are poorly integrated, co-ordinated and developed. The combination of the design and supply chain specialists can, with a few major projects, revolutionize the cash flow cycle and result in products that are stocked at the buying company's site and paid for when they are used (such as Kanban or a vendor-managed inventory system). The possibilities are almost endless and an improving supply chain is a major competitive weapon to any producer in the quest to satisfy customer profitably.

In summary

This chapter has outlined and presented the importance of designing and managing the supply chain for a business as a key part of operational excellence and the operation of international management standards conformity. The supply chain is vitally important to cash flow and achieving the goals of a business. The old belief that only rival companies compete is somewhat misleading; instead it is the combined efforts of all trading partners that is important to competitive advantage. Every requirement standard will contain reference to stakeholders and interested parties, of which the supply chain is one.

Any modern business will want to find and develop the right type of suppliers so that supplier businesses become thought of as just extensions of the factory. Suppliers can be integrated with the introduction of international management standards (which have a major part to play in product quality and superior environmental performance) and their efforts are directly related to cash flow and profitability so it would be illogical not to include them in business decisions to some degree.

The modern emphasis on risk management in recent standards supports the integration of suppliers to reduce business risks and to create a common focus for all supply chain improvements. A reliable and improving supply chain will support the strategic goals of any customer business as well as the final consumer of the product. Designers will benefit from greater knowledge about products and materials and suppliers will make better decisions when they understand the strategy and future intentions of their customer organizations. Businesses do not operate in a vacuum – even small businesses have complicated supply chains that need to be coordinated and developed to achieve the best possible performance for all businesses and the customer.

Seminar topics and examination questions

- What sources of competitive advantage can be developed with suppliers?
- How would a manager go about starting a supplier association?
- What are the benefits of an entire supplier chain using an international management standard?

- How can better product design support improvements as part of the ISO 14001 standard?
- Is a better product design likely to generate more financial benefits than worker teams conducting continuous improvement of manufacturing operations?
- What are the trends affecting customer tastes and expectations in a product market of your choice?

Notes

1 Christopher, M (2016) *Logistics and Supply Chain Management*, 5th ed, FT Publishing, London

2 Rushton, A, Croucher, P and Baker, P (2017) *The Handbook of Logistics and Distribution Management: Understanding the supply chain*, Kogan Page, London

3 Hines, P A et al (1999) *Value Stream Management,* Financial Times Prentice Hall Publishing, London

4 Kahn, O (2018) *Product Design and the Supply Chain: Competing through design*, Kogan Page, London

5 Hands, D (2017) *Design Management: The essential handbook*, Kogan Page, London

6 Weetman, C (2016) *A Circular Economy Handbook for Business and Supply Chains: Repair, remake, redesign, rethink*, Kogan Page, London

Developing a learning organization and auditing

11

Business improvements are made by people – the people who work for a business and are dependent upon it doing well for their own quality of life. The development of a learning organization with a culture of inquiry, collaboration and achieving improvements in business performance is a key competence for modern manufacturers – both in the design of products and the fulfilment of orders. Organizations that cannot or do not grow their learning capability will face an uncertain future as markets change and competition means it is more difficult to make a profit. A learning organization is a special environment which is energized, engaged and rewarding for staff. Staff are at the heart of the learning organization concept and are the only assets within a business that have the ability to innovate. Machinery does not have innovations because technology doesn't have the ability to think for itself (until artificial intelligence takes over anyway); products do not get better by themselves so worker engagement with the direction and imperatives of the business is critical. All too often businesses ignore the skills of their staff and fail to find ways of engaging them with improvement of themselves and the performance of the business. Ironically, many of these staff will have skills outside of work that call for greater creativity, innovation and team performance than the business asks of them. Workers will manage local sports clubs, they will work for charities and help out, some will even be reservist military staff – each of these hobbies has a lot more empowerment than their employer allows them. So it makes sense to nurture and develop workers to create and sustain a learning organization culture because a lifetime of innovation could come from every worker (a career lifetime that could result in a contribution that spans 50 years!).

World-class organizations understand this key learning organization capability and competence and use it to generate a great customer experience whilst allowing workers to enjoy the company of other great workers in a workplace that is innovative and sees nothing but opportunities to improve. Toyota Motor Corporation once led with this headline on the front of their annual accounts: 'How we saved $1.5 BN'.[1] The report showed how operational and design staff had combined with suppliers to find this amazing level of savings despite almost 50 years of conducting problem solving on their journey to TQM. And the business has continued to problem solve and improve its team performances in car assembly, truck assembly, house building, sewing machine assembly and many other sectors. The power of a learning organization cannot be understated and businesses that learn adapt and change at a greater rate than those that rely on a handful of workers to conduct improvements.

LEARNING OBJECTIVES

At the end of this chapter, you should be able to:

- explain why the development of a learning organization is critical for the exploitation of ISO standards and competitive advantage;
- describe the key features of a learning organization and how they contribute to business improvement processes;
- explain the different types of audits and why they are important as a means of feedback to the business (and as a means of initiating improvement).

What is a learning organization and why is it important?

Learning as individuals or in groups is a very human activity and happens almost naturally where people get together to work towards an organizational goal or to solve problems. Organizations are just a formal grouping of people who share a common purpose – to satisfy customers profitably.[2] The skills of a learning organization are inextricably linked to the organization's most essential asset – knowledge. Every organization must learn to improve and change effectively. There are many different types of learning that must be enacted in any business and ISO standards can help structure and provide meaning to why and how workers learn:

- **using standards to learn how to do things right:** each conformance standard contains requirements for organizations to adhere to and benefit from surveillance audits;
- **using standards to learn how to do things better:** each conformance standard is a compilation of best practices for organizational managers to design and improve effective control systems;
- **using standards to do things completely differently and to innovate** using an effective understanding of the business context to fundamentally challenge how a business delivers on its purpose and objectives. This could lead to wholesale changes in the business model, automation, outsourcing and many other forms of innovation.

ISO standards support learning at many levels and with many forms of the plan–do–check–act cycle at the team level, departmental management level when attempting to improve towards business goals, and at a strategic level to identify business gaps and where to take the business in the future. Learning, and improvement from learning, is implicitly and explicitly stated for most requirements standards. Proof must also be provided of continuous improvement activities and new standards must be introduced as a result of making improvement. Each improvement must be evidenced in order to conform with auditing processes and procedures that feed back gaps in the conformity of the business with the requirements standards. Much information for learning is generated by the organization's contextual analyses as well as planning and feedback provided in the form of customer issues and the layers of auditing that organizations shall undertake as part of the conformance process.

A learning organization has been defined as a process which results in changes to organizational routines and codes of conduct over time[3] and is different to (but includes) individual learning approaches.[4] If a business relies on individuals then it is exposed should the employee decide to move to another employer organization. Learning organizations can rely and draw upon the skills of all employees and are less exposed to the loss of key staff. For some authors, learning organizations are a metaphor rather than a distinct structure where employees learn 'processes for continually generating, retaining and leveraging individual and collective learning to improve performance of the organizational system in ways important to all stakeholders and by monitoring and improving performance.'[5] But whatever view is held, the development of a learning capability is necessary to compete in modern markets and to design new products for customers that the business does not even know it will serve yet.

In this process of constant knowledge creation, a learning organization will 'consciously and intentionally devote significant mentoring/coaching to the staff. The investment is to ensure that individual learning and continuous improvement are embedded and that groups of workers continuously transform the entire organization by making improvements each week.'[6] The improvements as a result of learning are based on the effective use of knowledge management skills to acquire, disseminate, refine, and implement changes and to develop reflections on what works and does not work in the business.

The definitions of a learning organization vary widely but essentially any one will include:

- learning results from an organization's and staff experiences;
- it is a process of continual accumulation of knowledge;
- it leads to knowledge exploitation for performance improvement purposes;
- it happens at the individual, group, organizational and inter-organizational levels;
- it results from social interaction;
- it is based on effective and open communication/discussion/controlled experimentation by staff within a culture of openness, trust and respect for all employees;
- it is supported by top management and high levels of empowerment for staff to find new knowledge and to employ this knowledge to improve performance.

Therefore, a learning organization is constantly building knowledge, assimilating it or deleting it, then moving on. Learning organizations can therefore be characterized as organizations where all staff continually expand their capacity to use information and experiences to help their employer improve its performance.

Peter Senge,[7] the Harvard professor and guru of the learning organization approach, offers five key features of such a high-performance business:

- **Systems thinking**, which involves thinking about the business as a single entity (like a single living organism that must interact effectively and profitably with its context) and changes to the business must align with the needs of the external environment of the business. Change must therefore be undertaken only when the impact of such change on the whole organization is known. If performance is to be optimized, then all thinking must be at the 'business level' rather than thinking in terms of functional or business department interests only (known as silo thinking).

- **Shared vision** is a process of communication, convincing and focusing staff on a clearly articulated view of the future and what organizational capabilities are needed to be effective in the future.
- **Common mental models** of how the business works and should work are important as they unite staff on what value the business delivers and how, now and in the future. These models cover the processes that deliver the vision.
- **Team-based learning** and the collection of staff experiences and learning is important as there are significant synergy effects of groups.
- **Personal mastery** answers the 'what is in it for me?' question and allows individuals to master their processes, to go beyond being mere operators of a process (how to) and move to a stage of 'knowing why' the process works and the technicalities (precision) needed to fully exploit knowledge for better business results.

Senge's features of a learning organization therefore offer insights into how best to engage with an ISO conformance requirements standard and build the infrastructure to support the standard and exploit the most from it. Learning is a core principle of all ISO standards; the guides help managers and workers to understand key practices that assist learning and requirements standards determine what evidence is needed to prove conformity. ISO standards therefore demand that senior managers learn and conduct formal feedback reviews, workers use learning as a part of an outcome of improvement activities, and requirements standards themselves will be periodically updated by experts to demand new processes and proof of improvement.

ISO standards and the learning organization

A learning organization is therefore a business that has the capability to recognize, understand, make sense of and take appropriate action based on learning. Learning is embedded in all ISO standards and procedures explicitly and implicitly. There is little point in conforming to a standard unless continuous improvement is stimulated, and businesses can improve to become more profitable and to enhance the reputation of the company amongst interested parties and stakeholders. The ISO standards support Peter Senge's learning organization concept and his need for a common mental model with high levels of team learning for innovation and problem solving and a clear vision of growth for the business and its employees. Personal mastery allows individuals and small teams to optimize processes by learning the most about them so that change becomes fluid and uninterrupted.

The learning organization model is very powerful and adds a new dynamic capability that other approaches to modern manufacturing do not. Other manufacturing awards tend to be given based on a single point in time, whereas an international standard will cover many years of auditing and require managers (especially top management) as well as all employees and interested stakeholders to demonstrate that there is a continual and ongoing approach to managing business effectiveness and learning from the standard itself.

The importance of auditing

Every ISO conformance standard demands that the organization 'shall' be audited. For the purposes of this book and the standards that are reviewed within it, an audit is a system audit. It is an activity which focuses on a management system to verify (by examination and objective evaluation) that all applicable elements of a system are appropriate and effective to ensure conformance to the requirements clauses of a given standard. As such a quality management system audit of ISO 9001 will examine all the clauses (or a selection of clauses) to test the system and provide a report back to the certified (or certifying) company.[8] Professional managers who understand the relevance and importance of audit for improvement do not find these audits to be intrusive, threatening and costly – they are all learning opportunities which, if designed effectively, will give a constant stream of updates to the operational and management teams.[9] There are three different forms of audit which tend to be conducted by different people at different intervals.

First-party auditing

This is conducted by 'competent' internal employees, often on areas of the business that they do not control, and the frequency of audits can be daily. This is the base level of control needed by a business to ensure that clauses of the conformance requirements standard are checked and reported upon. The audit is designed to test the operating system of the standard by selecting a particular area, such as a review of the process that ensures controlled documents are managed and revised. The report will detail whether the business has all the necessary evidence (documented and observed) to comply with the standard. Naturally, no organization relies on one layer of auditing.

For a first-party 'staff' audit, an employee may (as an example) be given a task to investigate the training records of staff working in the goods inwards department. The competent employee would therefore go to the human resources department and select the training records of those employed in goods inwards, then ask the members of staff who are doing the work on that particular shift whether they have been trained and when the training was last updated. They will also observe the staff conducting their normal role. This form of testing is very cost-effective because it involves staff checking other areas of the business than those in their own area of responsibility. It is an important feature; because it is conducted so frequently it provides a form of daily control. This type of audit allows many members of staff to do small amounts of auditing each day and for lots of controls of the organization to be tested. As a result of the audit, the employee will write a brief note of what they found and note any non-conformities. A non-conformity happens when the practice of an organization (in reality) is at odds with the demands of a clause. This variance must be dealt with and countermeasures enacted as a result of continuous improvement activities. It is a means of learning because it shows that the organization is not conforming to a standard that it holds in very high regard and importance. Such first-party audits are valuable when conducted in the spirit of honest and open learning rather trying to catch staff out. Seeing audits as positive support for staff makes working life easier as improvements and corrective actions are undertaken. These changes can result in massive changes to the quality of working life of all staff.

Second-party auditing

This is conducted by an organization such as a customer or supplier and they test the system (and its implemented performance) as an assurance that all processes and tasks are working effectively, and the company conforms to the latest standard of 'best practice'. Buyers from customer organizations use this as a form of quality assurance review with the certified business and for supplier development activities. This process is typically conducted annually but not all customers will use this form of supplier interaction.

A second-party audit is often conducted less frequently by a customer or supplier and conformity audits help assure the customer that all the necessary (and often contractual) processes are in place and working (practised and evidenced). It is typical that customers will spend one or more days on site and will have predetermined what areas of the organization they wish to test and probe. Typically, the areas that most customers like to look through include the operations and quality control processes, including how continuous improvement is managed to help with the continuous improvement processes. Customers typically do not want to see the problems the organization may have with other customers but do want to see that robust processes are in place. Often this is conducted by the buyer from the purchasing department of the customer organization and is done to provide confidence that the supplier has all the necessary processes in place to maintain a very good level of customer service.

Third-party auditing

This is conducted by a competent and independent (hence 'third party') organization that has the processes and conformances itself to assess and conduct surveillance audits of a named standard. Third-party auditors conduct annual reviews of the system in quite a substantial amount of detail. They do not tend to tell the certified company what they intend to look at and every three years they are obliged to do a very deep audit. As standards are revised and updated, the third-party auditors will ensure the company maintains its conformance levels. The formal report of these businesses tends to be reviewed by top management in a very thorough manner as it forms part of the management review and objective-setting process of the company.

Third-party audits tend to attract a lot of attention as they are quite special events and many members of staff will be involved. A third-party audit is conducted by an independent organization that is deemed competent by itself holding an ISO certification. This certification pertains to the way in which independent auditors will come and scrutinize a business. Conforming to an ISO audit standard is important because it gives credibility that the independent auditor will provide unbiased advice that is beneficial to the company and will help them maintain their certification as well as ensuring the third party is itself working to 'best practice' auditing practices. The third-party audit is embedded in all ISO standards and is a primary trigger for gap analysis, which is conducted in the form of improving business systems when the organization is being certified, and for post-certification purposes, primarily to identify non-conformances. Whereas the first-party audit is conducted daily, and the second-party customer audit may be conducted periodically, the third-party audit is conducted annually over a number of days, with a very deep and rigorous testing of an organization system every three years.

External auditors are not enemies; they are friends who are trying to help a business to get better. Nobody gains from polite advice or ignoring aspects of organizational performance that must be improved. The reputation of the certifying body depends upon their rigorous approach and a positive relationship they build with senior management, which itself will allow improvement to take place. At the very minimum the annual management review of the effectiveness of the ISO standard and systems, procedures and practices as well as the general report that comes back from the third-party auditor is vitally important for strategic planning, objective setting and setting the agenda for continuous improvement activities.

These (up to three) levels of audit and their different frequencies provide levels of control that support an effective management team in directing and making the business better. No managers can ignore this imperative and because the independent third-party audit is accompanied with a large invoice for the service, it is typical that the third-party audit is actioned and the recommendations adhered to. Third-party auditors will also come back every year and the first thing they will do after arriving on site and being welcomed is to review the outstanding non-conformances from the previous visit. Third parties can also conduct certification processes for an applicant organization. Please remember that the ISO never conducts such assessments – its remit is to develop and publish standards only.

The outcomes of an audit

The audit process itself is a great opportunity to learn and ask 'why?', and a formal audit will typically result in a written report that shows all of the strong and positive aspects of an organization that were observed and evidenced as working effectively; it will also cover other areas where improvement could or must be undertaken. An audit is a systematic process that is conducted independently and is focused on gathering objective evidence that a business has processes that meet the clauses of a given standard. The objective evidence and its evaluation will test the extent to which an organization meets the standard and report documents will explain any shortcomings to the audited company management (the report is a vital source of feedback and a learning opportunity). That is to say that the conformance standard and all that is deemed that the company 'shall' conduct is being fulfilled. Naturally audits look for conformation and will note deviations or partial fulfilments, which will be reported to management and top management of the certified company (or certifying company). These are essentially gaps that must be closed in order for the company to be deemed worthy enough to retain a certification. These forms of feedback are:

- Areas of good practice and performance worthy of note.
- A non-conformance is where the practised evidence and observations show there is a deviation or variation between what is required of the standard and what is practised:
  - **A Conformity** is a statement that the objective evidence collected supports the fulfilment of a conformance clause.
  - **A Minor Non-Conformance** (MNC) concerns an aspect of management practice that is a system weakness or minor issue that could result in a major non-conformance if it was unaddressed. Each minor non-conformance is a symptom of a poor implementation and therefore an opportunity for continuous improvement to redress this system weaknesses via a corrective action activity.
  - **A Major Non-Conformance** (MJR NC) is where objective evidence reveals the absence of or a significant failure to implement and/or maintain conformance to the requirements of the applicable standard. This could include the absence of any evidence to support the conformance to a key clause or any situation that would, based on the objective evidence collected, raise significant doubt as to the capability of the management system to achieve its stated policy or customer objectives. Such a failing demands significant and instant response by the company leadership and staff.
  - **An 'Observation'** (for want of a better word) is included in a report as an item of earnest and honestly presented advice. It does not represent a non-conformance but is an area of good practice that should be considered by the management team concerned.

Again, it must be noted that an audit report would be better termed a learning opportunity and effective counter measures introduced by a learning organization will bring all non-conformances and observations to nil.[10] At this point, audits will take less time and improvement activities can focus on adjustments to the system and not the use of staff to correct weaknesses.

Auditing and ISO standards

There are two major auditing documents for managers to be aware of. Each details the specific responsibilities of an auditor (either a competent internal auditor or a third party).

ISO 19011 is a document that provides guidance on auditing management systems. This standard is used particularly for the effective design and operation of a company-based 'first-party' internal audit programme and its elements of success; it also covers external audits (second and third party). It includes the principles of auditing (Table 11.1) and practical advice on managing an audit programme and conducting management system audits (form, frequency, layering and such like). It also provides guidance on the evaluation of competence of the individuals involved in the audit process and teams of auditors. It is applicable to all organizations that need to plan

Table 11.1 Principles of auditing

Principle	Meaning
Integrity	Acting with professionalism.
Fair presentation	The obligation to report truthfully and accurately what has been investigated.
Due professional care	The application of diligence and professional judgement in auditing and reviewing results of an audit.
Confidentiality	Ensuring that all information is controlled and secure.
Independence	Ensuring the audit process and report is impartial and objective in analysis and conclusions.
Evidence-based approach	The assurance that reliable and reproductive audit conclusions can be achieved through the systematic validation of evidence in the audit process.
Risk-based approach	An audit must include due consideration of all risks and opportunities when scheduling, conducting and reporting on an audit.

and conduct internal or external audits of management systems or manage an audit programme in order to conform to a standard.

The remainder of the ISO 19011 document, applicable to all organizations that need to plan and conduct internal or external audits of management systems or manage audit programmes, starts with the elements of the scope, normative references and terms and definitions used. Key terms use the definition of an audit as systematic, independent and a documented process for obtaining objective evidence and evaluating it objectively to assess fulfilment of a clause. It is conducted on an audit client (a company requesting the audit of its management systems). An audit programme is all the arrangements for a planned audit to be conducted at a specific time with an audit scope as the 'extent and boundaries' of thc audit. For an effective audit, there needs to be a set of audit criteria to be used for reference and against which objective evidence will be compared. Objective evidence is the provision of all records and statements of fact that are relevant to the audit criteria. Risks are considered to be uncertainties that represent deviations from expected performance and/or deficiencies in the information/evidence collected.

Competent auditors are those with the ability, knowledge and skills to achieve the intended results of an audit. These individuals (by themselves or within an audit team) will assess processes, results and the effectiveness of conformance standard fulfilment. Evidence may also be collected by **technical experts** who provide specific knowledge or expertise to an audit team but are not auditors, and there may also be **observers** who accompany an audit team to watch it rather than act as auditors. The remainder of the ISO 19011 auditing guideline focuses on the logic and systems:

- **Section 4** covers the principles of auditing.
- **Section 5** presents the considerations for businesses, which include setting the objectives for and evaluations of an effective audit programme. It also outlines how to establish, implement, monitor and review the audit programme.
- **Section 6** covers the practicalities of initiating, preparing for, conducting, reporting and distributing the report and its follow-up actions.
- **Section 7** provides guidance on the competence of auditors including determining competence, establishing auditor evaluation criteria, selecting the most appropriate auditor methodology, conducting the evaluation, and managing/improving auditor competence.

Figure 11.1 Signs of a poorly implemented system

Poor competence – less accurate and less useful findings.

Inconsistent collection of data – staff feel they did not get a chance to explain or support the audit. Staff see it as personally critical.

Being nice – the auditor writes what would be politically acceptable rather than factually correct. Poor integrity.

Methodology is unclear and therefore hard to repeat.

Non-conformances are not followed up and the management system remains with potential for failure.

Bad scheduling – lack of available staff and data not at hand.

Poor collection of evidence as a result of an inferior methodology leading to a feeling of inconsistency or opinion rather than objective fact.

Rushing the audit and compromising on thoroughness.

Rushing the report so good and targeting advice for the business is missed. Poor reflection on the evidence.

The report contains errors or is ambiguous.

This document is invaluable for businesses and sets out a rigorous programme that supports systematic and independent learning opportunities that are evidence based and will help the business limit its weaknesses whilst building upon 'best practices'.

Whilst many writers believe that the most important audit is that of the third party, the first-party audit remains a much more frequent and useful control. It means that the management system and management review process are timely and a lot of system tests have been conducted by staff who are competent and therefore many more learning experiences can be generated. Frequent first-party and annual third party-audits are very powerful when combined and integrated with a detailed management review and goal-setting cycle.

ISO 17021 is a standard of auditing which contains the principles and requirements for the competence, consistency and impartiality of bodies providing audits and certification. Such certification is provided by third-party conformity assessment bodies. These documents contain technical and organizational requirements that cover general legal and contractual protocols, the structures that must be in place to undertake certification, resources, and the competences, records and informational requirements for evidence, confidentiality etc. The document also outlines the process and management system requirements of a third party or Certification Assessment Bodies (CABs). Such organizations must also adhere to guidelines concerning impartiality, confidentiality, complaints and appeals, public disclosure and the use of management systems by CABs. In addition, there are further supporting documents for each major specific standard (such as Environmental Auditor Competence ISO 27021-part 2 or Quality Management Systems Auditor Competence ISO 27021-part 3 etc). These additional guidance documents contain information on general skills with specific reference to the conformance standard and even competency specialisms with these – so the part 2 guidance will provide guidelines for competency to audit ISO 14001 with respect to specific activities for testing the fulfilment of emergency preparedness clauses as well as specifics on the expertise to assess 'emissions to air' or 'releases to land'.

The standard – the conformance standard for certifying bodies – has the normal scope, normative references (of which one is the ISO 17000 series) and a list of terms and definitions. These include the term 'Certification Audit', the qualities of a good audit, the terms client, auditor, technical expert, observer and guide roles, as well as the types and severity of nonconformances.

Clauses 4 to 10 provide detailed requirements:

- Clause 4 outlines the principles of impartiality, competence, responsibility, openness, confidentiality, responsiveness to complaints and the risk-based approach.
- Clause 5 details the legal and contractual, management and impartiality, as well as liability and financing of CABs.
- Clause 6 provides the requirements for the organizational structure and control mechanisms.
- Clause 7 defines the requirements of competence, personnel and records and outsourcing procedures.
- Clause 8 provides requirements for information, confidentiality, and information exchanges with clients.
- Clause 9 covers the pre-certification, planning of certification, initial certification, conducting audits, the certification decision, and maintaining certifications. The requirements also include the management of complaints, appeals and document archiving.
- Clause 10 is the final section and covers the management system requirements for CABs.

The process of an audit

The process of conducting an audit is never left to chance. Audits represent effective testing of a management system and the learning that results can be used to improve the business and by all levels of staff. Learning about gaps and weaknesses in conformity helps to repair deficiencies but it also prompts additional reflections by all concerned about why such gaps exist and what needs to happen to close these gaps. A professional and planned approach to an audit (by the auditor, auditee and any observers etc) needs to be pre-planned, well executed and integrated with company-wide learning so that improvement priorities can be well understood and the appropriate counter-measures undertaken. Typically the certification body will undertake the following activities once they have been shortlisted and awarded the contract to certify by the client:

- agree a date to visit the client for the purpose of the audit;
- preparing for the audit and staff needed (of the correct competence/methodology);
- conducting the opening meeting with the client management and reviewing the clauses of the conformance standard sought;
- performing the necessary document reviews while conducting the audit of the management system;
- communicating during the audit;
- assigning the team roles and responsibilities of guides and observers for the auditor;
- collecting and verifying information (triangulation);
- generating and synthesizing the audit findings and levels of fulfilment of the clauses of the conformance standard applied for (such as ISO 9001);
- preparing the audit report conclusions;
- conducting the closing meeting with the client.

If successful, a client will achieve conformity, become certified and will be able with permission to display the ISO logo. Certification is therefore the provision, by an independent CAB, of a written assurance and certification (resulting in a certificate) that the management system in question meets and fulfils the clauses of a specified standard.[11] The process from then on is similar to the certification audit but is performed as a periodic surveillance audit to assure the business that it retains the levels of fulfilment needed to hold the certification. These are conducted annually with a deep audit every three years. It is also highly possible that a new revision of the standard will have been introduced or is undergoing review by a technical committee and therefore the client will need to make plans to transition from an old revision to the new one.

Audits and learning

There can be no more powerful system of conformity than the ISO system, which allows the ISO itself to develop standards with experts through its technical committees and for these published standards to be managed by certification bodies. These bodies then ensure the standards are met and have no interest in awarding certificates to businesses that do not meet the full intent and clauses of a standard; if they did so then the reputation of the certification body would be called into question. CABs are the police force of the ISO in operational terms and the ISO is the governance structure. The two systems work well together and local expert CAB help for businesses is married with the 'best practices' of the latest conformance standard revision. These both help businesses learn and continue to manage their knowledge and exploit the benefits of being certified.

In summary

This chapter has presented the learning organization approach and the role of ISO standards in the process of stimulating change and positive improvements for a conforming business. The learning organization, in a culture that is positive and collaborative, unleashes significant staff innovations and reinforces the power of a structured ISO approach to making positive changes that impact on the performance of the firm. Such impacts include the improvement of the design process as well as processes that help fulfil customer orders. Learning that occurs between the operational teams and the issues they face when making products is vital for designers to improve their designs so that products take less time to build, it takes staff less time to become competent at making products, and design optimization can happen (with regard to quality, health and safety, the environment, and the overall productivity of the firm). To be able to see the fruits of improvement activities is very motivational and can stimulate the team to rise to even higher forms of innovation. Audits provide an unbiased review of the firm and are submitted in an honest manner – the purpose of the audit is to show more ways to improve. Any competent top manager or team leader will greet such advice warmly – it helps them to know more about the organization and how better to manage it. Without learning, the future of an organization is significantly undermined and any form of competitive advantage will result from luck or will be short-lived. Learning is built into every requirements standard so that businesses have the necessary processes to continuously improve using the skills of the workforce.

Seminar topics and examination questions

Here are a few questions to test the 'grey matter':

- Why shouldn't the ISO do certification audits?
- Can a member of a client staff really be unbiased and truly competent in conducting an audit?
- Should companies just declare they meet a standard without being audited?
- In what ways does the development of a learning organization capability support the pursuit of competitive advantage by a business?
- Is being a learning organization necessary before a company starts to implement ISO standards or will it become a learning organization as a result of implementing ISO standards?
- How do you know whether a business is a learning organization or not?

Further reading

The best source of information for the reader is to visit the main ISO website and the website of the national body for their country. These websites are packed with great information about the process and technicalities of certification. The websites of CABs should also be visited as there as so many case studies and snippets of good practice that can be found when researching which certification body can help a business in its journey to gaining certification.

Notes

1 Toyota Motor Corporation (1994) *Toyota Motor Corporation Annual Accounts*, TMC, Nagoya, Japan

2 Pisano, G P (1994) Knowledge, integration, and the locus of learning: an empirical analysis of process development, *Strategic Management Journal*, **15** (1), pp 85–100

3 Levitt, B and March, J (1988) *Organizational Learning*, *Annual Review of Sociology*, **14**, pp 319–40

4 Argyris, C and Schon, D (1978) *Organizational Learning*, Addison-Wesley, London

5 Drew, S A W and Smith, P A C (1995) The learning organisation: change proofing and strategy, *The Learning Organisation,* **2** (1) pp 4–14

6 Pedler, M, Burgoyne, J and Boydell, T (1991) *The Learning Company*, McGraw-Hill, London

7 Senge, P (2006) *The Fifth Discipline: The art and practice of the learning organization*, 2nd ed, Random House Publishing

8 Tricker, R (2016) *ISO 9001:2015 Audit Procedures*, Routledge, London

9 Cochran, C (2017) *Internal Auditing in Plain English: A simple guide to effective ISO audits*, Paton Professional

10 Hewitt, D and Ainslee, V (2018) *Quality Management Systems: A guide to ISO 9001:2015 Implementation and Problem Solving*, 2nd ed, Purple Parrot Publishing

11 Accreditation is the formal recognition by an independent body, generally known as an accreditation body that a certification body operates according to international standards

Leadership and international standards 12

Introduction

A common feature of all international management standards and all management books is the importance of effective organizational leadership for businesses to become high-performing, highly reliable and learning organizations that are capable of improving on a daily basis. Even though the term 'leadership' is perceived to be critically important, it remains a confused subject area and there is very little agreement on what it is and which model is best (despite over 100 years of organizational research). The requirements of an 'international management standard' are very transparent and clear in terms of 'conformity requirements' and what organizational practices need to be operated and controlled for all forms and sizes of business (in terms of sales value and employment) and different national cultures. However, businesses that operate with the same number of people, the same technology and similar customers do not always behave in the same way and are not the same the world over. Each business will have a national culture which impacts on business practice and more importantly it will have its own organizational culture and 'way of doing things around here'.

Although business culture can evolve, it can also be designed and shaped by the business leadership team in terms of behaviours and investments in the organization and its ways of working. Understanding the concept of leadership is therefore vitally important in order to understand how to harness the power of an international standard for superior business performance. It is a major influence on how the business works and a major element of every international management standard as explicitly identified in the new high-level structure approach. Leadership will determine what is implemented and how new working practices that conform to standards requirements will be operated, with many degrees of freedom in how a business achieves this conformity with its unique cultural approach.

LEARNING OBJECTIVES

At the end of this chapter, you should be able to:

- define leadership;
- explore the key characteristics of an effective leader;
- define followership;
- explain the implications of introducing international management standards for business leaders.

Leadership and management

The first lesson in leadership is that it is not the same as management. Management implies a level of control of tactical operations (working in the short term), whereas leadership involves greater vision, a higher purpose and set of goals that creates 'followers' who want to adapt and achieve more. Both management and leadership are necessary for organizations to perform at their full potential and one cannot exist without the other. Visionary leaders are great for organizations to aspire but rarely achieve their goals without capable managers to carry out their vision. These businesses operate in a 'dreamy state', with the danger of too much management and not enough leadership leading to employees feeling they are being micro-managed, unempowered, alienated from the goals of the business (even having a feeling that no goals actually exist) and generally having an organization-wide feeling of frustration. Workers like to see what authors call 'the big picture' and most want to play a role in a business achieving its business goals. Leadership at the top of an organization will always be effective when integrated with managers and/or self-managing teams that deliver today's products and services for existing customers but also grow by spending some time working on making the business more ready for future competition. From the leadership view, operational stability provided by a systematic approach to managing processes (as embodied in an international management standard) is necessary as it provides a platform upon which to create visions of the future. It moves away from constant firefighting and gives leaders the 'head space' to think through key issues such as what skills will be needed in the future to compete effectively and where customer trends are headed.

All businesses face a complex and uncertain environment so it is important to understand the link between business leadership and operational management. Past models that worked during the early years of a business (or were introduced during a more stable time period) may not work effectively in the future and may have undetected problems even today. It is the role of leaders to think through how a profit will be made in the future and what models will be needed to survive and thrive, as well as adaptations to the existing operating model. The point that leaders think through the 'fit' of the current business operating model and future needs almost implicitly accepts that there will be a difference between the two and leadership will be necessary to help staff migrate from the current to the future model. It is also important to understand that leadership is associated with key business positions and titles but also that it can be determined by what is happening at the time so that experienced, skilled and empowered staff can act as leaders to solve issues and support the long-term direction of the business. Therefore leaders:

- have job roles where leadership is expected;
- can be situational and lead when needed but do not have this as part of the formal job role; the leader of an emergency procedure or business continuity process may not be an executive director (where leadership is expected) but will lead when one of these situations happens, such as an information security breach;
- have a clear understanding of the situation and a vision of the future;
- have the ability to communicate the vision (or future state) of the business to their teams and other stakeholders;
- are listened to within the organization and judged on the consistency of their behaviours;
- will express the benefits of change and answer the questions of every employee as to why change is necessary and how it impacts on me;
- serve as powerful role models for staff and their behaviour determines the culture of the business; if culture is 'the way we do things around here' then leaders 'walk the talk' and reinforce the values of the business;
- enthuse organizational staff and others to follow them and make them want to participate in shaping the positive future for the business by engaging in change;
- share information and visions (or models) of the future to enthuse staff and to stimulate greater idea sharing and constructive criticism;
- see differences of opinion and diversity as healthy aspects of a modern, dynamic and adapting business.

To some, leadership can be summarized as the 'intelligent use of power' to steer groups in the right direction for the business to succeed. Management is the 'intelligent use of power' to govern and improve business processes. Leadership and management must combine to create high performance. The concept of power is quite important and with power comes responsibilities – certainly within an international management standard these responsibilities are clearly articulated. The leadership of an organization must drive performance towards a new and better business that can thrive and use its operational excellence (ie processes) to innovate and deliver superior performance over its competitors.

Leadership over time

In the early 1900s, large-scale factories (mass production manufacturing systems) began to emerge and, at the time, engineers dominated and held the power in all aspects of company leadership and management. These early professions cherished specialist engineering knowledge, especially industrial engineering, and there were few models of leadership and management that existed to guide these new factory designs. With relatively inexperienced and comparatively low-skilled workers compared to today's workforce, jobs were deskilled and an autocratic model of leadership was adopted. Essentially, the autocratic approach suited these early days when it was felt that workers were not capable of engaging with leadership issues and were untrusted by leaders. With long product lives and undemanding customer markets there was little to motivate leaders to engage with the workforce. In fact, the workforce was viewed with distrust and where possible automation was used to remove workers in favour of 'less troublesome' technology.

Over time, the autocratic model proved ineffective when market competition increased and it was not possible to 'rule over' all staff. A more human approach to leadership and a greater engagement of the workforce was needed; an approach which relied less on key individuals to determine everything for a large and complex organization. During this process of change, rigid and specialist business departments were transformed through greater use of teamwork, beginning in the 1940s when companies started to experiment with teams as a means of improving productivity and began to emphasize the relationships and social dynamics of the workplace.[1] Greater democracy was practised as the dynamism of the markets changed and became more volatile. The purpose of working in teams was to combat slow and bureaucratic decision-making processes, which worked against the needs of the market, in exchange for more responsive business processes. It was impossible to lead using rules and positional power alone – the market conditions demanded greater reactiveness and adaptiveness. Leadership styles therefore changed to embrace greater levels of staff engagement. The British and Europeans embraced this approach much more quickly than US industry where paternalism flourished (America still benefited from large markets for products and high automation). The Europeans, motivated by religious and other factors, started to lead by engaging the workforce, often through working with trade unions and other forms of worker representation.

The trend from the early autocracy to models using greater attention to and involvement of the human resources has continued from the 1960s to the advent of Western TQM models of leadership in the 1980s. With an even greater intensity of markets and current contemporary views that leadership must be more democratic, workers have become more 'engaged' with the business they work for.

Although these previous paragraphs have painted a 'broad brush' change and migration to a holistic leadership model that attempts to create a business where staff can contribute, it would be wrong to suggest that this evolution has resulted in the demise of previous models, with many businesses remaining in the autocratic mode. The approach an organization takes, along with the behaviours of its leaders, is a decision and practice that is specific to that business. It may be perfectly fitting that an autocratic approach is used in safety-critical environments and a more democratic approach is needed for businesses that require high levels of innovation. International management standards do not advocate any specific approach to leadership but instead leave such matters to the organization that wishes to work to or become certified to a certain requirement standard and how a business ensures its conformity to that standard.

According to John Adair (1973),[2] leadership models cover three overlapping activities: operating at the task level (achieve the task), at the team level (build skills) and at the individual level (develop core skills and competences). A leader could operate a highly autocratic organization and still introduce all the practices necessary to achieve task and individual needs and conform with a requirements standard, but so too can a more democratic leadership approach. Nevertheless, the key point is that leaders must understand the levels at which they engage with their own workforce in order to support the business to achieve its goals. Investing in people skills is critical, as this process creates both effective organizational learning and valuable tacit knowledge[3] about how best to enact change.[4]

Generic leadership types

Many different types of leadership style have been determined over time, including:

- **The autocratic leader** is a person in the middle of a structured set of relationships with staff, akin to the individual being in the middle of a cartwheel with each spoke coming out representing a direct relationship with a subordinate. Subordinates must therefore report back to the leader to approve any action to be undertaken. This form of leadership places great stress on the individual leader to 'rule over' each subordinate.
- **The democratic leader** is one who prizes staff engagement with key business decisions and deliberately seeks to generate consensus across all staff in order to make decisions that are likely to embed and sustain because everyone wanted them to be introduced.
- **The charismatic leader** can be an autocrat or a democratic leader but has a personalized and energetic approach to the leadership model whereby personality and the natural characteristics of the individual infect the organization and create a set of behaviours that staff follow. Charismatic leaders are often entrepreneurial and the founders of a business.
- **The situational leader** is one that holds leadership responsibility only during specific events or for a temporary period of time.

What can be seen by this simple typology of leadership is that leadership involves both **task behaviours** (setting goals for instance) and an attention to **relationship behaviours** (inclusivity and engagement of staff or treating them as business assets that are best controlled and ruled rather than engaged). These skills are necessary to develop a technical understanding of where a business should be headed and are also attentive to the emotions and relationships that will adapt within the business. These skills will be needed for effective change management during the introduction and use of a requirement standard.

Leaders will create a goal or vision for the organization and use persuasion or dictatorial skills to ensure compliance of the people who follow them; this is often referred to as 'followership', where workers follow the intention and strategies of a leader. Leadership style is therefore important because it helps to add meaningfulness for followers. Leadership style also sets the tone for all change within an organization and will also include organizational rituals and symbolism. Such symbolism could include the use of large individual-occupancy offices for leaders, leaders who wear suits, not uniforms, and leaders that have separate car parking and luncheon facilities at the factory – these all signify that leaders are different and 'more important'. The latter are trappings of leaders who want to be differentiated and this symbolism reinforces the distance of the leader from certain types of work and most employees (these are typical trappings of an autocratic leadership style).

Other leaders of a more democratic nature will stress inclusivity. They will eat in the same canteens as staff, they will have 'open door' policies for staff to come in and talk about work issues, and they will lead regular business updates and 'all staff' conferences/forums. Understanding these stereotypical types of leadership is important because they define much about how an organizational leader will design and enact an international management standard. Choosing the right style is important and, interestingly, the leadership style will be reflected in what followers see and therefore perceive as important.

Most international standards will require senior leaders to think through how best to use teams or reflect upon the effectiveness of current teamworking arrangements. If teamworking is to be encouraged so that teams collaborate to learn and improve, then it is important that the right words and leadership style are combined to reinforce these key aspects of getting the most from teams. Inconsistencies between the style of leaders and their behaviour will soon be exposed by followers.

Followers and followership

Central to the concept of leadership is the twin concept of 'followership'. Followership presents the view that organizational staff and others will follow leaders for a number of reasons but primarily because they believe in the leader and the vision they have established. The leadership choice of style will be reflected in their treatment of followers:

- The **autocratic leader** will develop staff who rely exclusively on the decision making of the leader; subordinates may also be given tasks to do but are comparatively un-empowered. Followership is based on the positional power of the leader and followership will be based on 'rules' and an acceptance that the leader has the right to determine everything for the subordinate. Resistance or questioning of the autocratic leader will typically result in sanctions and even disciplinary action levied on the subordinate.
- The **democratic leader** will deliberately seek engagement of subordinate staff and will exercise various levels of staff empowerment so that staff remain engaged and committed to a jointly determined outcome or course of action. Autocratic leaders see democratic leaders as weak, whereas democratic leaders think autocrats are stifling their subordinates, who never mature to take their own decisions and have to create 'reports'.

- The **charismatic leader** will stimulate loyalty because followers enjoy the individual's leadership style and personality. Such leaders also have followers that enjoy high levels of fun at work and the excitement of working for the charismatic leader. Charismatic leaders use relationship building to support loyalty and will often be situational in their decision making. On occasion they will be autocratic because they passionately care about an issue and on other occasions they will let followers take decisions. Often charismatic leaders will operate cliques of staff and surround themselves with 'their team', which can be de-motivational to other staff.
- The **situational leader** will empower or centralize the leadership prerogative based on the decision/s that the leader faces and also on whether they believe the followers are competent and sufficiently skilled to make the correct decisions.

Followership is an important aspect of any international management standard implementation. Organizations tend to operate with a few leaders and many followers so it is important to reflect upon the leadership style and culture of an organization. Being overly autocratic when the business needs greater levels of empowered teamworking will limit what can be achieved by the teams and will slow the implementation and commercial exploitation of an international standard. There is much for leaders to reflect upon and many guides to help interpret any requirement standard.

Features of the leadership process

Up to this point in the chapter, the style of a leader has been discussed in very general terms, but it has been presented to allow the reader to draw their own conclusions about their organization or leaders they may interact with. There is also another dimension of leadership, which is a process. The leadership style of an individual will determine how the process is implemented and how it is controlled but the process of leadership is very important because it translates business needs and talent management into effective change for the future prosperity of the business and all its employees. The main stages of the leadership process include:

- **Developing a vision** for the business by scanning the environment and using available data/mental models to develop an understanding of where the business is going and what it will look like when it gets to this ideal vision.

- **Establishing values** that envelope the business and what patterns of behaviour are considered legitimate and acceptable within the business. In this sense, democratic leaders will promote the values of openness, transparency, inclusivity, engagement and team-based ways of working. Autocratic leaders may emphasize specialist skills, organizational elites, and teamworking within strict boundaries of responsibility.
- **Creating structures to communicate** with staff and external stakeholders in a manner that allows meaningful information to be shared within and beyond the business. The autocratic leader may restrict and control commercially sensitive information to only trusted subordinates, whereas the democratic leader will often promote all meaningful information to all relevant staff in the business in the belief that workers will make better decisions and greater followership will result.
- **Setting the standards for the way in which staff behave** towards each other and external stakeholders, and setting standards that determine what is acceptable (and importantly what also is deemed unacceptable).
- Leaders also, by their deliberate intents and observed behaviour, **shape the culture of the business** in the way they work, are seen to behave, and how they enact discipline when needed. If an organizational culture is the function of the way in which 'we do things around here', then leaders have a pivotal and direct role in establishing the business culture.
- Inevitably, through autocracy or democracy, **the leader will prioritize certain initiatives over others** and provide resources so that such interventions and programmes of improvement are successful. The level of democracy of the leader will determine the extent to which such initiatives may be originated by subordinates.

These basic facets of leadership are supported by additional activities that support effective leadership practice, including:

- The degree to which **teamwork** rather than individual specialists dictates the management of engagement with decision making and how change is in enacted.
- The level of **empowerment** delegated to subordinate staff to determine the actions needed to reach the vision of the organization and allowing staff to allocate (often scarce) team time to their own self-determined courses of action.
- The extent to which all staff can act to **profitably support the customer** (customer orientation) and solve problems/identify opportunities to better serve the customer.

- The **formalized and informal change model** promoted by the organization and its leadership for staff to enact effective and prioritized change.
- The extent to which staff **embrace the ideals of operational excellence and Total Quality Management** (**TQM**) and use these approaches to systematically improve processes and customer service. Such an approach is linked to skills and the ability of teams to engage in problem solving to **harness learning for improvement** and better corporate performance.
- Leaders also determine the **legitimacy of working across departmental and company boundaries** to manage processes that include interactions and improvements with suppliers, regulators, financiers, the local community and such like.

These process features and enabling activities (such as TQM) create a framework for leaders and this knowledge is important when working with standards that outline what is considered to be contemporary 'good practice'. Up to this point in the chapter, the leader has been portrayed as varying in attitude and style towards their followers but essentially concerned with achieving a task or goal for the business and having an approach to managing internal relationships with workers.

Leadership focus: staff and task

There needs to be a balance between relationships with staff to enable better learning and a better quality of working life, and the main task of generating a profit from effectively managing production processes. In effect, tasks represent technical issues and relationships support the social and interpersonal aspects of leading change. Blake and Mouton (1964)[5] were among the first authors to promote a range of approaches that blend a focus on achieving tasks with an approach to the workforce. They termed their work the **Management Grid** (although it is termed a management grid it can also be used to assess leader behaviours and attitudes). The grid uses two graphical axes – the first represents a concern for people (ranked from low to high) on a vertical axis and the second dimension is a low-to-high rating for attention to the task of workers (plotted on the x-axis). From these two dimensions, Blake and Mouton derived five key leadership positions:

- A high concern for people with a high focus on completing the task of delivering products to customers was referred to as **team management** because staff are involved in running the business and feel valued by the business and its leaders.

- A high concern for people and a low concern for completing the production task was termed **country club management**. Such a position cannot be sustained for long because demanding customers and a competitive marketplace will soon see the demise of the business. The country club approach is a comfortable working environment but is not particularly high performing.
- A low concern for people and a high concern for completing the production task was labelled **task management** but this suffers from a lack of attention to the human learning and developmental aspects of a business. The style of managers and leaders is autocratic.
- A low concern for people and a low concern for completing the production task was termed **impoverished management** and achieves little actual outputs for sale and low levels of investment in staff skills and learning. The leadership and management approach involves a lot of compromises and delivers poor performance and poor sustainability results for a business. It is the worst of all the five positions identified by the authors.
- A medium concern for people and a medium concern for completing the production task was termed **middle of the road** management and achieves only partial success with the workers and partial satisfaction of customers.

The grid and research analysis is old but important because it shows that leaders need to deliver tasks and generate a profit but must provide additional attention to the development of staff skills (operations and design staff as well as all of those that support them). Plotting leadership behaviours in this manner helps to identify the strengths and weaknesses of the leader and what can be done to optimize performance as well the social and knowledge management processes. Most international management standards represent investments in processes, tasks and people so, despite the age of the work, Blake and Mouton's grid is a good way of viewing the corporate leadership approach and what it could do to support greater performance or worker engagement.

The Hershey Blanchard lifecycle[6] is another model of a similar type to the Blake and Mouton grid. The model suggests a number of leadership styles based on task and relationship approaches to form four styles of leadership. These styles are important because they show what strategy a leader or a manager can use when working with followers. These options include:

- **Delegating style** has a low-task and low-relationship style wherein the leader allows the group to take responsibility for task decisions. The style is best applied to mature teams and established businesses.

- **Participating style** is equivalent to a low-task but high-relationship style of leadership which is based on shared ideas and staff that are engaged with major business decisions. The group approach is good for staff that have yet to become autonomous and are learning about how best to work together. In the future these staff are likely to become empowered and almost autonomous.
- **Selling style** concerns a high-task and high-relationship style and is where the leader deliberately tries to sell their ideas to the group of subordinates. The subordinate 'followers' may well be competent but may be resistant to change so selling ideas is a viable strategy as a means of aligning and engaging those upon whom the leader is dependent to change the business.
- **Telling style** is an autocratic and high-task, low-relationship style where the leader removes any subordinate autonomy in favour of telling subordinates what to do. The style works well with teams that have just been formed and those that need guidance.

These situational styles of leadership to engender more effective followership suggest that leaders can move between styles in order to achieve the outcomes they seek and that leaders can change styles within the same day. The Blake and Mouton approach implies a deliberate and deeper routed position that is less amenable to change. Hershey and Blanchard do not advocate any particular option as superior to any others and their situational leadership model is a very useful approach to introducing international management standards. This form of assessment is also very important when at the early stages of assessing the usefulness of an international management standard or early in its introduction. Leaders may have to sell the implementation to certain colleagues and must also delegate activities so that the most effective business processes can be introduced. An effective leader will be aware of these different strategies and will adopt the best one for each follower group.

The role of leaders within any business is critical. After all, it is leaders that set direction. Leaders set the tone of the organization and control significant organizational resources to invest in the future of the business and the knowledge of all workers. An understanding of the styles, behaviours and strategies available to the leader is vitally important if they are to effectively engage with change processes and major transformational activities involving international standards.

Leadership and international management standards

Leadership is integral to all international management standards and is explicitly identified in the latest high-level structures of all international standards. Leadership is a vital element of a business operating model and a good international management standard will not operate effectively if there is a disengaged leadership team or insufficient attention is paid to the role of leadership when implementing or sustaining conformity/certification to a requirements standard.

Leadership is needed well before a standard is actually enacted because leadership style can be an inhibitor to competitive advantage in the marketplace, profitability, and the retention of talented staff. More importantly, leaders play a key role when businesses face highly competitive and uncertain times. During times of uncertainty, followers like to see where the business is going and how they fit into these future plans. Leading during such challenging times requires a competency in understanding the challenges facing the business and clearly showing an awareness of the present state of the business and its shortcomings. This is similar to a self-audit and requires a significant amount of self-reflection and brutal honesty by the leader. If an international standard full of good practice is to be implemented effectively and deliver results, the leader must assess themselves and their role in such a change, as well as monitoring their words and behaviours too!

The leader must also convince the organization and followers that there is a rational and robust analysis of the trends and future expectations of the business and its stakeholders. Knowing the present and future states of the business reveals a gap which needs to be closed in order to remain effective and viable in the company's chosen markets or to prepare to move into new sectors. Such analyses also cover the importance of introducing and certifying to a given management standard. If a market and customer base is moving to a future time when environmental credentials must be developed, then a leader will be able to identify what management standards could support a transformation to greater environmental control (see ISO 14001). Such an approach is a strategically justified implementation of a standard to support the longevity of the business and to help it to exploit opportunities and prosper.

The application of an international standard will help a leader to determine the answers to many of the business issues that need to be addressed in order to take full advantage of the new standard and make it a useful addition to the competitive arsenal of the firm. These questions include: where is the business now? What are the key changes needed and how do we focus the efforts of all staff to generate results that are impressive (or essential for survival)? Are we prepared and ready for change? What old routines must be broken to prevent going back to old ways of working? How can the change requirements and solutions be cascaded throughout the business? Who should be involved in and informed about change? Who should develop and lead projects and measure progress? One of the biggest advantages of using the high-level structure of a standard is that it outlines 'what good looks like' (best practice) and provides a means of visualizing how much better the performance and working environment of the business will be when the standard has been implemented. The standard shows the real enormity of the challenge to gain conformity and this gap will give an indication of the time needed to implement everything necessary to meet the needs of the requirements standard.

Leaders will also be expected to align the entire organization and its membership (including external stakeholders such as suppliers) to the new strategic needs such as deploying ISO 14001 throughout the supply chain to ensure that the business operates using the latest best practices for all the products and services that it buys. Setting internal goals and objectives for a standard as part of understanding the context of the organization and the needs of its 'interested parties' is a major and highly important set of analyses which combine to justify the implementation of key management standards.

The actual decision to implement a standard may also have resulted from numerous staff research activities and suggestions from staff; this allows the leadership to engage the workforce in a meaningful and empowering manner. As the workforce were part of the early identification of the need to use a standard it is likely that there will be less resistance to change.

The implementation of an international management standard is a period that calls upon a lot of leadership time. The early stages of implementation call for a great deal of reflection by the business leaders about the organization, its goal setting, and the frequency and quality of feedback, audits and performance indicators. These system structures and their effective design are squarely leadership responsibilities. The leadership team of a medium-sized company can expect to spend a lot of time reviewing the 'shall' clauses (or requirements) of any standard and then designing processes that achieve these 'shalls' for which the right type of evidence can be presented to auditors.

Beyond thinking about the business, leaders will also spend a significant amount of time thinking about and reflecting upon the necessary leadership styles that will be needed to promote the importance of the standard for the performance of the business. New leadership skills will be needed to reduce the diverse effects found with the old models and old ways of behaving, instead transitioning to a more proactive leadership approach whilst being mindful that this may also take time (and practice).

As the design and implementation of new policies and practices are introduced, the leadership team will also need to ensure resources and the alignment of company-wide activities so that the change programme can be optimized without causing inter-group or inter-departmental conflicts, which can arise when attempts to achieve the measures for one business department cause disadvantages for another. Significant time and mentoring of the staff engaged in the structural and process change is necessary to achieve an effective standard implementation and leaders will be called upon to support such activities.

The building of new processes that conform to a requirements standard demands good management that is supported by positive leadership. Designing new ways of working can be stressful for the worker and management teams so leaders have a responsibility to monitor progress and offer support to staff and workers who may benefit from such an investment in the relationship with their leaders.

Interventions to introduce new processes or to modify them (or even get rid of some processes) can be traumatic for staff. People are programmed to enjoy the status quo and change is uncomfortable, so progress must be monitored and staff will need to be encouraged and rewarded for their efforts. The leadership team are critical to the positive reinforcement of progress and what it means for the goals of the business.

When the basic structures, policies and processes of an international management system standard have been introduced, then the leadership team cannot rest and instead must prepare themselves to receive open and honest feedback in terms of pre-certification and other audit reports. These will be factually correct and the leadership team may be forgiven for feeling a little deflated if their expectations of achieving a good result are unrealized. The grounds for gaps will be presented by the auditor (or third-party company) and these will be logical and fact based. This feedback is typically the first independent assessment of the business and it tests the quality of solutions and processes introduced by the business to conform. Additional activities aimed at raising staff morale will be needed to urge the teams to invest more time into closing any audited gaps and build robust systems that can withstand a robust audit. It is difficult to see such internal or external third-party criticism as positive initially and, after weeks and months of hard work to achieve a system that is considered effective, to receive feedback that there remain items of non-conformity can be hard to take on board. But international management standards are founded on the twin concepts of improvement and learning, and this will be the first of many such cycles. Ironically, each cycle brings new opportunities to improve and add to the robustness of the systems and processes in place at the business. At the beginning, though, feelings can be a little raw and staff can be in denial that the systems they have introduced still need to be improved; the business leader must help to maintain the commitment of all staff to the introduction of the strategically justified and business-critical management standards.

Over time, staff will 'get' the audit system, as the business moves from nothing (no standards) to standardized processes and then further progressing on to improving processes. They will see these opportunities to gain feedback as useful and will learn how to present their systems in a clear and concise manner (and present auditors with lots of verified data, all available on demand). Senior business leaders should promote such a professional approach and recognize the efforts of all staff in making audits efficient and a genuine positive learning experience.

When standards are embedded and systems enter the surveillance and sustaining mode of implementation, the role of the senior leadership team can change to support greater coaching and new analyses to assess the organizational context can be deployed to empowered staff around them. With effective and steady systems in place, the international standard takes less time to manage and more time can be dedicated to finding staff innovations.

Inevitably, after a number of years, the standard itself will be revised by the ISO and a new standard with improvements or new additions may be issued; the business that holds an existing certification will have a number of years to transition from the old version to the new one. Such a radical change will require leadership and a significant period of learning and assessment to see how the new standard will impact on existing business operations.

At present, the high-level structure has a significant number of major clauses that demand senior leadership attention:

- The terms and definitions section of a standard will need to be studied and understood by the business leadership so that they use the right technical terms when explaining the standard and creating a narrative for all workers.
- Exploring the context of the organization is a very important leadership-based activity. In the past, the management of many international standards was the role of a lower-level manager, whereas the modern approach is to require clear leadership involvement. The new requirements of the high-level structure emphasize leadership and its mandatory engagement to drive the implementation of a standard for a business.
- Exploring the context of the organization also implies the business leaders, individually and as a group, will consider issues from internal and external stakeholders and sources of change. Consideration must be given to social, legal, political, technological, environmental, and ethical changes in the way businesses conduct their affairs. Such stakeholders will include government regulators, economic trends and data, market information and competitor analyses, banking reports, trade union reports and technology providers, which will be instrumental in shaping the decisions of the leadership team.
- The planning and support clauses represent activities that leaders will be expected to review and endorse. Allocating scarce resources, especially human resources, will often need higher leadership authorization and a significant business plan that is presented to the senior leadership team.
- The business operation clauses concern the value-adding processes and the bulk of staff in the factory; these processes use technologies, materials and the skills that support the competitive advantage of the business so will attract a significant amount of senior leadership time.
- Performance evaluation is a mandatory requirement for leadership engagement. Understanding performance and trends of organizational processes is important and allows a leader to identify performance gaps.
- The leadership team will spend a significant amount of their time working on business improvements (business leaders add value to the business by conducting and supporting business improvement teams). As such, senior leaders tend to sit on improvement committees and champion key projects.

A simple and cursory review of the high-level structure approach shows that leadership is vital in setting business direction, determining the pace and scale of change expected to deliver good business results, and having a good awareness of what conformity means. The leadership of an organization will also go through a personal learning journey which may well lead to a greater range of strategies being used and a consistent use of a management style that followers like, respect and enjoy.

The roles of the senior leadership team, and leaders at all levels including situational leaders, have a pivotal and critical impact on the implementation of a standard, as well as its ongoing management. Whilst all standards require a total approach to the organization and the engagement of all staff, the senior leaders represent the calibre of staff who can initiate change and motivate staff to achieve more than can be imagined. A good standard will unleash the power of staff and will support a 'world class' leadership team. A standard will provide the knowledge of what to do and the senior leadership team will provide the answers to why and how to enact the system using learning processes to ensure it remains a vital part of the business's solution to customer needs.

In summary

International management standards are based on good practice and are designed by experts for the ISO and commercial application. It is entirely logical that these standards will have implications for the way in which businesses should be led and managed. It must be noted that international management standards are applicable to all businesses of any size and therefore do not autocratically demand a specific way of leading; however, the modern standards do reflect the modern needs of commerce. The modern environment is one that is competitive, highly changeable and where resources are limited, hence employee skills are key to business adaptiveness and performance.

Whilst international management standards will not dictate any particular leadership model, they do have certain implications for the best practice of leadership. Standards demand that leaders have a greater appreciation of business stakeholders and operate with effective communication processes that engage all employees and interested parties (suppliers, customers, local stakeholders in the success of the business and others) that promote the business. The new leadership model also means that leaders must be aware of risks and must act accordingly to protect the business and its interactions. As such, requirements standards (and guidance standards) require a business to enact certain processes that will shape what happens for managers within the business and will set certain pressures on leaders to behave in new ways and to become role models. Being a role model means promoting and exhibiting the right behaviours for staff and stakeholders to see and engage with. There are many requirements within the high-level structure approach that have implications for the way in which leaders lead. These include:

- a greater emphasis on leading standards rather than just managing tasks or procedures;
- a strong emphasis on demonstrated learning and improvement of business processes;
- a requirement to show (through documents and other verifiable means) conformity with key processes such as business communication, the promotion of the business goals and objectives, and such like;
- a requirement to show how 'interested parties' who have a stake in the performance of the business are engaged with the business;
- requirements concerning staff competence and skills;
- greater attention to risk assessment and a holistic approach to business leadership and management;
- a demand that reviews of the auditing processes are undertaken and related back to organizational learning and improvement.

These aspects of international management standards are supporting more effective leadership and the supporting guide standards provide a wealth of advice for leaders of all types within a business. Such advice and the learning from conformity with any given standard will help leaders to make sense of the future and to harness the transformational power of organizational learning. It is highly likely that modern international management standards will improve the skills of leaders throughout an entire supply chain so that businesses have a bright and more secure future.

Open-minded leaders with a holistic view of their task of transforming the organization and its performance to be 'future ready', will inevitably use cultural inventories and analyses of readiness and competence in change management. These analyses will also include the ability of staff to identify the need for change and sustain improvements to the organization. These are fundamentals of a great business, one that can harness interoperable requirements standards to deliver outstanding performance.

Seminar topics and examination questions

The key questions concerning leadership qualities and styles that can be used to rethink or practice for examinations include:

- What are the penalties for adopting the wrong leadership style?
- How does leadership style support more effective learning processes?
- How do international standards (the high-level structure) impact upon the role of the leader in a business?

Further reading

There are many great books and textbooks concerning the subjects of leadership, organizational behaviour and change management. Many of these books cover identical subject matter so the reader is well advised to conduct searches for recently published works in these subject areas.

Notes

1 Wilkinson, A, Redman, T and Dundon, T (2016) *Contemporary Human Resource Management: Texts and cases*, Pearson Publishing, London
2 Adair, J (1973) *Action Centred Leadership*, McGraw-Hill, London
3 Leonard-Barton, D, Swap, W and Barton, G (2014) *Critical Knowledge Transfer: Tools for managing your company's deep smarts*, Harvard Business Review Press, Harvard, MA
4 Snook, S, Nohria, N and Rakesh, K (eds) (2011) *The Handbook for Teaching Leadership: Knowing, doing and being*, Sage Publications, Thousand Oaks, CA
5 Blake, R and Mouton, J (1964) *The Managerial Grid*, Gulf Publishing, Houston
6 Hershey, K H and Blanchard, P H (2013) *Management of Organizational Behavior: Leading human resources*, Prentice Hall of India

Implementation, resistance to change and sustaining change 13

Managing the business change process is important. Without the pressures of a dynamic market, organizations tend to stagnate and stop learning or changing. A dynamic market puts pressure on businesses to learn but also to translate that learning into change and improvement. In business it is often said that 'If you stand still, you will lose the competitive race' and this may be more relevant today than at any other time in industrial history. This statement implies that unless you are changing and improving you will be surpassed by your competitors. Throughout this book, the plan–do–check–act PDCA cycle has been emphasized;[1] it is the basis of continuous improvement and is a form of change that is embedded in every ISO standard. But change is not easy to conduct, so there is a need to understand the process of change for practitioners to take advantage of each implemented standard and combinations of standards in the workplace.[2]

LEARNING OBJECTIVES

At the end of this chapter, you should be able to:

- see why businesses must change and how to prepare and plan for it;
- understand the importance of continual improvement;
- understand some of the key models and approaches to change;
- identify reasons why some staff resist change;
- understand how to sustain change and relate these methods to continued improvement of ISO standards.

Innovation and change

Innovation and change are intrinsically linked. For an innovative organization, there must be some sort of change; after all, innovation is something new. To prevent organizations from becoming obsolete or falling behind competitors, change is essential, but it does not always come naturally.

So, what kinds of things effectively motivate or force an organization to change or innovate?

Well, there can be internal and external motivational factors; for example, external factors could be technological advances in the field that force an organization to embrace them or become obsolete, or customers' needs/wants/requirements may change. An internal factor could be that the organization faces technological issues when implementing processes and needs to upgrade or change in some way. It is these change triggers that result in an organization working towards innovation as a solution. One of the first attempts to describe the types of innovative businesses that exist was presented by Everett Rogers, who identified five types of organization, from innovators to laggards (and followers, who are less innovative and follow others once an innovation has happened).

Rogers' technology adoption curve

Communication expert Professor Everett Rogers promoted his ideas concerning the 'diffusion of innovators' in the 1960s, and developed a theory on how people approach innovation.[3] His model is useful in understanding how organizations will embrace a new innovation, such as a new ISO standard or revision, depending on their basic organizational traits:

1 **Innovators:**
   - these are organizations that fully embrace the innovation and are willing to take risks;
   - typically these are profitable businesses and relatively young in comparative years of trading to the other categories;
   - only 2.5 per cent of cases fall into this category.

2 **Early adopters:**
   - this group of companies adopts the innovation the second fastest;
   - they are typically also younger than the categories that follow;

- they tend to be more looked upon as industry benchmarks by the other categories;
- 13.5 per cent of cases fall into this category.

3 **Early majority:**
- this group is more conservative at adopting the innovation compared with the former categories, taking longer to embrace it than innovators and early adopters, but they are open to innovation;
- they are not typically benchmarks;
- 34 per cent of cases fall into this category.

4 **Late majority:**
- this group adopt the innovation later than the sector's average adopters;
- they are highly sceptical towards innovation;
- typically organizations in this group are led by less educated and less intelligent managers and are less profitable;
- 34 per cent of cases fall into this category.

5 **Laggards:**
- this group is the last to adopt and embrace innovation;
- they are very conservative and change averse;
- they tend to be the oldest of all the categories, with more focus on 'traditions';
- they have the least financial profitability;
- 16 per cent of cases fall into this category.

Plotting these categories of innovation adopters, we get what is known as Rogers' bell curve, as shown in Figure 13.1.

It is important to understand this in the marketplace, as change does not just affect those working in organizations; it is not always embraced by the public. Understanding consumer groups can assist an organization in calculating what point in the market they have reached and where their saturation point is.

Whilst the unbroken line (bell curve) on the graph (illustrated in Figure 13.1) represents the **innovation adopter** categories, the dashed line is the market share. If there is complete adoption of the innovation then they reach 100 per cent of the market share but it is clear here that not all will embrace or want to adopt such changes. This can be said of the workforce

Figure 13.1 Rogers' bell curve of innovation adoption[4]

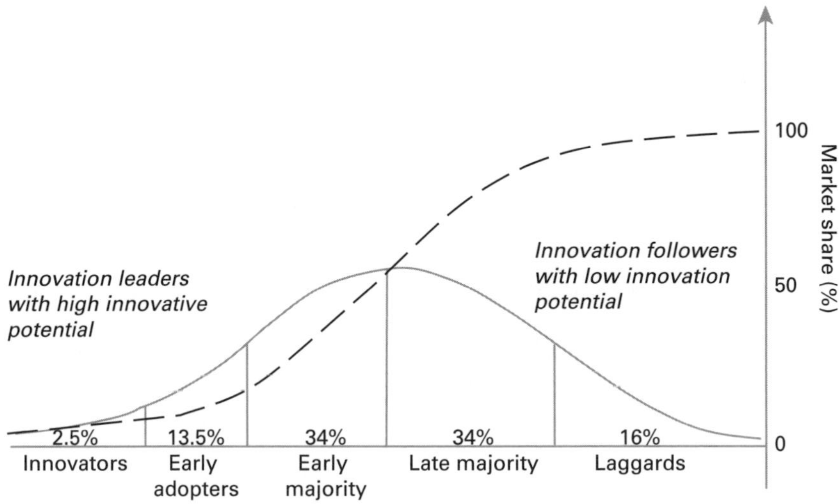

too, and so these innovation adopter categories are important to understand. That is not to say that each of us will always fit into only one category; people can move back and forth in terms of how (and if) they embrace innovation. The model is a very effective means of showing how a new ISO standard is adopted and that **early adopters** and innovators will be the first organizations to win new business by having the standard as a differentiator. Laggards will embrace ISO standards as a defensive mechanism when all other companies in the sector have it and they face conditions when customers demand the standard. Laggards are typically led by poor-quality leaders who have not detected the importance of the standard and how it can help a business.

Organizational change and transformation

It does not matter at what stage of Rogers' model a business is, it is impossible to avoid change when working with ISO standards. It is important to note that certification and surveillance audits demand evidence of change. Whilst ISO standards are applicable to all types of business, the ISO and other national bodies do not promote any specific approach to change. When organizations start to change internally to improve their operational processes and to become more efficient and productive, they typically find that they encounter resistance from staff to this change.

Figure 13.2 Typical symptoms of change programme failure

- Staff are not engaged
- Change is a fad
- We are tired of change
- Lack of communication
- We have had so many failed projects that I am apathetic to it
- Poor understanding of need for change
- The change means you need to learn a new language and words
- Change means job losses
- No business justification
- Change is negative for me!
- It doesn't feel right
- It was tried before and did not work then
- Management are not trusted
- Other companies have experienced failure of the same programme
- Change feels imposed
- Change is demanded so management can look good
- No one listened to our concerns
- Management consultants are justifying their fees by demanding that we change
- No one has told me how my job will change
- I cannot be bothered to support it
- You want to change my job but you don't know how to do my job!

An often-cited statistic – of very questionable academic evidence – is that 70 per cent of all general change programmes fail (these are change programmes that are not guided by a process of certification). There can be a number of factors that influence why change programmes fail or why resistance to change is generated, as highlighted in Figure 13.2. Most reasons for failure (behind the expressed symptoms of change failure) come from a lack of staff engagement and a lack of imperative. In short, staff do not understand why they need to change and hence resist it, as they see it as threatening and forced upon them without any way that they can engage with it.[5] After all, let's face it – most of us do not like change in whichever form it arises, as it forces us outside of our comfort zone.

Engaging staff is particularly important and a lot of attention to awareness raising and justifying a change is key to successful adaptation. Not just that – staff are innovative and will know there is a better way of managing the business and satisfying customers profitably. After all, our families and lifestyles rely on a successful business making money.

Change does not always come about as part of an improvement plan though; sometimes change is imposed on an organization due to its environment and the changes to the industry sector, or as a result of competitor strategies. Changes in conditions can sometimes be sudden but will typically be gradual, as it takes a long time to enact new regulations and laws, or to develop new technologies. An example could be predictable change, such as advances in technology that can quickly make old manufacturing systems obsolete yet could be seen coming (and hence prepared for)!

ISO standards promote and require all staff to keep up with best practices and plan for change. So, most importantly, it is how change is introduced, adopted and managed that is important for an organization. Careful planning and engagement minimize potential employee resistance. Up to this point we have been discussing change in this chapter as negative, but in reality change does not have to be such a challenge or a sudden abrupt upheaval if it is planned and adaptations deployed in a thoughtful manner that empowers and supports employees and also meets an organization's needs, objectives and targets to remain competitive and 'in the race'.

Enabling change – reducing resistance

It is easy to see why any change management plan must involve all human resources and most interested party stakeholders (even though they are external parts of the business teams). Change that is empathetic to the current culture within an organization will be more effective than disruptive approaches that disturb the values of a business. The ideal scenario would be where staff align and embrace change and contribute to the new ways of working whilst focusing on the future, seeing it as an opportunity rather than a threat or an inconvenience.

Resistance to change must not be mistaken for healthy conflict or the genuine need for more communication by staff. Constructive criticisms are fine – this is a good sign of staff learning and the genuine inquisitiveness of an engaged staff. Staff need to understand the change at hand so that they can embrace it and align themselves with it rather than resisting it. Resistance to change (Figure 13.3) and other barriers slows the ability of a business to respond to the triggers to change.

The most important two aspects of change are that a business continues to deliver high levels of added value to the customer whilst managing change in a managed and sympathetic manner which respects staff and other interested parties. Sometimes organizations will enlist external consultancy assistance to help manage the change approach and keep an objective perspective on the process. Whether 'in-house' or supported by an external consultant – the change must support the future needs of the business.

Figure 13.3 Signs of resistance to change

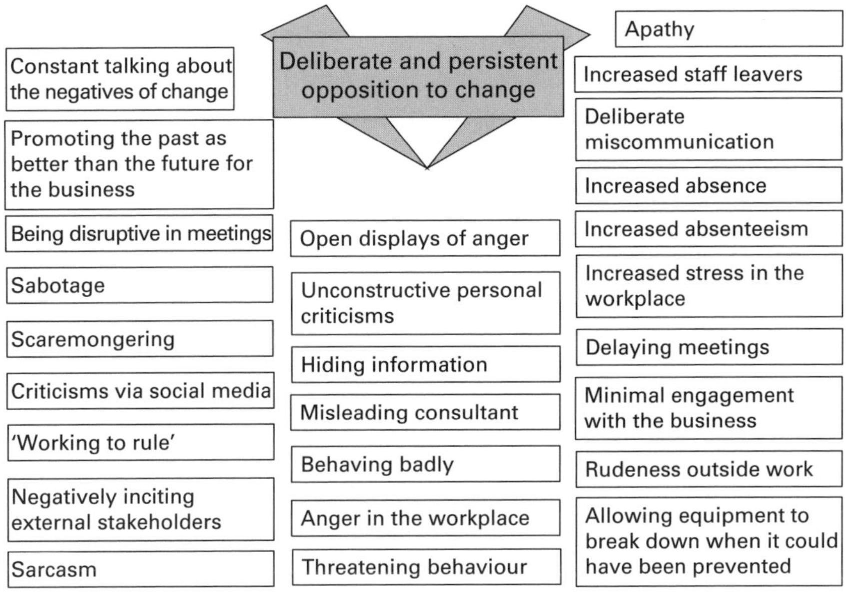

Change management models

Change management is a bespoke activity that blends the need for change with the culture that needs to be built as a future competitive capability and the behaviours of staff that reinforce the positives of enacting change in a proactive manner (not a knee-jerk reaction to changes in the context of the organization).

Lewin's approach to change

The psychologist Kurt Lewin[6] is considered to have pioneered a three-stage process change model. This fundamental approach involves the following three steps:

1. **Unfreezing the existing way of working:** changing or challenging the current status quo, which could be:
   - **a.** inertia or mindset of people within the organization;
   - **b.** current culture such as behaviour and belief systems;

   c. apprehension around learning a new skill;
   d. feeling of inadequacy or an inability to upgrade knowledge, which results in what seems to be an unwillingness to change and adapt.
2. **Changing and implementing the changes needed to improve performance or effectiveness:** implementing the changes taking due care to:
   a. ensure the changes are made at the right time;
   b. communicate, encourage and support staff.
3. **Freezing and codifying/standardizing the new way of working** (some refer to this as re-freezing): changes are further embedded and stabilized and at the same time celebrated.

During the first stage (unfreezing), communication with employees is critical. It is here that staff should be able to raise concerns and thoughts around the proposed change in a safe environment. It is the manager's role to use this platform stage to adequately and sensitively explain the reasons and approach to be harnessed around the change, to alleviate any employee anxieties, and to nurture motivation within the team for the proposed change plan. Change can be scary and initially, whilst change is in process, can feel like it is destabilizing, so this unfreezing stage is important to set the foundations for the change to ensure that the workforce is mentally prepared and therefore will be more resilient during the shift. After all, change is critical to the survival of an organization and hence of employees' jobs, and this too can be used as a motivation during this stage in the process to overcome any inertia or defensiveness towards the changes proposed.

Having set the foundations for change, an organization can move on to step two in this process, which is implementing the change. Here it is critical to keep open the lines of communication and support with staff who are impacted by the change. Some may take longer to adapt than others, requiring more time and patience to learn a new skill, for example. All this needs to be constantly and sensitively monitored and managed. Typically, fear and insecurities within the workforce can arise, leading to unfounded rumours which have to be quickly dealt with to prevent them from sabotaging the change. After all, old habits and patterns are being challenged and replaced and it is this transition period that is the most destabilizing. However, once through this stage, the final step comes into play, which is freezing. This basically means that the new mindset, skills and behaviour are now being integrated into the operational processes, but further work needs to be carried out in this third and final stage to crystallize and embed these changes.

Bridges' transition model

William Bridges[7] is a well-known change consultant who developed the Bridges' Transition Model. It consists of the following three transition stages:

1. Ending (or letting go):
   a. This stage happens when the news of change is disclosed;
   b. It is here that people can go through a range of emotions such as shock, uncertainty, fear and anger.
   c. Some may resist the change here as they are not comfortable moving out of the familiar comfort zone they have been working in.
   d. It is important that whatever people are going through in this stage, it is recognized and acknowledged in a sensitive manner to assist them in accepting the change concept.
   e. Encouragement, understanding and communication are critical here.
2. Neutral zone:
   a. For those who have gone through stage one, they often find themselves in a state of confusion, uncertainty or stress as the new ways are learned.
   b. Whilst adapting to the new processes, equipment or systems for example, in this stage staff may prefer to go back to the familiar old ways, systems, processes or technology. Productivity may be poor and so it is important to support and communicate, giving feedback and positive reinforcement.
   c. Managers must encourage staff here in order to boost their morale and alleviate anxiety or scepticism around the change.
   d. Some staff, on the other hand, may feel empowered and happy with the change/s.
3. New beginning:
   a. Here people feel energized, due to having learned new skills, for example, and being able to see the fruits of their labour.
   b. It is important that in this phase change is maintained.
   c. Success stories and celebration of good practice should be implemented here to help keep everyone on track until the change becomes the new norm.

This model puts a positive spin on change by focusing on the transition rather than the change and has similarities to the work of Lewin. Bridges' focus on transition helps empower those going through the 'transition' rather than focusing on change, which can feel like it is being imposed upon them. Transition also implies a more gradual and manageable occurrence. For each of the three transition phases, it is understood that everyone is different and hence can take more or less time to transition from one stage to another. Those who embrace the new ways move through these stages at a quicker pace than those who do not feel so comfortable for whatever reason.

Kübler-Ross's bereavement curve

Elisabeth Kübler-Ross developed what was known as 'the change curve' to better understand and explain the grieving process of terminally ill patients. It is very insightful as a means of understanding how people behave during organizational changes. Her model has five chronological emotional states for people participating in change, and has since been adapted many times, becoming widely used in the field of change in general. This model typically covers seven emotional states on the rollercoaster curve of emotions that those facing change and uncertainty go through. It highlights how these emotions can affect morale and confidence over time and, as a result, performance, in this instance in the workplace.

Change means the end of something that one is familiar with or that one takes for granted; it is, in a nutshell, 'loss', and even though this can and does happen in the workplace, it does not mean that employees do not experience the grief emotions discussed by Kübler-Ross. The reality is, any unexpected change comes as a shock to those it affects, and it is important to understand and appreciate this along with the other emotions that those in the workplace are likely to experience when assimilating such news and working through it. The emotions of fear, anxiety and thoughts of uncertainty can plague some, and how an organization implements and manages change can make such emotions worse. Being aware of these emotions is critical for organizations managing change such as the implementation of standards in the workplace. Knowing that these are normal reactions and emotions is helpful not just for managers but for those going through change. How one announces and manages change can minimize these emotional states that negatively impact on performance.

Whilst not all change is bad, Kübler-Ross's model outlines the most challenging emotional states that people find themselves going through.[8]

The list of the seven emotional states below has been modified from her original curve:

1 **Shock about the need for change:**
   a. This is when news of change comes as a surprise.
   b. This state occurs in response to the announcement or the manner in which the change is broken to individuals.
2 **Denial that there is a need for change:**
   a. People do not want to hear about the change.
   b. Individuals may try to block this out by finding evidence that it is not and cannot be true.
3 **Frustration:**
   a. This is a state where people experience anger.
   b. Here the realization of how things will be different is made.
4 **Depression:**
   a. Some find it difficult to know how to cope with this and their mood can become low.
   b. This can be as much a physical thing too, with some having low energy levels.
5 **Experiment and pilot studies:**
   a. Acceptance of the need to change has now been internalized.
   b. People start to slowly engage with the new situation they find themselves in.
6 **Decision:**
   a. A greater feeling of positivity comes here.
   b. People may start to engage proactively in developing new skills, for example, and figuring out how to work in the changed environment.
7 **Integration and embedding into customary practice:**
   a. Here changes have been integrated.
   b. People feel a new sense of satisfaction, morale and confidence that has a positive impact on their performance.

The model is very relevant to continuous improvement and large-scale organizational changes, and many management authors have promoted its utility as a means of understanding how workers see and greet changes in business practices – such as the adaptations needed to introduce and sustain an ISO standard. It is worth noting that the Lewin model fits neatly with this 'emotional states' model despite its age and simplicity. The major contribution of the Kübler-Ross model is the need to engage staff and understand that their mental states (and what they need from a supportive leadership team) will change over the duration of a transformation programme. Sometimes high levels of clarity are needed to outline the case to introduce an ISO standard, whereas other stages require coaching of staff and mentoring to nurture the correct behaviours or to explain how best to exploit a change and engage the workforce. The model adds an emotional needs dimension to the simplicity of unfreezing and refreezing a business system.

Kotter's implementation plan model

Professor John Kotter of Harvard University is a change management guru and identified an eight-step model towards change after carrying out research on organizations (Figure 13.4).[9] Kotter's work has been highly influential and many world-class and high-performing businesses have used his model or adaptations of it.

The eight steps lead an organization systematically through steps that may be time-consuming but which mitigate serious 'resistance' issues. The framework is easy for organizations to follow and each change step is prepared for before implementing the actual change process. The eight steps are:

1 **Create a sense of urgency:**

   a. The sense of urgency is needed to convince staff that change is necessary and must be undertaken!

   b. Carrying out a type of Strengths, Weaknesses, Opportunities and Threats (SWOT) analysis whereby:

      i. risks, weaknesses and any threats are identified that can harm the organization if change is not taken on board;

      ii. opportunities and strengths are also understood so that they can be harnessed and built upon.

   c. Opening communication around the issues at hand so that staff can discuss their thoughts and as a team understand the issues better and what needs to be done.

   d. Listening to customers, supply chain and other stakeholders is also important here and where necessary involving them in the change.

Figure 13.4 Kotter's eight-step model for organizations going through change

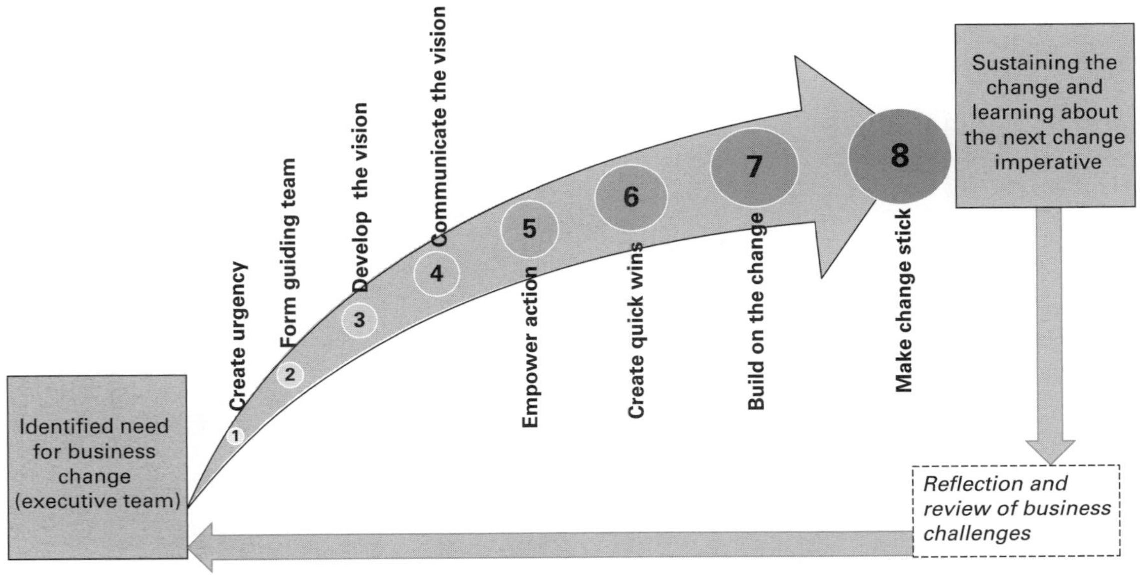

2 **Form a guiding (coalition) team:**

   a. Identify and bring together those who can assist in implementing the change and will work together and in a committed manner to get through the ups and downs of change.

   b. It is important here to bring together a diverse team that can influence the different levels, areas and functions within the organization.

3 **Develop the future business vision:**

   a. Change needs to be understood fully before implementation. After all, if those who are driving the change within the organization do not understand the vision behind it, how can they communicate it effectively to others?

   b. The change vision, values, strategies, initiatives and plan must be clearly set out and all in the guiding team must understand it before going to the next stage.

4 **Communicate the vision widely:**

   a. Here the vision for change must be communicated clearly and concisely to employees. It is these employees who become the organization change army.

   b. The vision communication must include how it links to staff activities and training.

   c. Concerns of employees should be listened to here and addressed honestly.

5 **Empower staff to take action:**

   a. Rewards can be put in place to give incentive to change.

   b. Constant monitoring should be carried out here to ensure that any resistance to change is identified and resolved.

   c. Any barriers to change must be removed so that action can be enabled.

   d. The organization must ensure that there are adequate resources in place to empower employees to make the change.

   e. The change vision must align with the organization's objectives.

6 **Create quick wins to prove that change is good and is working:**

   a. Creating quick wins for the organization helps build confidence in the change and a sense of satisfaction.

   b. Creating short-term goals makes it more manageable to achieve the long-term goal, with staff feeling less overwhelmed.

   c. Introducing target rewards here again adds not just incentive to change but also satisfaction and pride.

7 **Build on the change to improve again and roll out change across the business:**
   a. By consolidating on quick wins, an organization finds that they quickly progress towards the overall change they are trying to implement.
   b. Sharing success and good practice here is important.
   c. Focus on continuous improvement to sustain and accelerate change.

8 **Make the change stick:**
   a. Here the change that has already been implemented now needs to become a part of the culture of the organization, effectively institutionalizing it.
   b. New employees that come on board now become part of the new changes and for them it is normal; they do not know what went before and this helps it become the new norm.
   c. Celebrating and communicating the success and good practice creates pride and satisfaction and helps to maintain the change.

The model is very logical and grounded in research, but many critics have suggested staff will get fed up with a constant 'sense of urgency' for change and will often become disillusioned with constant calls for change. The model has had significant success and is a viable model for organizational change, especially to frame and convince staff that ISO standards are important and will support the future prosperity of the business. However, the change model does help to understand the stages of a successful change and is drawn from research with successful businesses. It is widely accepted by industry as a good and effective means of understanding corporate change programmes and how best to embed them as customary practices.

Hoshin Kanri, also known as policy deployment

When implementing change within an organization, it is important to engage with staff at all levels and ensure that they understand the strategic direction of the organization and are aligned with it. Sometimes staff misalign with a change initiative, leading to lower performance and even excess costs, without a performance improvement at all. However, when all employees are aligned, high performance results. So how can this be achieved? Well, many Japanese 'world class' businesses and others around the world have applied the principles of TQM to planning and change. This process is known as **Hoshin Kanri**, which translates as 'compass-setting management' and is a reference to a navigational compass that shows the way in which the business is headed. It relies on 100 per cent staff engagement. Hoshin means 'direction' (or shiny compass needle) and Kanri translates to 'administration' (or execution through 'control logic') and the combination of the two is all about ensuring that an organization's strategy and objectives are carried out in the operational processes in such a way that everyone is pulling in the same direction to produce outputs.

Policy deployment (as it is more popularly known) uses the same basic principles of the ISO and uses Deming's PDCA cycle but for setting business goals. The alignment of staff on a common business direction of change means that the future needs of the business become the very reason why improvement and changes are needed. Imagine that! Everyone in the organization is working towards a common goal and everyone is involved with projects that will help the business get there. So, everyone has an important change project to conduct to protect the livelihoods of everyone! Policy deployment is a systems approach to change that is facilitated using a step-by-step planning process that focuses on the vital few projects that will make the business better as well as supporting other forms of continuous improvement.

The seven steps of the policy deployment process are:

- **Step 1:** Establish the organization's strategic vision and its long-term plan for the next five years:
  - This stage is conducted by the top management of a business three months before the annual budgeting cycle begins.
  - Here the current status of the business and its policies, procedures and gaps in performance are shown.
  - Evaluate where the market for the business will be in the next five years. Compare with the vision, goals, and targets of the business and the performance levels expected in the next five years (what the business must achieve to survive).
  - Communicate the five-year vision and express the difference between now and the performance requirements as a challenge to the business management team:
    - to improve quality performance levels by reducing defects by 50 per cent;

  - to reduce the current order to shipment time by 30 per cent;
  - to reduce the costs of production by 10 per cent from this year's performance level.

- **Step 2:** Develop breakthrough objectives through strategic planning:
  - This action is conducted by top management.
  - This process is to refine and test the objective challenges for the business within a three- to five-year planning period (so breaking the five-year objective into an annual objective, a year two objective, etc).
- **Step 3:** Define and develop annual objectives:
  - These objectives allow an organization to move to a focus on the next year of business – such as a 10 per cent reduction in quality defects, a 10 per cent reduction in order fulfilment time and a 2 per cent reduction in costs.
- **Step 4:** Cascade the annual objectives and goals to different parts of the organization:
  - Here objectives are shared amongst relevant departments/teams from the top management to the middle management.
  - The annual challenge targets are shared widely and discussed by top and middle management to gain clarity and ensure the objectives/goals are relevant and improvements are prioritized against top-level priorities.
  - As the objectives are shared from top management down the management structure, they become more and more focused and detailed (hence the processes that go into achieving the priorities).
  - Middle managers must agree on what key projects (the vital few) will be started to radically improve business performance and achieve the targets of the challenge set by top management. In this broad process of discussion, some conflicts may arise when a project could disadvantage a department. These conflicts are reported upwards to top management to resolve. An example could be to use suppliers from a cheaper country, but the operations and quality departments may raise concerns that this will cause problems. This matter would be reported to top management, who will rule over the decision and may rule out buying from such sources. This stage encourages a back-and-forth approach to the system that is known as 'catch ball', whereby the managers refine change projects without compromising on achieving the outcomes expected by the top management.

- Upon agreement of the key projects, this step makes use of the Hoshin planning matrix, known as the x-matrix (see Figure 13.5), onto which any selected project is written. At this point it is recognized as a legitimate project and must be resourced and the management processes put in place.

- **Step 5:** Implement the plan:
  - At this stage – timed at the beginning of the new financial year so that monies can be put aside for these important projects – the projects are executed and improvements (change) carried out. The groups meet frequently and report their process to the whole middle management group, typically every month.
- **Step 6:** Regular reviews carried out:
  - This typically is monthly and is used to assess if the plan being implemented is on target or if corrective actions need to be carried out to keep it on track to deliver its results.
- **Step 7:** Annual (or half-yearly) review carried out:
  - This is a more detailed review than that in the previous step and is conducted by top management.
  - Once again, this review allows an organization to adjust to the system and react at the point in the year before the top management conduct the next cycle of the process and look forward another five years.

For the purpose of clarity, the x-matrix is a one-page document that is typically utilized in lean management (see Chapter 5). The matrix helps to ensure that the organization's strategic initiatives (which are at the centre of the matrix) align with the long-term needs of the organization. It is a methodical tool that uses a five-pronged approach for identifying the activities that are critical to the organization, and effectively maps what is needed to improve. The four quadrants at the centre of the matrix are the four compass points outlined in the first four points below, along with the fifth point referring to the right-hand side of the matrix:

1. **South** represents the **long-term goals** or breakthrough objectives (3–5 years), shown as step 1.
2. **West** represents the annual objectives (**mid-term goals**) and how far an organization is aiming to improve/change, shown as step 2.
3. **North** represents the top-level improvement priorities and what processes are needed to achieve them. This is effectively a to-do list on what needs to be carried out in the **short term,** shown as step 3.

Figure 13.5 X-matrix used in Hoshin Kanri (policy deployment)

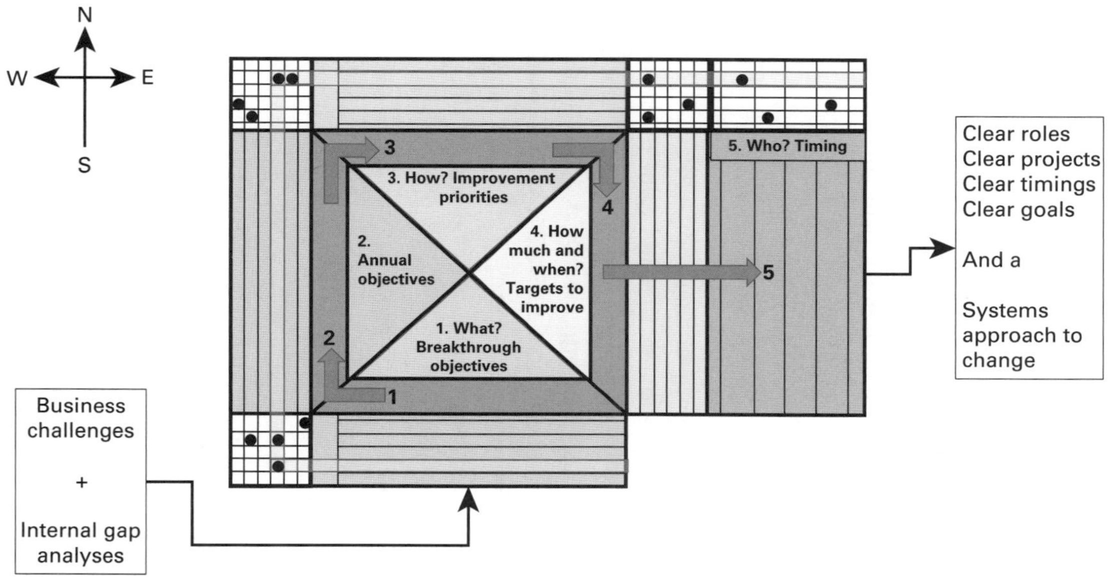

4 **East** represents the targets (or key performance indicators (KPIs)) and how much is needed to make these improvements and when. It is at this point that the plans are typically shared with stakeholders for feedback and hopefully agreement. Shown as step 4.

5 This element of the matrix shows when the project will start and stop as well as who is part of the team (and the leader of the team).

Having mapped out these four steps, the corners of the matrix are typically coded (using dots) to assist the users' quick and easy visualization of what the dependencies (as shown with the dotted line in Figure 13.5) are between the actions that are mapped. Those responsible for implementing and carrying out this change/improvement plan are recorded in the fifth section under resources. The most important information in each section is prioritized by recording it closest to the centre.

For a deeper discussion of the policy deployment process, refer to Akao (1991)[10] or Casey (2011).[11]

The policy deployment planning approach assists organizations in identifying and deploying resources that add value to the operational processes. This involves senior management, middle management and implementation teams to continuously feed into the PDCA cycle[12] so that there is open and transparent communication of relevant data/information to continuously improve and effectively communicate. This whole approach to change helps minimize risk from lack of growth, enabling an organization to be more agile, with an approach that identifies opportunities and risks and uses this to continuously improve. The process is conducted annually and has many features superior to the traditional practice of Management by Objectives (which is applied to individuals in departments rather than the full population of managers). Harnessing the creative potential of the entire management population is very important and serves to promote consensus and mutual agreement about what needs to be changed within a business. By having a significant input from the senior management team in determining the business in its future predicted competitive context, the policy deployment approach is 'future focused' and challenges managers and workers to enact improvements before they are needed (and to prepare the organization for its future predicted competitive environment). The use of a system-wide PDCA model built into the logic and practice of policy deployment means it is fully compatible with the ISO approach to standards. It can be no surprise that this approach is widely used by world-class and high-performing businesses. It also helps a business to remain at the innovation and early-adopting stages of the Rogers innovation model. Furthermore, by deploying the implementation of change to those who actually do the job, the sustainability of improvements is also enhanced. The policy deployment approach is therefore a very powerful, if under-used tool for linking the strategic importance of improving a business to meet the demands of a future expected market with the engagement of all workers in meaningful improvements to take the business to this next stage of competitiveness by building the capabilities now to be able to compete in the future.

Sustaining change

Change has been portrayed in management literature as uncomfortable and fraught with worker resistance. These difficulties can be overcome when there is a need for change coupled with a structured methodology that can be used to guide employees. Change does not have to be uncomfortable even in a fast-moving world. The modern, dynamic world means that staff should be more engaged with change and integrated with the business and its future. Voicing concerns, apprehensions, anxieties and fears should be 'normal' and greeted with encouragement and praise/recognition for efforts and achievements. The need for urgency of change must be clearly communicated but can only be executed by competent staff who are trained and always engaged in some form of change process.

Ongoing monitoring and reporting of results helps ensure that an organization stays on track. It can be no surprise that ISO standards assist with this process and provide a structure to evaluate gaps in performance, including, amongst others:

- the mandatory elements of reviewing 'the context' of the organization;
- the requirement 'shalls' associated with performance measurement;
- feedback from third-party audits;
- feedback from internal audits;
- the elements of ISO standards that require reflection and to seek out 'best practice'.

The US change management organization Prosci conducted research over 14 years with 900 organizations located in 59 countries, and developed five key steps to help employees support a change strategy.[13] The model they developed was termed the ADKAR model (Figure 13.6).[14] The model puts people first in the change process and involves the following steps:

1 Awareness:
   a. Employees must be aware of the need for change.
   b. This must be communicated effectively by managers.
2 Desire:
   a. Employees must have the desire to make the change happen.
   b. Including employees (and stakeholders) in the change vision helps bring everyone on board and gives an opportunity for all to contribute and feel a part of the process.
3 Knowledge:
   a. Employees must be given the knowledge about how to change.
   b. Here new skills development/training is carried out.
4 Ability:
   a. Employees must have the ability to implement new skills.
   b. Employees must have the right behaviour to change.
5 Reinforcement:
   a. Reinforcement by managers and the system must be carried out here to ensure that change is sustained.
   b. Rewards are helpful here as well as the sharing of success stories to embed change and make it stick.

Figure 13.6 The logic of the ADKAR model

Again, ISO standards support the ADKAR model in that they promote employee engagement, widespread communication of change requirements, and extensive training in the skills needed for the current business and also for the future needs of the business. The heavy reliance of ISO standards on improvement and responses to non-conformances found during auditing means that ISO standards and the ADKAR approach are also well suited.

The ADKAR model provides an overview of individual and group learning so as to enact sustainable change. The model shares some characteristics with the Kotter and policy deployment process approaches. Again, the need to demonstrate an alignment of skills to ensure workers are competent to compete in the future is an important feature of this model. This model therefore answers the critical question that workers have, which is, 'What is in this for me?' When the answer to that question is 'nothing', then workers will often find ways to resist a change, whereas if the investments in the workers are seen to help them to better take part in strategic business change, to 'own' the change process and also to become more valuable through greater skills training, then resistance is often low, which means the organization can become more adaptive.

In summary

Modern businesses do not enjoy a competitive advantage simply from their products or their technology, because these can be copied and technical knowledge can be acquired. What differentiates a great business is the leadership and teams (or people) within it. Humans drive innovation and champion change. If they are well integrated into the design and operational business processes, staff will have faith in top management, leading to change becoming customary practice, with staff embracing and helping to drive the change rather than moaning about it when it occurs.

It is important to remember that change brings opportunities if the right mindset is harnessed by staff. It is imperative that there is a good rapport between management and staff, otherwise change will harbour fear. After all, employees are an 'interested party' and that is why international standards promote an approach to change that is based on collaboration and mutual respect.

Effective, sustainable and high-performance organizations know that they can never invest enough time in applying the skills of the workforce to improvement and change opportunities. ISO standards support the identification of such opportunities in all manner of forms, from health and safety (ISO 45001) and quality (ISO 9001) to environmental improvements (ISO 14001) and standards that protect the business and ensure customers are never let down (ISO 22301).

This chapter has presented some of the modern approaches to change management to help make sense of change, why staff may resist, and what mechanisms can be employed to guide and systematically deploy resources to ensure change is effective. None of the models reviewed are offered as a panacea or the only way to conceptualize change, but they are useful; they are also process approaches to change that require the engagement of and significant communication with the workforce. As with all major investments, the best change model is one that fits the organization, is sensitive to the cultural way of 'doing things around here', and is inclusive for all staff to take part and work on projects that are of strategic importance to the future of a business.

Seminar topics and examination questions

Here are a few questions that may help provoke some thoughts:

- Will the process of the 'control of documents' contained within most standards just end up slowing all change programmes?
- Can resistance to change be pre-empted?
- How can external 'interested parties' contribute to more effective change management?
- Do empowered workers replace the need for good business leaders?
- Is there any such thing as a universal model of effective change management?

Further reading

The topic of organizational change is saturated with bestselling books. Lewin's work is seductively attractive but is better as a description of continuous improvement and how to make changes in daily operations. It is clearly linked to continuous improvement and the work of Masaaki Imai.[15]

Kotter's model has dominated most business approaches until recently, when many companies switched to the policy deployment approach.

Here are some other good books and resources for you to consider:

Bechtel, M (1995) *The Management Compass: Steering the corporation using Hoshin planning*, AMA Management Briefing

Bleistein, S (2017) *Rapid Organizational Change*, John Wiley and Sons, USA

Franz, J and Liker, J (2011) *The Toyota Way to Continuous Improvement: Linking strategy to operational excellence to achieve superior performance*, McGraw-Hill Education

Liker, J and Meier, D (2007) *Toyota Talent: Developing your people the Toyota way*, McGraw-Hill Education

Lundin, S, Paul, H and Christensen, J (2002) *Fish! A remarkable way to boost morale and improve results*, Hodder Paperbacks

Spencer, J (1999) *Who Moved my Cheese? An amazing way to deal with change in your work and in your life*, Vermilion Press

Notes

1 Bicheno, J and Catherwood, P (2005) *Six Sigma and the Quality Toolbox: For service and manufacturing*, Picsie Books, Buckingham, UK

2 Smith, R et al (2014) *The Effective Change Managers Handbook: Essential guidance on change management body of knowledge*, Kogan Page, London

3 Rogers, E M (2003) *Diffusion of Innovations*, Free Press, New York

4 Ibid

5 Maurer, R (2010) *Beyond the Wall of Resistance: Why 70% of all changes still fail – and what you can do about it*, 2nd ed, Bard Press

6 Lewin, K (1951) *Field Theory in Social Science: Selected theoretical papers* (ed D Cartwright), Harper & Row, New York

7 Bridges, W (2000) *The Character of Organizations: Using personality type in organization development*, Davies-Black Publishing

8 Cameron, E and Green, M (2004) *Making Sense of Change Management: A complete guide to the models, tools and techniques of organizational change*, Kogan Page, New York

9 Kotter, J (1996) *Leading Change*, Harvard Business Publishing

10 Akao, Y (1991) *Policy Deployment for Successful TQM*, Taylor and Francis, New York

11 Casey, D (2011) *X Matrix: Strategy deployment and execution process for breakthrough business performance*, Lulu Publishing

12 McCarthy, D and Rich, N (2004) *Lean TPM: A blue print for change*, Butterworth-Heineman, London

13 Prosci (2018) *Best Practices in Change Management*, 10th ed, Prosci Learning Center, Loveland, CO

14 Hiatt, J (2006) *How to Implement Successful Change in our Personal Lives and Professional Careers*, Prosci learning Center, Loveland, CO

15 Imai, M (2012*) Gemba Kaizen: A common sense approach to a continuous improvement strategy*, 2nd ed, McGraw-Hill Education

Conclusions and looking forwards 14

We began this book by stating that every ISO standards implementation is a learning journey for a business that, when implemented effectively and in conformance, builds levels of new competence with each standard that is embedded into customary business practice as well as generating significant benefits. The ability to operate multiple standards and gain benefits from inter-operability is huge. The modern international standards are far from being the 'bureaucratic monsters' that early standards were depicted to be and deforestation to produce vast quantities of paper-based documents is no longer needed. Modern standards are sympathetic to the needs of the modern business and now offer greater value and utility for all interested parties.

It is, therefore, a great surprise that international standards are rarely taught at technical colleges and on university degrees. Every student leaving a school or any person entering a business must be able to work within standards. Awareness of such standards is mandatory if the new employee is to contribute effectively to the business. This book was designed to raise awareness and allow managers to select the most appropriate combination of standards to suit their businesses, and for students to get involved with standards before they join industry and commerce. To be an effective manager, now or after graduation, depends upon a knowledge of standards and the precision of working to the latest documented best practice.

Standards are revised every five to ten years and then are updated (with a period of transition from the old standard to the new of around three years) so standards evolve to remain relevant to modern business. So, if an international standard provides the skeleton and architecture for processes within a business, it is important that businesses exploit them to their fullest[1].

Again it is no surprise that most 'world class' businesses are certified to ISO and sector-specific standards (such as TS 16949 – the automotive sector standard for quality management systems).

The effectiveness of management standards for business

International standards, when effectively implemented, enhance value in the following ways.

Increased value: future roles and responsibilities

There are some distinct implications for businesses and competition in the future. The standards we have reviewed (the most popular combination of standards) imply:

- new value in the 'top management' role;
- new value in the role of middle managers;
- new value in the role of teams and team leaders;
- new collaborations with 'interested parties'.

The value of a senior manager comes from their ability to set direction and conduct a strategy. These members of an organization are leaders and employees look to them to set the priorities and culture of the organization. Senior managers therefore think about where the business is heading and where it needs to be in the future. So the value of senior managers means they must not get too embroiled in the daily running of the business other than coaching and mentoring lower levels of management and team leaders.

ISO standards demand that top management undertake significant new responsibilities as business leaders charged with thinking about the organization in its context and where the business needs to go to meet competitive, regulatory and other forces that impact on the business and its ability to make a profit. Prior to the new generation (Annex SL) standards, it was possible for top management to abdicate their responsibilities and make a single business manager the owner of a standard, but the top management must present themselves as credible leaders who play a key role in standards implementation and post-certification.

The value of middle managers (often called departmental managers) comes from their ability to know what best practice is and how to change business systems. These managers must collaborate to optimize customer service, and are the best system architects for the overall management of an international standard. They determine how fast a business will change to become aligned and achieve its strategic goals.

ISO standards rely heavily on middle management engagement – these managers set the processes to meet the clauses of a standard and ensure conformance with the documented procedures. They are equally important members of staff and are a source of competitive advantage when they work as a team.

The introduction of ISO standards also creates a new value from the teams and team leaders of a business. This level of the organization has the highest number of staff and therefore the greatest number of potential contributors to innovation, process improvements and, of course, high-performance customer service. Teams deliver goods and control the daily operations of the business. When operational staff are trained, competent and motivated, the positive business culture becomes infectious and teams can achieve more by innovating and owning their part of the production process. These staff are as important as the middle managers and senior managers – they are also instrumental to delivering the profits that the business will need to manage its cash flow and survive. So, in summary, modern standards have reassigned the roles of employees and allow them to directly add value and contribute to the success of an organization. The combination of great staff and effectively implemented international standards is a powerful one, especially when the organizational culture promotes collaboration for success, innovation, and respect for each other.

Increased value: ISO at the heart of the organization

Having an ISO standard, and the 'shalls' that an organization must deliver in order to be certified, provides a means of engaging with the different levels of staff as it forms a structure that supports and harnesses innovation. Furthermore, if a business believes that its suppliers should be partners and organizations should work together, then using common standards means that internal staff could be deployed to suppliers and customers to help them develop. Such deployments are good for business – when staff work with suppliers it helps the supplier to access expert knowledge and aligns the supplier with your needs. Developing customers is also a positive activity and no customer can ever know too much about a supplier in order to help them. Also, customers who enjoy working with suppliers are more likely to favour them and:

- provide valuable information about the strategic direction of the customer and its markets;
- support the supplier and therefore reduce the possibility that a competitor will win business with the customers;

- help the supplier to lower its costs;
- possibly open new opportunities to the supplier in terms of engagement with the product design process or encouraging the supplier to do more for the customer and even create new products.

Customers and suppliers are only two parts of a full ecosystem of interested parties. ISO standards offer a means of engaging with the knowledge of the local community, investment communities, regulators and such like. The new relationships and promoting the organization to think more broadly about business are important. The future has fewer opportunities for mega businesses selling a simple product – the future will probably indicate:

- small businesses are critical to most economies;
- there is less scope for mass production of goods and instead products will be made in the smallest possible batch size;
- businesses will look to add more value (differentiate rather than cost-lead) and will create more complicated products that may be more bespoke;
- customers will want to do business with 'the right type of supplier';
- the digital economy will become more important;
- securing and retaining the best staff will be a premium for businesses;
- workplaces may change from large factory buildings to much smaller or shared facilities;
- the time from product concept to actual prototype will collapse;
- networks of companies will be formed that will work together (locally and internationally) and will compete as a group;
- innovation will be a highly prized competitive weapon and such innovations will come from staff and new relationships with other organizations (such as universities, machine providers and such like).

The competitive world of the 2020s is far removed from the early days of industrial manufacturing when the Model T Ford of the early 1900s had few options (no options in the colour of the vehicle). Most vehicles in production will have changes made to them every six months, that is mainly from the suppliers to the vehicle assemblers (over 80 per cent of the final vehicle is supplied to the assembler). The automotive supply chain is no different to those of aerospace, fashion garments, food production, construction and many others. These supply chains perform because processes are controlled, standardized and improved on a daily, weekly, monthly and yearly cycle. At the heart of the delivery of existing products and design of new ones are well-managed and effective processes that conform to ISO standards. So ISO standards will have more meaning and utility in the future than they already do today. And ISO standards apply to all organizations regardless of size, location, sector, age, and production technology employed. Standards are so much more than a document – they are the blueprint for businesses to be or become successful.

Value from design

ISO management standards clearly rely on an effective product design process (especially ISO 14001) and compressing the time from concept to prototype then onto actual production will be key to successful competition in the future. Businesses that cannot design their own products will never be able to remove costs and wastes from the actual product design. Getting deeper into the design process by building an internal competence of working closely with a designer will become important and will unlock new opportunities. The ability to design products (and services) with anyone across the world has many implications and opportunities. ISO certification helps to identify the right type of supplier to work with and also – for internal design departments – has the management clauses that support a seamless integration of the design process with the production system. The ISO management clauses structure all information going into, and archived from, the design process, it standardizes documentation, and has the same improvement potential for design processes as it does for manufactured products. So, ISO-certified design processes will be critically important in the future too.

Value from diversification

Manufacturers today rarely earn a living from just selling products; today a product usually has a service bundle wrapped around it. You may purchase a car using a lease agreement, or a manufacturing company may rent you the chairs they make for your offices and take them back after a number of years. The engines on an aircraft may also be rented. This means a manufacturer must produce the best products and not sell them but rent them to customers, resulting in a monthly return of revenue to the manufacturer to pay the bills. The new service of leasing and maintaining products is a lucrative revenue stream and a manufacturing business must learn how to be a combined manufacturing and service business. ISO management standards can aid this transition and Annex SL allows a business to interpret what is needed to add such services in a systematic and effective manner. With over 22,000 standards in the world, the number of new standards being created will diminish as the years progress because most management systems will have been addressed by a standard. Also 'best practices' for each existing standard are unlikely to change radically for the majority of standards so organizations will be able to spend time optimizing their business processes (and conformance).

The value of multiple standards

The world's most popular standard is ISO 9001 quality management system requirements and Annex SL has created a means of writing standards that are interoperable, so the future is likely to see much easier implementation and management of certified standards. Many ISO 9001-certified businesses have, voluntarily and for business reasons, combined the standard with ISO 14001 environmental management systems and now these two standards require less effort to co-exist. Furthermore, interest in ISO 45001 occupational health and safety creates a trilogy of standards that engage staff, help them to be safe and help the business to deliver for its stakeholders, customers and the planet. These standards could be regarded as delivering successes. The future is likely to see new standards that protect successes and these include information security and business continuity. These five core standards have all the necessary management best practices to build high-performance and highly resilient systems and organizations. Such a combination of standards is a positive move and will be greeted well by many interested parties who benefit from the long-term success of the organization. With this robust jigsaw of safety, quality, environmental quality and resilient standards, any business is well equipped to exploit new business opportunities and use the 'sand cone' model to perfect its product offerings and customer service. Such perfection is necessary to make the best use of cash flow and profitability.

A sand cone of standards?

The 'sand cone' model was explored in Chapter 1 of this book. It presented a layered approach to mastering key business processes which enhance business performance. The model commenced with an attention to the safety of the workforce and then moved through quality and others until a business had mastered all the necessary competitive capabilities to survive in a dynamic and competitive market place. We can return to that model now and link the competitive capabilities with ISO standards. The latter is exactly what world-class businesses have undertaken and deployed to their supply chains. The keys to competitive success and the rate of learning within a business may well derive from the use of international management standards within a culture that is essentially total quality management in nature.

The model commences (the foundation) with the discipline of creating and sustaining a safe and healthy workplace for staff so that they attend work and engage with the company's improvement processes. The discipline of ISO 45001 implementation and conformity is a means of conditioning all staff (leaders and operational) to Annex SL and the many benefits of a systems approach, standardized processes and continuous improvement. It also answers a very basic question, 'what has my employer ever done for me?', with the answer that it has '...created a safe workplace and a good place to work within which you are valued and respected.' From here, the quality layer changes the focus of staff by adding the tools to improve operational processes so they are safe and of good quality.

Naturally, 'waste' in processes will reduce and the operational performance of the business will improve (including the delivery of quality products) allowing both a lean approach and Six Sigma methods to be introduced. From this point, the business can assure its environmental sustainability credentials, processes and the next generation of cost savings. Throughout each

Figure 14.1 The modern 'sand cone' of standards

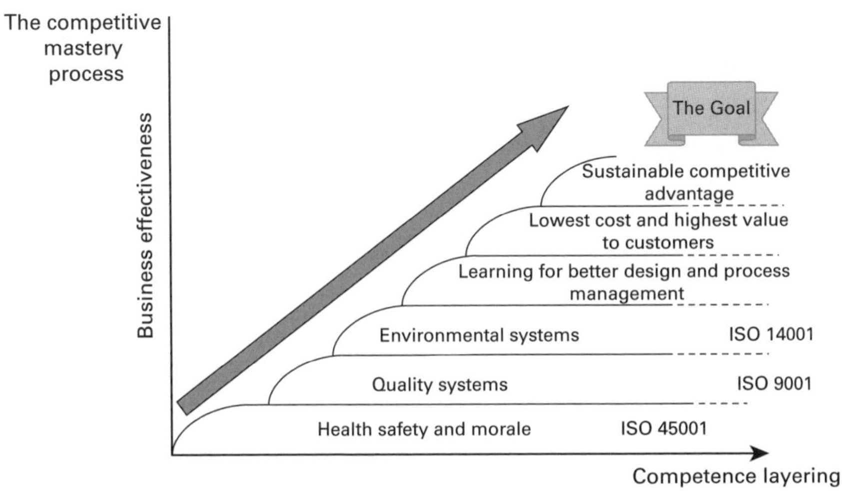

layer of the competence model, designers of products and engineering layouts have a major role to play to support the business. Few improvement activities are as important as designing the workplace layout for greater ergonomic comfort, redesigning a product to make it easier to make, product designs that use less material and have less depletion of natural resources yet still offer the same functionality, or products which feature sustainable materials. The combination of great designs of products that are delivered without delay is a capability that will service any business well – now and in the future.

We started this book by emphasizing that business must make a profit and must search for operational excellence in order to adapt and survive in the modern competitive marketplace. Effective management of cash flow is also at the heart of a high-performing business. These book chapters have also explored the role of certain ISO standards in establishing a safe, quality-assured, environmentally friendly and secure working environment. This book has also highlighted the critical role of the design department within any manufacturing business. Great people working in a great environment to improve reliable processes is key to ensuring all workers are engaged to support the future of their employer and can do this through the use of (but not necessarily certification to) ISO standards. Without standards, the world would be chaotic and confusion would reign in terms of determining which businesses have good management systems and which do not. Those that do not pose a substantial risk to any supply chain and a failure of such a supplier to deliver is likely to delay or stop an entire supply chain of companies. International standards add value to a business and therefore require an engaged leadership team that play their part by championing the use of standards and ensuring all workers participate in standardization and improvement of business tasks and processes. ISO standards represent the latest knowledge of good practice in a given subject area and the content of all standards is invaluable when seeking to use a given standard to help improve the competence and competitive capabilities of any organization.

Final words

This closing chapter explains how ISO standards are necessary weapons for any modern manufacturer. They are more than just a list of requirements – standards are a blueprint for organizational success. That success relies on good leadership and engaged staff, thinking about the business and how to position within a clear set of business-justified objectives and goals. It relies on standardized processes that allow workers to deliver the best products they can and to use reactive and proactive improvement to ensure the business performs better tomorrow than it does today. Also, a business that is humble and believes it can get better will listen to feedback and will demand the harshest of audits so it can learn more about how and where to improve its systems. Such an approach relies heavily on all staff enacting the PDCA cycle – top management, middle management, team leaders and their teams. If the modern environment is a competition where only the fittest will survive, then ISO management standards will go a long way to ensuring that survival by building the necessary organizational capabilities to learn, change, improve and adapt to new markets, regulatory and general trading conditions.

Good luck on your journey!

Note

1 Heras-Saizarbitoria, I (ed) (2018) *ISO 9001, ISO 14001, and New Management Standards*, Springer International Publishing

APPENDIX
Further help for professional and university students

Student life can be very hard and stressful. This is such a pity as these years should be some of the happiest of your life. Lectures concerning international standards, quality, design, operations management, supply chain management and others are highly relevant to professional careers and are learning opportunities that can (if embraced) set the student up for the rest of their working lives (in big companies, other employment or self-employment). As such we have added this small section for the modern student to make the most of their education experience.

Making the most of this book

This book presents a lot of summarized information and that is why there are signposts to further reading. There are some really great websites and also YouTube channels that deal specifically with international management standards, implementing standards, specific standards, interviews with technical committee members and such like. These are well worth returning to periodically as they have many golden nuggets of information that will help you learn and revise. Many have case studies too, which help bring this subject to life, such as the application of standards or what it is like to be an auditor.

Lectures

You should always take notes in your lectures because the human brain is not that good at recalling what happened in the early weeks of a course. To get the most from a lecture you should think about its theme and what questions the lecturer is answering when they give the lecture. Identifying what the lecturer is trying to convey in the forms of key questions is insightful and will help you to revise effectively and think strategically about topics and potential exam questions. For example, a lecture on ISO 9001 is presented using the theme of Quality Management Standards (QMS). The lecturer is likely to answer the questions:

- What is the ISO?
- What is a Quality Management System?
- What is ISO 9001 and its history?
- What are the features of ISO 9001 and the high-level structure?
- What are the benefits of having ISO 9001?
- How do companies implement ISO 9001?
- Who are the critics of the standard?
- How does ISO 9001 help implement the sand cone model?
- How does ISO 9001 help the modern business?

These types of questions (ie the what, why, how, who, etc) are best presented in a mind map for each topic. We find that those students who take the time and thought to use such an approach find that it is a great way of summarizing information for use later.

Seminars

Seminars, which can also be called tutorials, are used to expand upon lecture topics and these should NEVER be missed. There will be a lot of seminars that have case studies and remembering the case will help you when revising because you will remember what the case did and how they did it. Seminars are also a great environment for class discussion and exploring the subject area and you will find that it is your chance to actually interact with the lecture content in a meaningful way. Seminars bring the lectures to life. You should always prepare for a lecture and engage during the seminar and be disciplined to write up a small page of notes at the end. These notes could again be structured using a mind map and you will find they are easy to capture if done straight after the seminar when the content and discussion is fresh in your memory. You will also find that if you do your best to interact and engage in seminars (and where appropriate in lectures), then content becomes easier to remember and you will be become more confident with it.

How to write an essay

Even students that have done many years of studying can make simple mistakes that cost points by not being effective at writing essays. There are many books that help students do this, such as: *Essay Writing Skills* by Jacqueline Connelly and Patrick Forsyth (Kogan Page, 2012); Peter Redman and Wendy Maples' (2017) book entitled *Good Essay Writing (Student Success) 5th Edition* (Sage, 2017); or Janet Godwin's *Planning Your Essay (Pocket Guide) 2nd Edition* (Palgrave Macmillan, 2014). It would be wise to at least try to get the gist of the key points to help you maximize your marks. The key is to always read and re-read the question and spend time planning your essay before launching straight into it. That way you will stay on track and not go off on a tangent discussing things that are interesting but not relevant to the question.

Model answers

Students often forget that the quality assurance process for most universities and colleges includes the use of an external examiner. An external examiner is a member of staff employed at another university or college who is an expert in the subject area. The role of the external examiner is to ensure the course is a good one and covers the subject materials that would be expected as well as being of a standard that would make them equivalent to any other university or college (at that particular level). They will also see many of the submitted essays and the examination scripts to make sure they are marked fairly and in line with standards operated by all other universities.

The external examiner will also (well before the students are given the essays or the examination scripts) have seen the essay and exam questions together with model answers that are prepared and submitted by the lecturer. A model answer contains all the definitions, arguments, and analysis of a perfect answer to any question that has been set. Students need to think on this. What would be in the model answer of any question from any lecture or associated seminar? To help narrow down the questions you may like to develop your model answer and it might well be worth thinking about the 80/20 rule. The 80/20 rule states that – in general – of the 100 per cent of different questions that could be asked about a subject, about 20 per cent of those questions will appear around 80 per cent of the time. Hence looking at past exam papers is a worthwhile activity too. If you want to try this out then get a piece of paper and allow yourself five minutes to write down all the possible questions that could be asked on the subject of ISO standards development (for example). After five minutes combine ones that are essentially the same question.

Next you could look for questions that appear more often than others and see how a model answer would be structured. If you keep writing model answers for every question you will begin to notice patterns and start to see how similar some of the responses to certain types of questions are. This will help you write better essays and better examination answers.

The key aim of an essay or examination plan is to maximize the marks you will be given and that means providing a written model answer! Again, practice makes perfect.

Revision

Revision is an important process. Sadly many students will try to memorize everything they can or take a question they think is coming up and repeat and repeat and repeat it. When it doesn't actually come up, this strategy is not that good or effective. To know the subject in a better way is actually what is needed rather than placing all your eggs in one basket (too risky). Therefore you will find, if you want to be successful on an international standards course/module:

- **Mind maps** from lectures/seminars will be very useful and will help you recall key points.
- **Past papers** are useful to start getting you into the right frame of mind for an exam and to familiarize yourself with how questions may be phrased. You will need to think about drawing a mind map for the question or putting together an essay plan.
- **Revision cards** that have mock questions on them are useful and can be a lot of fun too.
- **Revision in teams** – remember you are competing against yourself – can also be fun and will stretch you to answer questions that others come up with. You will also find that discussing questions/topics in groups will help you formulate ideas into coherent language that you can use in exams/assignments and which can assist you in a deeper understanding of the subject.

Examinations

Examinations are stressful and pretty inhumane periods of time. But students often fail to prepare, which is a great but sad way to fail. Complacency and lack of engagement (or attendance) at lectures/seminars only exacerbates this. For some reason, students seem to forget that lecturers at university have set the exam and whilst they cannot tell you what the exam questions are, they will be guiding you during seminars/lectures to ensure you will be able to answer the questions that are coming up. Hence we cannot stress enough the importance of attendance.

Another major issue that students have is in answering the wrong question by not reading the question thoroughly or by running out of time. Students should check the regulations for their specific exams but time-saving tricks include focusing on the aspects of the question that will score the most marks. The best introduction in the world probably won't score highly but definitions, arguments for and against, and analysis will. So sometimes it is best to just start with a simple introduction and maximize on adding value (hence gaining marks) during the exam by spending time on the parts of the question that will score you the most marks. The conclusions and ending can also be quite simple and short.

Plan your time and allocate a bit of time to read the question and make a few notes to help you structure your answer. Structuring your answer will mean you will have a systematic way of scoring valuable marks. With a structure you can also plan your time; this is the third biggest source of students failing to get their expected exam results – behind failing to revise effectively and not answering the right question! Plan your time! And give yourself a few minutes to read through your answer to add in anything that comes to mind that will increase your score.

The use of tables (if permitted) is a great way to summarize lists of items such as the elements of the high-level structure Annex SL where you show each major clause and explain the major elements of the clause. Or a diagram may save a lot of time when discussing the introduction of a new ISO standard (again if diagrams are permitted). But do remember to explain the diagram in words – just showing it is insufficient!

The only other recommendation we can offer is to enjoy your course and engage with the content and lecturer/s and just do your best. Best of luck!

Nick and Tegwen

INDEX